GORDON I

MUSINGS
OF A
BLACK PUDDING
MAN

To my small but talented family and many excellent friends

...... always make sure you have a good bed and a comfortable pair of shoes, because if you're not in one you're in the other

© Gordon Lomax 2002

Front cover "Bury Black Puddings"
by kind permission of
Chadwicks Original Bury Black Puddings Ltd.

All other Black Pudding photo reproductions by
Alan Spencer
Bury prize-winning photographer

Published by Gordon Lomax
Printed and bound by Short Run Press Ltd, Exeter

INTRODUCTION

This English adventurer and upwardly mobile Briton was nurtured and raised in that black pudding bastion of old Lancashire, Bury. A place where gossip was the glue of life and example influenced the rest of Great Britain.

After university (where he was kicked off the debating team for constantly agreeing with the other side) and serving Her Majesty as a National Service pilot, his more physical years were spent as a sports devotee, businessman, columnist and broadcaster. At the BBC he presented his own programmes ranging from cricket to politics while rumpling many a producer and editor with his offbeat freelance contributions.

How old is he? He's not yet so elderly that he doesn't buy green bananas and not so young that his receding (nay, vanishing) and greying hair does not challenge deathly muscle spasms. Indeed, so buoyant is he by nature that he knows for certain the world won't end today because it's already tomorrow in New Zealand where his son Kenneth, daughter-in-law Adrienne and granddaughters Niki and Beth live.

Thoughts of the Day flow consistently from him on an hourly basis ....

"If the world was a logical place it would be men who would ride side-saddle."

"Today you are immersed in moral ambiguity - tomorrow who knows?"

"He who doesn't remember the past, is condemned to forget where he parked."

"When women throw themselves at me, why do they always miss?"

The exercise of providing a miscellany of light-hearted thought-provoking words make him happy and prevents him from experiencing amnesia and deja vu at the same time.

Since leaving "normal" life, he and his wife Jytte, an unorthodox Viking who forsook raping and pillaging to enjoy the more subtle perversions of Britain by gaining a black belt in proof reading, have managed to live in various flickers of paradise such as Spain and Florida. Life now ranges from solving the vagaries of imperfect golf swings, playing grindfest clay court tennis, writing creative punctuations previously unknown to man, and partaking in pineapple passion awareness weeks.

As a columnist he is forever on patrol ready to overcome readers with satire and handcuff them with metaphors. He knows where to find Cliché Close, Banality Boulevard, Drivel Drive and Pabulum Parade. They all lead off Gigg Lane, the home of the Shakers, where most things that later proved useful in life were learned on the terraces.

ALSO BY THE AUTHOR

100 Ways To Better Tennis Thinking

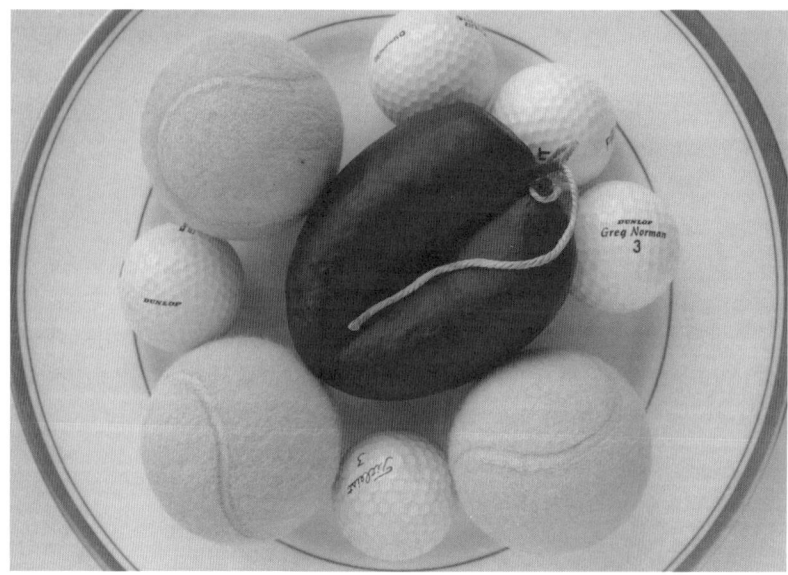

BLACK PUDDING COUNTRY

I tasted my first black pudding at precisely 1.27 p.m. (I remember looking at the clock in the old Bury market) on a cold gloomy 1946 November afternoon. At the time, it was a dank Lancashire town riddled with old fashioned natural fibres, that shrank, stretched, felted and matted, pilled and faded, and finally, withered and rotted away.

To warm the cockles of my heart, my granddad thought it was about time he treated me to the famed Thompson's local delicacy which my parents had forbidden me to eat. "You never quite know what it's made of," said my mother. "You'll come to no 'arm," said granddad. The occasion he'd chosen was just before Bury's football match against Barnsley at Gigg Lane. he rightly thought that burning mustard on a hot black pudding was just the thing to warm me up and prepare me for the feet freezing conflict ahead.

The memory lingers still of muffled football supporters having a competition among themselves to see who could devour the most horseshoe rings of black puddings. One of them, who ate seven, was the type of man who had decided not to slim specifically but share his surplus with adjoining areas of his body. It's surprising how food just seems to taste better when it's being consumed outdoors where totally indescribable creatures can destroy all hygiene requirements.

I learned that the celebrated Bury Black Pudding had to be plump and not resemble an emaciated pepperoni salami. I was warned that a BBP was not a "banger". I discovered that a BBP had the same air of mystery as a haggis.

Although first made by Assyrians, the black pudding was referred to in Homer's Odyssey .... "In the same way as a man having filled the stomach with fat and blood, stands in front of a great fire and turns it this way and that, in his eagerness to get it roasted." The black pudding was brought to England by the Romans, whose recipes were highly spiced as recorded by Apicius, a gourmet of AD100. The Anglo-Saxons reproduced it; the British adopted it; some industrial towns refined it, but Bury developed it to a level of excellence previously unknown.

Basically, the black pudding is made of fresh pig's blood, suet and seasoning enclosed in an intestine. Mustard is optional but absolutely essential. Indeed, 'Mad' Ossie, my granddad's friend and local purveyor of (according to him) "the finest black delicacy in town," claimed he had a hole in his sock because he couldn't take the heat of the mustard! Ossie, whose dubious recipe went with him to heaven, insisted you "might" take groats and pearl barley, tie them loosely in a bag and boil until cooked, place in a large tub and add seasoning, flour and chopped onions. "And don't forget to mix it well, while it's still hot." Adding cubes of white pig's fat cut into quarter-inch squares, the blood and stiffening the mixture with oatmeal completed the mix.

The concoction was then divided into pudding fillers (old shoes when Ossie ran out of intestines) allowing 6 to 8 pieces of fat to each pudding. After being tied up firmly the puddings were boiled gently for about 20 minutes or until Ossie returned from the Dog and Partridge.

What my granddad knew and my parents didn't, was that a BBP was full of energy and contained significant levels of protein, iron, phosphorous, magnesium, zinc, potassium, calcium, riboflavin, thiamin, dietary fibre and vitamin B12. What my parents knew and my granddad didn't, was that a BBP had high levels of monounsaturated fat, a surplus of sugar, too much sodium, an excess of carbohydrates, way too much cholesterol and should be eaten in moderation. Quite clearly my granddad, to whom I was devoted, won on points.

As a young man I occasionally had sliced and fried black pudding as a starter to a meal. Later still, I was introduced to a wonderful main course. Layered Black Pudding consisted of slices of potatoes, apples, onions and black pudding baked in the oven and topped with nutmeg, thyme, black pepper and mustard sauce. Yummy!

As my granddad said on that cold day with a rosy smile .... "Who could want for anything better? That should put a bit o' bant in you." It was clearly a food from hellfire kitchen to ensure that the rain lapping around the damp ankles of a Lancashire lad soon dried up.

Now that Thompson's are no more, my granddad, had he been alive today, would have relished the fame and glory of Bury's food from heaven resting on the shoulders of Chadwick's Black Pudding Company.

Long may it continue.

AND SO TO BED

It is my proud privilege to present the first masculine medical News For Men. It is the most significant step for the so-called stronger sex since the invention of that most suggestive object, the electric nose-hair trimmer. A device which overnight wiped out worldwide hair sprouting from noses like summer asparagus.

Researchers at my old stomping ground, Sheffield University, have discovered at long last, that men need sleep. This profound revelation was based on the fact that men have hormones which produce chemicals so that they can take control away from our brains. As proof, men produce a hormone that makes them unable to see dust, cobwebs and smears on glass, and another that compels them to watch instant replays on TV. If a man is watching a Premiership football match, a polar bear in drag could amble into the room and the man will not notice because his hormones are forcing him to watch, possibly for the fifth time, David Beckham fall down in slow motion.

Women do not produce this hormone, but they do generate one that compels them to rearrange furniture, and another one that causes them to believe they can improve their appearance by using a tiny brush coated with bitumen to improve their eyelashes.

One researcher from the Wicker valley area has stated that men produce a hormone that causes them to develop muscle mass, which they need to perform masculine tasks that are biologically necessary for human survival, such as operating a remote control. The catch is, men produce this hormone only during a deep sleep. If they don't get enough sleep, they become quite logical but flabby.

If you don't have the chiselled physique of a male underwear model it's not because you have the same exercise habits of a hibernating mammal, it's because you're not getting enough deep sleep.

It is suggested that to change your lifestyle you need the support of your spouse. Imagine the scene.

Spouse: "Darling, could you take out the recycling, mow the lawn and help me move the furniture around the living room until I finally decide that I like it best in its original location?"

You: "I'd love to Sandra, but I need to get some deep sleep so I can build my muscle mass."

Spouse: "Well, I suppose that is medically more important especially as those folks in Sheffield seem to know what they're talking about."

You: "Thanks my darling. By the way, your eyelashes are very attractive."

As everyone knows, it's a full-time job being a wife's husband.

Things would be far better if there was a TV exercise programme called "Muscle Mass For Men". It would be similar to other exercise presentations, except that instead of annoyingly perky over-muscled women prancing around to repetitive music, "Muscle Mass For Men" would consist of 6 to 10 uninterrupted hours of a man sleeping in a recliner. I can envision a nationwide chain of MMM Fitness Centres equipped with state-of-the-art beds. Fitness conscious men could spend entire weeks at these centres watching golf on TV providing it wasn't too exciting, and countless football replays while secreting vital hormones.

Before long the muscles of enthusiastic men are going to be so massive that the males of this world may have to move up to a larger potato crisp bag to provide that new physique with adequate nutrition.

But even the manliest man can become sick or injured. If the new MMM needs medical treatment the answer is to try and fix the problem yourself in order to save you being charged an arm and a leg by frequenting the private health care system. Simple home remedies like duct tape on a chest wound can work wonders. If you have a painful corn on your toe you can do what a retired Norfolk farmer did .... "I shot it off with a .22 rifle." The surprising thing was, in spite of his neurons not being fully connected at the time, it worked out fine. The corn vanished but so nearly did his foot. That is why those hard working Yorkshire researchers recommend ...."For foot problems, it's easier to take aim with a pistol."

Of course, nobody is suggesting that you should attempt such a task without any preparation. First of all men, you should sleep. Deeply.

ARE BABIES AND PLANES COMPATIBLE?

Air travel is lots of fun isn't it? That's what I was pondering over as I was removing my clothes during a security check at Gatwick Airport, which I have now learned is located on the north coast of France. For some reason I had been singled out by the security people for an intense level of security because the baby just in front of me started crying. Perhaps it was the look on my face the baby didn't like.

I cannot imagine terrorists accomplishing any dastardly deed if they're just behind a baby. They would be enmeshed in cooing at the baby, making faces at the baby and snatching lethal objects out of the baby's mouth. The terrorist would be in state of shock. "When did you plan to commit the act of terror?" "I was just wiping the sticky fingers substance off my jacket when, totally inadvertently, I dropped the hand grenade."

Nevertheless, I was picked out not for the first time. On a security check some years ago at Manchester Airport I was strip-searched before boarding for Copenhagen. My mother-in-law never quite forgave me for not acquiring my duty free allocation because of the delay. Apparently it was my Manchester accent that caused the problem. Somehow I had IRA overtones in my bearing. It might have been the shillelagh I was carrying or the shamrock in my buttonhole that triggered suspicion. I'll never know.

The other travellers - all of whom, frankly looked suspicious to me - accelerated through security. I was ordered off to the side where a man told me to remove my shoes, belt and the contents of my trouser pockets, which he handed to a woman, who without a word, walked off with them. It is surprising how security passes dangling on chains from necks, pour forth signs of immense power. I was hoping that these were security personnel, as opposed to thieves who had worked out that, these days, air travellers will do anything they are ordered to without question. "OK, Mr. Lomax. I'm going to ask you to put your left hand in, take your left hand out, do the Hokey Cokey and shake it all about." When the man who wrote that song died, they put his left leg in the coffin and things started to go downhill from there.

Next, the man told me to hold my arms out so he could scan me. This meant I had to let go of my trousers which, being beltless, began to slide down, an occurrence that I am sure had been recorded in my Terrorist Suspect Profile on computer somewhere. "Use Extreme Caution When Trousers Are Lowered."

They finally let me pass to the gate but not before asking me to hold out my arms to be scanned yet again, while all the other passengers looked on no doubt wondering what kind of low life terrorist I was. The thought did cross my mind that airlines would love to eliminate passengers so they can rid themselves of all these precautions and therefore improve the service.

It was embarrassing but I have to admit that it gave me the security of knowing that if anything remotely suspicious had occurred on the flight, my fellow passengers would have beaten me senseless with their in-flight dinner rolls. What did occur on the flight was the small boy sitting directly behind me, decided to kick the back of my seat for sheer fun for what seemed hours. A polite request to the boy's parent holding a baby, to insist her child desist, fell on deaf ears.

An intelligent person, or even a reasonably bright toadstool, would know that one lone woman cannot possibly look after a potentially delinquent child and a delicate baby with menacing potential. And, on top of that, all the supplies the baby needs including a special chair seat, clothes, liquid food, nappies, industrial-sized bales of wipes, stuffed frog, stuffed tiger and a stuffed object of doubtful origin that the baby insisted on clutching while shouting "Da-Da" at a decibel level that drowned the aircraft's engines. The total weight of all these supplies was hundreds of times the weight of the baby.

This is why famous explorers never travelled with babies. If Columbus had set sail for America with a few babies on board, his ship would have sank long before reaching the Azores.

Worse still, do you know what a baby does on a plane when its brother has just stopped kicking a passenger's seat? It stands on its mother's lap and sticks its head over the seat in front, so it can get maximum range when it shrieks. On baby-intensive flights, like the ones to Mallorca, you see shrieking babies heads constantly popping up all over, like jack-in-boxes from hell.

The trick for keeping your baby from screeching is to come up with a new activity each time the baby gets bored. As a normal baby gets bored every 15 seconds on a 3-hour flight, you have to come up with 720 different activities. By the second hour of the flight your standards have reached rock bottom. Whatever baby wants, baby gets! Baby insists on biting the flight attendant on the ankle - that's OK. Baby wants to lick the toilet seat - that's gross, but just about OK. Baby demands to crawl towards the cockpit - that's definitely not OK.

Talk about a plot twist. That initial move towards the cockpit by the crawling monster had two effects. For some reason I was mistaken as a terrorist father, and with my previous pre-boarding record I didn't stand a chance. I was immediately pinned down between the floor emergency lights by the flight attendant seeking retribution for her sore ankle. To add insult to injury, the baby was then sick all over me. In generous mood, I put it down to a change in atmospheric pressure.

As situations like this occur on nearly every flight, it's a wonder that babies are not accommodated in special seats out on the wings with parents being conveniently seated so they can see, wave and coo at their offspring. On the other hand, an airline just for people with babies could be a commercial boon. The renamed SAS (Scream And Shriek), would not have seats. Everyone would roam around the floor. The pre-flight safety routine would consist of how to get a large foreign object out of a child's mouth. The in-flight meal would be sticky jam toasties eaten off the floor. As there would be no formal toilets on the plane, little changing shelves would be strategically placed between the windows. The sole flight attendant dressed in full protective clothing would encourage parents to "tie a knot in it" or "sit cross-legged as long a s possible" throughout the flight. A nose clip for each parent would replace the standard issue packet of mixed nuts to offset the repulsive air emanating from baby waterworks and bowel movements. If the noise reached a certain decibel level and minds were becoming a little fuzzy, plastic tubes would drop down from the ceiling to dispense chloroform to the parents.

I definitely won't be on one of these flights. In fact, I won't be on any flight to anywhere. I'll still be in security assisting with their investigations into my alleged terrorist activities. One good thing could come out of this. If I lie down on the airport security detector perhaps I'll get a free MRI scan.

IN .... OUT! IN .... OUT!

Another stunning morning on the River Thames with just enough fog for mystery. I'm in a boat facing backward but looking forward to the day. So peaceful, so relaxing.

"Number three! Get with the stroke!"

This is the place to be.

"Roll that oar when you cross your knees and drop the blade in square, number three! Let me see some backsplash!"

Was that an otter that popped up near the river bank?

"Length number three, length!"

I'm the number three man and this is no scenic boat ride.

The competitive sport of rowing has a long and glorious history that's not been terribly tarnished by my being a minor footnote to it. I'm rowing because of the need to impress my station commander with my attitude and physical prowess. He's a rowing nut and I want to become a pilot. I have to impress him before my attempt to dazzle a future flight instructor is put to the test.

I deprive myself of sleep so that I can be at the boathouse by 5.15 a.m. to avail my anticipatory body of this wonderful career opportunity. Carrying a boat 17 metres long and nearly a metre wide on your head resembles eight ants attempting to place a wooden ruler in the water. The boat is known as an eight man shell because if the four rowing the port side and the four rowing the starboard side died through their exertions, the boat would wash up downstream like a huge conch.

Most of you I know have worked on rowing machines at home or in the gym, but in your situation you've no one shouting at you or even a cause for which to live or die. A further difference is that the machine doesn't have an oar that, if you don't get it the right way at just the right moment, can lock in the water. In rowing parlance this is called "catching a crab." On such an occurrence the worst thing that can happen is that the oar smacks you hard on the side of the head.

Another element the rowing machine doesn't have is a coxswain (pronounced: Evil Little Man). The coxswain, invariably an educated anorexic, is the only person who can actually see where the boat is going and, therefore, the only person allowed to give orders on the boat other than the exhausted and demented stroke when you're four lengths behind. Coxswains are neurotic individuals who don't feel fulfilled unless they can boss people around. They usually sit about at home reading "The Decline and Fall of the Roman Empire" while drinking a very pale lager. Their job definition is to notice every single flaw in your rowing technique and personal character, and exploit them to the full. An ELM's aim in life is to give your thin skin a tough time.

As a rower you have three duties in relation to the coxswain:

1. Never row at stroke as the appalling stench of garlic will affect your timing.
2. Choose a position as far from the ELM as possible.
3. If you can't, wear earplugs and look very interested.

The ELM is aided and abetted by a coach in his dotage who performs the singular feat of cycling along the embankment looking only sideways whilst shouting crude epithets through a battered megaphone. If they both do their job right, about 75% of the potential crew will have dropped out and the remaining glazed fools will be ready for their first race. The rowers will be as one, all slapping water in unison.

"You're making good progress but you've a long way to go yet. Remember to stretch and take "lonnnngggg" strokes. And that means you number three!"

We've heard it all before. On race day as the wind freshens, we're threatened with the ignominy of sinking but fear and our ELM now steering in a psychopathic condition: "They can't win if we sink 'em first," ensure our survival. That's how wars are won. And this is war. Just ask any trainee pilot.

I don't know how many "lonnnnggggs" I did in the race, to the number only my aching back and blistered hands can testify. Suffice it to say my efforts ensured I was soon at one of Her Majesty's airfields with another tortured soul in the cockpit.

"Keep her level! Level means level, Lomax!"

Some things in life never change.

FIRST LOVE

During my fifteenth year in Bury, that gutsy (or gusty in a Pennine wind) town in north-west England, I fell in love with D.M (little c) K. I have no idea where she is today, if she is at all, but her name will not be revealed in this piece in order to protect the innocent.

Why? Because a gentleman doesn't kiss and tell - not even for oodles of lolly!

At my Grammar School there was a code of honour about such

matters. It wasn't pounded into me by some teacher in my first year. It's a truism one picks up along the way. Either you're a cad or you're not.

It's not that D.M (little c) K and I had anything to hide. Technically I never kissed her. Never knew the softness of her hand. Never, in fact, exchanged even a few words with her. Ours was an eye to eye contact of the tenderest, yet lustful type. First love liaisons in Bury were Augean dalliances of the intriguing kind.

I insist still, that her name shall remain cloaked behind initials. The printed word especially today, reaches far-flung places and the intent here is not to embarrass D.M (little c) K or her children and grandkids, if there are any. Perhaps, with productive speed, even a great-grandchild.

Although it's hard for my wife to believe it, I was an excruciatingly shy lad with an aptitude for stammering when talking to members of the opposite sex. My beetroot face masked my adolescent acne. With such afflictions how was I to let D.M (little c) K know that out of all the dozens of girls in light blue blouses and grey skirts, she was the pick of the bunch?

Nowadays teenagers with crush problems have it much easier. All they need do is "let it all hang out" either verbally or in advice-to-teens columns in which so-called experts dish out direct advice. As I read the letters in my dotage, I'm astounded at the frank tone of the letters and the advanced maturity of the problems. You would never have found letters like that in the Bury Times during the days of my teenhood.

Even in those days, I guess I could have written directly to the object of my desire, but what if my billet-doux was intercepted or worse, spurned? Oh, the humiliation, I would have to emigrate to a wild and nefarious place like West

Yorkshire.

My plan became obvious. I always went to school on my bicycle. So, with puncture excuse at the ready, we would have to share the same bus home. It was to be an eye-catching accidental deliberate Bury Corporation vehicular meeting. The plan was simplicity itself. I would sit across the gangway and D.M (little c) K would turn towards me and for a few lingering seconds she would embrace my yearning, burning eyes. That was when I discovered that young love (or old love for that matter) is a condition of the mind that often strikes when the mind is not in very good condition. The bus proved not to be my transport of delight.

D.M (little c) K smiled and waved at me. Or so I thought. The rapture and hormonal adjustment soon evaporated when I realised she was acknowledging the boy sitting next to me. The stop before mine they both jumped off and arm in arm went their whispering way.

My lowered confidence was only slightly repaired three weeks later when I discovered during idle boyish chatter, that D.M (little c) K smoked. How could she? My cap which had been set was withdrawn immediately, after all, even in those days of innocence, I knew that kissing a smoker was as seductive as licking a dirty ashtray.

Not long after, D.M (little c) K left school and we never saw each other again. Or did we? Do we pass one another today without realising it|? D.M (little c) K wouldn't know me now with balding head and greying hair but maybe she would still see the smoulder in my eyes from that long-ago afternoon.

You've got to believe that's just some ageing man's wistful thinking. The girl I'm married to extinguished that torch years ago. Honest.

MUSICAL CULTURE

It has been suggested, even by so-called friends, that I'm the kind of cultural moron who sits around all day watching TV with a beer in one hand and the remote control in the other. This is a downright lie. Sometimes I have a drink in both hands and copious quantities of ice cream and chocolate at my side as I flick from channel to channel.

No, seriously, I happen to be a highly cultural individual. I've been involved in tour groups that walk briskly past some of the world's finest works of art. I personally own multitudes of CD's I don't play and voluminous quantities of books I don't read.

I graduated swiftly from piano lessons to voice production. It cannot be said that my music started as a hobby because I was singing my lungs out before I knew how to write or even walk. I was cooing tunefully and with chesty vigour in the delivery room in 1934 Lancashire.

Knowing that musical talent is a prerequisite in the music business, I asked myself: "What is the real spiritual driving force behind my music?" I reluctantly came to the conclusion it was exercise. A conclusion arrived at due to the impressive chest measurements of male opera stars, not forgetting of course, the ample dimensions of their female counterparts.

Should I be serious or popular? Should I scat or be content with an amen spiritual? Whatever it was going to be, my music had to have soul. my music had to have feeling and statement.

Fortified by several school singing prizes, I auditioned with my first band nearly fifty years ago. The band was called The Gutter Rats. The musicians had these little plastic rats all over the stage, and they wore sunglasses even a night, which I figured was a sign that either they were extremely cool, or they suffered from DT's. Man, they were BAAAAD!

The second band I tried to join didn't even have a name, I asked them where they played and they said, "In Geoff's Dad's greenhouse." I pitied the demented plants even more than the crazed glass. My enthusiasm evaporated when the band asked me a really important question: "What do you like on your chips?" As I was the only one in the band old enough to drive, our first gig never happened.

Ever persistent in my search for musical excellence I turned to composing. Inspired by the King of Swing, Benny Goodman, I settled on my hit formula. With a chord structure of C, A minor, F and G, I was on my way. Words with the theme of love and sensuality were added in a poetic haze.

What went wrong? I can only put it down to lack of exposure in the right way.

Still persistent I turned to opera. When I told my friends I was aiming to sing at La Scala it was as though I was planning to quit these precious isles and become a smelly Greek goat herder. "Oh! That's nice," they said. Some of them I've not heard from since. Such are the burdens of culture.

My friends consider that the artistic themes opera embodies aren't presented in a manner that is intellectually relevant for the modern listener. Their objective criticism arrives at one solid conclusion. Operas are written in a foreign language. I must confess that I'm forced to ask myself how in the world can the operatic world be expected to reach a modern audience if the lyrics aren't written in English.

Please don't misunderstand me. I'm not saying that the devotee can't enjoy opera. I'm just saying that 99% of other people say they're wrong.

It was while seriously rehearsing my introductory aria that an okapi died in Denmark from stress triggered by opera singers. Apparently, this rare African mammal was in a zoo located nearly 300 metres from a park where opera singers were rehearsing. This poses the question: "Could opera in sufficient doses, also be fatal to human beings?"

If opera music proved fatal it would surely be time to think about requiring that some kind of government health warning be prominently displayed on Luciano Pavarotti. "Second hand opera" would have to be studied to see what effect being in the range of hummed and whistled operatic melodies had on co-workers especially in poorly ventilated areas.

Although you can't take chances with the health of the public, it would be a sad state of affairs to ban opera altogether, along with ballet, non-rhyming poetry and any kind of sculpture that doesn't accurately depict naked women.

I realise after all my musical efforts that I'm now going to be harshly criticised by the zealous culture crowd. As I've still got the courage of my convictions (3 months for a badly rendered "My Way", and 4 months probation for not reaching top C), I realise that success in the music business is full of relentless demands for even better performances and achievements. My search for my ideal musical medium will continue unabated.

A TRUE FAUX PAS

The French are still convinced that we're making a bid for the hostile takeover of their language. They're trying to put up trade barriers against imported English words. So here I am nibbling my CROISSANT and sipping CAFE AU LAIT at LE COQ AU VIN as the protectionists in Paris seem to be suffering from what is known in France as LE STRESS.

I've always understood that as we are all in the European community, language interchange would be normal. Apparently not so. The French ELITE don't like the fact that you can order LE SANDWICH in LE MOTEL, or that a business can suffer LE CASH FLOW. They're equally alarmed that their fellow citizens are flying LES JUMBO JETS and reading LES BEST SELLERS. It's not really English that's created this CAUSE CELEBRE and it's hardly my fault that the French eat LE POPCORN, watch LE TALK SHOW and listen to LE HIT PARADE.

Words today don't have a permanent residence, and why should they in an increasingly internationalist world of greater cooperation? How can you regulate against an immigrant word? And, again, why should you? If your grammar is correct, use as many words as you wish from any source. That's the beauty of language. It's fluid. It's adaptable.

It's now over thirty years ago that the French began to do LE SHOPPING at LE SUPERMARKET. Now it's LE MICROCHIP that helps them do it. Why don't they invent their own words if they object to this Anglo-American cultural invasion? If they can't or they're too lazy, don't blame those across Le Manche.

Wasn't it the French who put their stamp on LAISSEZ-FAIRE economics? What L'AUTO is to Japan, LE BON MOT is to France.

My guess is that French intellectuals who are constantly reigniting the moniker war aren't really angry that their lives may be saved by something called LE AIR BAG. They're appalled at the insidious cultural creep by British business and

Euro Disney.

France is the country that gave us BALLET and what did we give them in return? Le DISQUE-JOCKEY. They gave us HAUTE COUTURE and we gave them LE JEANS. They gave us a GOURMET CUISINE and we gave them LE FAST FOOD.

For nearly a thousand years since William the Conqueror's time we have traded words in more ways than one and it would seem a pity to stop now. It would be more than a sad GATEAU, a curdled QUICHE or a collapsed SOUFFLÉ could stand. It seems strange that while we employ CHEFS, the French people are actually eating LE HOT DOG at LE SNACK BAR.

But before the word war becomes a FAIT ACCOMPLI may I remind a French conventionalist that when we only had underwear, you gave us LINGERIE. When we had mere flowers, you put them into a BOUQUET. When we had toilet water, you created PERFUME. You gave our beef and two veg its A LA MODE. You gave our soup its DU JOUR. You helped us know the CHIC from the GAUCHE. You let us turn a mundane meeting into a RENDEZVOUS.

In travel we have inherited the TRAIN, the GARAGE and the TAXI. While we gave you Scotch whisky and gin, you returned the compliment with an APERITIF and COGNAC. We really appreciate that we can eat PATÉ, COURGETTES, PIGEON and BONBONS in any CAFÉ, BRASSERIE or RESTAURANT, be it at a BUFFET or afterwards at the CABERET. Our women have been adorned with BRASSIÈRES and ROUGE for decades, while our homes are blessed with CABINETS and an antique BUREAU or two.

We do appreciate that France has always been among the AVANT-GARDE, but in this modern world of the internet and mass instant communication, and hence word proliferation, language barriers are simply PASSÉ. Any sane Frenchman reading this would see that the English language hasn't deteriorated because of its Gallic imports. I like to think of it as a mutual enrichment.

ARE MY MEMORY LAPSES DUE TO BRAIN SHRINKAGE?

Now, let's see. What was this column supposed to be about? Oh yes, forgetting things!

I'm now at the age when I forget seemingly everything. My natural state of being is that of someone who has smoked a substantial amount of high-quality marijuana. I wake up in the morning and can't find my glasses. I can't look for them because I can't see. So I frantically run around tossing things this way and that until my wife finds them for me.

Then I take off my glasses to have a shower. After the shower |I can't find my glasses. So I frantically run around until my wife finds them for me. I then take off my glasses to put in my eye drops. Afterward, I can't find my glasses. Sometimes I don't have to look for my glasses after putting in my eye drops because I forget to put in my eye drops.

On bad days I can't find my money or my car keys. I have a place to put them but this does little good because I don't remember to put them where I won't forget them. I walk in the house with money and car keys and ten minutes later they're gone. I have no more idea where I left them than a porcupine knows where it shed its last quill.

I once tore apart the house looking for our expensive camcorder before my next door neighbour finally found it. It was hanging in the garden on the rose trellis. The other day I was sorting through some computer information. What do you do call those things you store info on? Oh yes, floppy discs. I forgot where I had put them, got mad about forgetting, calmed down, then I forget I forgot them. I've now adopted a new approach. I turn on my computer, forget I've done it, turn left into the bedroom instead of right into the kitchen to make myself a cup of coffee, return to the study without the coffee and reply in longhand to a letter I had forgotten to answer.

Is my condition due to brain shrinkage or lack of enervating sex? I'd like to think it's the latter but deep down I feel it must be the former. According to my latest information university researchers did a study showing that as males - but NOT females - get older, their brains shrink. I was so relieved to read that as I thought it was just me! I'm now deliriously happy to know that when I go into a newsagent to buy The Times and some magazines, pay for them, then leave the shop without them ....I'm not alone!

I've always been dreadful at remembering people's names, but now I forget names instantaneously before they have permeated my ear canal. If somebody introduces himself to me at a social event, it sounds as though he's saying: "Hello, I'm Blah!"

"I'm sorry," I'll say, "what was your name again?"

"Blah," he'll say.

"Ah!" I'll say, hoping that a meteor will crash into the building before I have to introduce him to someone else.

Here's another symptom. I currently own four identical unused toothbrushes because every time I'm in the supermarket and walk past the dental section, my brain, which by now must be the size of a peanut, racks its tiny shrivelled self in an effort to remember whether I have a spare toothbrush, and it never comes up with a definitive answer.

As a frequent flier I hope that brain diminution in males doesn't extend to airline pilots. "Ladies and gentlemen, we are now approaching either Manchester or Munich." The university study also showed that as we get older we gradually lose our sense of humour. This is definitely true in the case of my oldest friend, whose name is ..... excuse me while I look up his name. OK, here it is. Denis Clutterbuck. We were remarking on the fact that when we were teenage males roaming around Bury in old Lancashire, we thought the most hilarious activities we perpetrated should now be punishable by death.

The brain shrinkage study makes me feel a lot better because now I know that I'm not getting stupid alone. Zillions of men are getting stupid with me as witnessed by ...

1. Golf
2. Bald head scratching
3. House of Lords
4. Viagra overdosing

This natural process is one not to be feared unless you are me. Most people start out with a healthy memory so they can spare some of it, but I was suspect even when at school. If you were absent-minded at Bury Grammar School it was deemed a mark of brilliance. It demonstrated that your mind was filled with things like the theory of relativity and the writings of Socrates, and that you couldn't be bothered with the minutiae of life like names, faces and the placement of items. But I was not an absent-minded genius. Although my IQ was high, my young mind was filled with important things like football and cricket statistics and the budding breasts of Line Renaud.

Later in life when I bought a book on memory retention

I did pretty well so I put my deficiencies down to the fact that I was forgetting things because I wasn't making any real effort to remember them. After all who cares where you put your glasses or car keys when the F.A. Cup final is on television?

What I need to do now at my advanced age is to establish an essential mental link that goes like this: Interest - Motivation - Attention - Concentration - Organisation. Hopefully one day I'll have all that memorised. Until then, I will make lists like these.

Hang car keys on hook in utility room
My neighbour's wife is the fat one, my wife is the thin one
The best place to make a mug of coffee is the kitchen

I believe one other solution to be for the government to recognise Older Male Brain Shrinkage as a disability. At the very least, we should have a law requiring everybody to wear a name tag. Sadly, older males would be exempt from this requirement because they wouldn't be able to find their tags. Everybody would therefore be called Blah.

I have many other views on this subject, but I can't remember what they are.

WHAT DO YOU DO?

There's a simple question that men ask each other that women avoid like grams of fat.

"What do you do?"

Four words. Four syllables. One question mark. A question, if you're a woman, that harbours a thousand conflicting emotions.

"How do you know?" I can hear women out there saying at this mere male.

Well, as the dutiful listening man, that's my long - and I mean long - experience of social contact between men and women.

Upon meeting, men say those four words at the shake of a hand. They're part of the male catechism.

"So Geoff, what do you do?"

"Geophysicist with the government. How about you?"

"Insurance, with one of the big boys."

"No kidding. Say, what do you think about ....?"

Asking people what they do is a socially acceptable prelude to deeper conversation, if you're a man. It seems to me that if you're a woman, it's a prelude to awkwardness.

Why? Because women have lost their common ground in the gender shuffle. Whereas men have always worked outside the home, most working women today belong to the second generation of the female workplace. Work has always defined men while home has always defined women. Historically, it would have been uncivil for a man not to ask another about his work. In contrast, it would have been superfluous to ask a woman.

At the end of the 20th century, with some at home but more at work, women seem in conflict not only about their roles, but also about how their roles are perceived. The question - "What do you do?" - is filled with connotations, innuendoes and emotions loaded with potential for guilt, envy, self-righteousness and even contempt.

I dare you to ask a woman: "Do you work?"

Of course she works. Being a woman is work in my view. It matters not whether the woman is a full-time engineer or pursuing a full-time career with kids and household, she's a working woman. What the question implies of course is: "Do you work outside the home?"

Some of the most conflicted are women who work part-time, managing to be home with their children after school. These women don't want to raise the question for fear they would have to answer it and be exposed as the lucky ones.

At a recent function I observed two women making conversation with the most trivial of talk. Weather, dieting and hair styles were the topics covered. Not an inkling of "What do you do?" It was obvious to me that BOTH these women were intelligent sophisticated people and one, at least, oozed ability from her very pores. Even I was intent on finding out what they did. Somehow.

Finally, honing in like an arrow on a straight path to its objective, one of the women came up with: "So what do you do when you're not at gatherings like this?"

I was agog with excitement. All was to be revealed. The answer might be from brain surgery to tennis.

"I'm a Professor of History."

Marvellous! At long last. They'd spent nearly a quarter of an hour boring each other with the superficial details of their lives when I could have been listening to an intelligent view of the past.

Needless to say, the occupation of her fellow conversationalist soon followed. As the Sales Manager of a leading pharmaceutical company she proved a fine ambassador.

I joined them and tactfully elicited their view on the what-do-you-do question. They agreed it was a discomforting question especially in a culture that seems to value working women and yet implying they're not doing enough for their family.

The entire episode seemed to sum up women's confusion about society's conflicting messages. It seemed as if the two women, in the initial stages, had forgotten one thing women, historically, do better than men - communicate.

It was an evening to remember. I admired every single word that came out of their mouths once the dreaded question was out of the way. My working mother would have loved every minute. I couldn't have felt better if I'd been their confidential hair stylist.

BORING BEYOND WORDS

I was sitting quietly, reading a newspaper, at Manchester Airport when the world's most boring people sat down next to me and started to talk so loud amplifiers became redundant. They had clearly learned to whisper in a saw mill.

First person: That's a big case.
Second person: You can hold a lot in a case like that.
Third person: Helen has a big one like that.
First person: Helen does? Like that?
Third person: Yes. It holds everything. She puts everything in that case of hers.
Second person: It's a big case.
Third person: She says whatever she has, she just puts it in her case and bingo, closes it up.
First person: Helen does?
Second person: That's a big case.

Just then another traveller walked past pulling a suitcase on wheels. This inspired a whole new train of thought.

First person (proud of the first sighting): There's one of those cases with those easy-run wheels.
Second person: Where?
First person: Over there, with those wheels.
Third person: Our Annie has one.

First person:	She does? With wheels like that?
Third person:	Yes. She says you just pull it along.
Second person:	Your Annie?
Third person:	Yes. She swears by it.
Second person:	She's all there with her coughdrops!

And so on. The thought crossed my mind that a possible explanation for some plane crashes might be that people like these were sitting close enough to the cockpit for the crew to hear them talk, and eventually the pilot, in utter despair, flies into the ground for his own peace of mind.

The sad thing is, these otherwise worthy citizens didn't know they were boring. Boring people never do. In fact - and certainly no offence - even you dear reader, could be boring. When you talk to people, do they tend to make vague excuses? "Sorry! Got to run!" If that happens in a lift, then you're really boring.

The nice thing about being a celebrity however, is that when you bore folks to death, they think it's their fault. A good example of this genre is Prince Charles who, when he speaks, everybody pretends to be fascinated out of sheer good manners.

Most people sadly lead a boring life of sluggish inactivity, reflecting how immobile and uninspired they really are. But a warning! Even if crowds listen to you with what appears to be great interest, that doesn't mean you're not boring. They could be pretending.

If people start yawning when you're talking and then fall asleep, you're evidently trying more than their patience. You're obviously overstaying your verbal welcome as you, in their eyes, have become as dry as dust.

Beware of the person who wants to sell you something or wishes to have intimate carnal knowledge of you. You will never be a wet blanket to them. The point is that you could be totally unaware that you're boring, This is why everybody should make an effort to avoid boring topics. Not everybody, of course, will agree on what boring means. Some might find collecting Dresden china boring, others might find it a fascinating hobby. To lots and lots of people any hobby is boring, agriculture is a drag, foreign policy is a bind, children's overrated achievements induce tedium and being buttonholed about the weather works better than a sleeping draught.

Take heart. Eliminate stale and stodgy matters from your mind and speech. Don't torment the people you meet with dull, repetitious matters. If you're surrounded by a gaggle of pandiculating people, you've definitely got problems. Be bright and invigorating in thought and word. Become a fast bore instead of a slow bore. At least you'll give the impression that time is passing quicker.

AN ALIEN IN BRA COUNTRY

All you women out there with even a shred of pity, I come before you today, shaken and delirious. I've just returned from Bra country! I'd good reason for being there. My wife's birthday was approaching and I thought it might be a nice gesture to buy something frilly and romantic.

To buy lingerie is one way for a man to redeem himself from the vagaries of a humdrum life. If chosen correctly, lingerie is the perfect gift. Done wrong and your beloved winds up looking like she belongs on a garage workshop calendar.

Buying lingerie can be a misery. It's a combination of red-faced embarrassment and assimilated arousal. It can take you back to your first date of eager tentativeness. In spite of the advocacy of women's magazines, lingerie is not normal clothing. Lingerie exists for one purpose only. To be, eventually, visible for a very short time. If it's visible for a very long time and, I'm trying to be discreet about this, then, it's not doing its job.

As England is a lady-first country, subtlety generally works best. Sadly, most men tend to go for the Fifi French maid look. You've seen it many times - the black garter belt with little hearts, and the bodice with a neckline that plunges so deep you have to go by submarine to reach the lowest fastening. The rest of the men, those who have the fashion sense of cement, go for either feathers or the type of clothing that makes their women look like fishing lures.

Most women, especially wives, don't like active lingerie but men are so intimidated when buying that they grab the first item to catch their eye, and flee from the shop. Only women who've bought see through jockey shorts for their sporty male will have the vaguest notion of what men go through when buying lingerie.

This afternoon I wasn't intimidated. I sauntered through cosmetics, turned left at the leather goods and there I was in Bra country, in the empire of intimate apparel. I felt like the stranger in a western who enters the bar and the man at the piano stops playing, the bartender reaches nervously for his shotgun and everyone else just stares edgily. Sweaty palms, rapid pulse and complete disorientation betray symptoms of malaria. Only completing a purchase and leaving the store makes you feel better.

Although I had a perfectly valid reason for being there, you could sense the rest of the customers thought my sole purpose was to fire my cramped and twisted desires. It made you conscious that every eye was focussed on this man with a cross-dressing or a lust-and-grab fever problem.

When it came to the nitty-gritty of sizes, I seemed to have octopus hands cupping in all directions. And why is it, that only two kinds of women work in lingerie outlets? Young women who know exactly why you are buying sexy lingerie and ignore that fact for the duration of the transaction, and the older woman who looks exactly like a close friend of your mother, and who, over coffee the next day, will tell of my need to indulge in low and unspeakable deeds.

My courage was rewarded. My choice was discreet and tasteful in a tone of pale apricot. I even gift wrapped it myself to enhance the romantic allure. I had climbed Everest. I was on top of the world and all for the woman in my life. The woman who is a real lady and makes her man behave like a gentleman ... at times!

BEACH LOVERS

We've come a long way since proto man frequented the seashore eating fish and coastal flora. In this modern age another human predator walks the white sands and dunes between the palms and the oceans. The wolf disguised as a beach boy. As an expert on such matters it falls to me to offer guidance on the species to the unsuspecting girls of the world.

For a GERMAN, beach domination is a serious business. Gunther's idea of fun is two circuits of his hotel and twenty minutes on the trampoline. His pectoral-clinging T-shirt and clasping G-string show off his athletic body, but the main fun on his Teutonic quest is monopolising all the sunbeds and delineating his territory. His mating call technique is more Vorsprung than Technik. He is beautiful and he knows it. He's also a touch infantile with a strong desire to strip off at parties.

Gunther uses women like gym equipment as toning muscles is everything, so sex becomes an alternative to press-ups.

    Spiros from GREECE is a totally different animal. The aroma of moussaka surrounds this short, dark type replete with pectorals, hair and medallions. Spiros is a flirt who always seems to live at home spoiled by generations of women. Out of the beach season he herds goats. He only falls in love twice a month and invariably promises to write but doesn't. He can't, even in Greek! Much like Pedro from SPAIN, Spiros checks his reflection in windows as he drops off one girl at the airport and waits in arrivals to pick up another. These beach boys are notorious massive mammary seekers and mix naivety with lingering looks and olive oil doused body language. They speak in clichés with lots of ..... "you are too bew-tee-ful" and "I've never felt like zees before." Spiros and Pedro have a basic need to conduct seven affairs simultaneously without interference.

    The Romeo from ENGLAND usually comes bottom of the Fun in the Sun League due to his passion-killer shorts and beer-reddened face. Frank's beanie hat tops his chain laden Union Jack T-shirt while he radiates fomenting duty free aftershave. For some strange reason, he thinks of himself as cuddly because he's strongly stubbled and drinks prodigious quantities of real ale. Bars and loud music are his natural habitat and he only sunbathes when the previous night's excesses leave him semi-comatose on the beach. His shouting and groping ensure minor success with the "birds", but basically he's a pack animal shining only in the presence of his mates.

    Sven from SWEDEN loves women deeply. He believes in free love in order to share a cosmic experience. His tan must be all-over and decorated with leather souvenirs. He does not interact, he just is. Scandinavians never pick you up, they simply approach you to explain long-winded and bland views on life and death, and thereby ruin a rock concert by talking a lot of nonsense about neocryptoquasi-Expressionism. Falling in love isn't in Sven's character as he believes in connecting without commitment. Sitting and staring into your eyes "touching spirits" betrays however, a latent high sex drive.

Hank from the UNITED STATES only talks and eats which lulls the opposite sex into a false sense of security. Vastly overweight, but seemingly totally oblivious to it, he considers himself a gift to women. His idea of fun is to eat all day, swim a little, then pick a "chick" and be in bed by nine. Grandiose schemes are always at his fingertips which translates into a fabulous dining out experience at the nearest fast food eatery with paper plates, plastic cutlery and finger-licking hamburgers and hot dogs washed down with ice-filled Coca Cola.

"I love women. I love their eyes, their laughter and enchanting figure. I just love love." Those words could only be spoken by a man from FRANCE. Pierre in his elegant understated shorts which mask his designer condom case, has little use for soap but uses body lotion, spray and perfume to mask his garlic. Being in the middle of a love affair with himself, he finds flirting wasteful, much preferring to use charm and arrogance to catch his prey. He's a lounge lizard seeking deep-throat relationships. Certainly Pierre is the only beach boy to teach a beach girl how to make love, eat oysters and clean ones teeth at the same time.

So girls, on this tender day as you book your package romantic break in some sultry hideaway, you're primed to recognise the wolf in many of its less subtle forms. Be warned though. Danger always lurks on the hot beaches of the world.

IS HAGGIS AN EXTRACT OF BAGPIPES?

Visiting anywhere north of Glasgow invites you to bring thermal underwear. Because the people are friendly I feel guilty, as I live in warmer climes, that I think of the region as a cold, frigid, freezing, subzero, arctic, polar wintry place characterised by low temperatures.

The towns have "Lach", "Bein" and "Kyle" type names which proclaim they "are where the sod meets the air." I feel there are lots of places "where the sod meets the air," but most of them don't get overfussed about it. But, I made my feelings known and I got letters from every resident of the Kyle of Tongue (a total of 62 letters). Most of the letters proudly defended the Kyle of Tongue and its citizens claiming they don't usually include a tourist as an ingredient in the local haggis recipe like some other places deep in the |Highlands, and their cousins in the Kyles of Bute.

After much debate several Kyle of Tongue political and civic leaders invited me to visit. They sent me information about the area as well as gifts of typical local origin, including a leather based haggis and a large plastic bag of peat. The problem was, which offering should I set fire to first. If you are ever, on pain of death, forced to choose between eating the leather based haggis or eating the peat, my advice is: Go for the peat, although it does taste like putrid frog spawn and defies my golden rule of never eating foods that are easy for reptiles and amphibians to hide in.

In contrast, the worthy citizens of Lach Nuthin also made me a generous offer. If I visit their burgh they would rename the local sewage plant after me. According to Bailie McCurdle this is a major honour in Lach Nuthin. "The system moves 6 million litres of sewage a day," he said, in a statement that tells us more than perhaps we want to know about the effects of eating peat on the human digestive system.

 Having my name fixed to the main building of a sewage plant is not the only reason why I'm attracted to Lach Nuthin. There are lots of exciting things going on up there. It's like Disney World, Rome and Shanghai all rolled into one, minus the hotels, the rides, the Coliseum and extract of rhino horn. But who needs attractions when you have Bagpipes Fantastic? This is a huge summer event in the area, judging from the Lach Nuthin Gazette which covers Bagpipes Fantastic in front-page stories with headlines the height of the late and great, Harry Lauder.

 As well it should. Because Bagpipes Fantastic is nothing less than the largest haggis inflating, bagpipes playing tournament in the entire Highlands which attracts thousands of spectators. When that many people turn out to watch haggis being stuffed under the duress of incredible noise levels, then you know you're talking about an area with poor TV reception.

 Bagpipes Fantastic looks very exciting. The Gazette ran a front-page photo of this year's winning team - three men holding a haggis that is way too fat to resemble any self-respecting bagpipes. The Gazette article describes one of the winning stuffers as "a haggis guide, seminar speaker and author."

 Yes! Haggis seminars. Don't tell me Scotland is not a great country. Lach Nuthin also plays host to the Frigid Toe. In a stark departure from the concept of Bagpipes Fantastic which is a summer haggis stuffing tournament, the Frigid Toe is a winter haggis stuffing tournament. It gets its name from the fact that, if you spend enough time walking barefoot through the snow in a Highland glen while casually stuffing a haggis, eventually your toes become frigid, then frosty, and finally, footless.

But there is much, much more to the Highlands. There is also the annual Porridge Bowl which I am sure is everything the name implies. The Bailie of Inverclack, Chatty McTavish, informs me that her town also boasts some powerful attractions, including "the largest oat processing plant in the Northern hemisphere," and "the widest selection of porridge recipes on public display."

So call me crazy but I'm seriously pondering a trip to Inverclack. I could use some excitement not to mention some fresh air, the appeal of Chatty and a new approach to porridge. Tasting peat and burning oats while stuffing haggis with my ice cold toes has a certain attraction for someone who has been accused of being two sandwiches short of a picnic. It's the high road for me!

NO CONTEST

If there's one thing my mother studiously tried to avoid in her life, it was letting her son fight. Fight in a ring with gloves on I mean. Of course, I realise that boxing isn't fighting. It's allegedly sport. A sport for men who smell like bus seats and roam in a world of hurt.

My mother's abhorrence to fighting had its origins in commonsense. She instantly appreciated that boxing was the last resort of people whose brains failed to function properly. To my way of thinking, boys and bullies seemed to resort to fisticuffs when problems needed resolving at school. Someone got a bloody nose and went home crying. Dads invariably invoked, "You're a man now!"

Not all boys fought. Some of the more intelligent ones

avoided confrontations with an intellectual vigour belying their gender. They were called sissies, and now they are captains of industry.

My mother didn't want me to be combative. She didn't realise that aggressive posing began with the way you carried books at school. To effect the correct posture you had to lean back from the waist as though you were about to perform the limbo, thrusting your hips forward with your right hip protruding slightly more than the other. Upon this hip, you balanced your books. Walking in this way had the effect of a steam roller, nothing dared get in your way, not even the terrifyingly tough girls my neighbourhood produced with such alarming frequency. Sleep disturbers I used to call them.

The more aggressive you were, the more you leaned and the more your eyes narrowed. As a child who was extremely tidy - just begging for a fourpenny one in the kisser - I decided to develop a mean-eyed look too, to enhance my virility. To this day my mother's words of disapproval ring in my ears. Nevertheless I survived fourteen years of school with no hint of a playground scuffle. I consider this an accomplishment second only to representing the school at six different sports.

My mother and I never saw eye to eye on the noble art. She knew that professional boxing is a rough-and-tumble world in which at least a third of the rewards go to the manager while corner people specialise in voodoo magic potions and problematical substances. A sport with more than a century-long reputation for brutality and corruption, and a myriad of snake-oil promoters preying on young hopefuls from the streets. I didn't realise boxing is the last thing that man clings to as far as our instincts go. I could only appreciate that the bright lights are on you as you enter the ring. It's mano versus mano. There's nobody to blame but yourself. You're alone and exposed out there.

At school I fought my first of only three fights. My left jab and fast feet helped on two counts. My nose remained unbroken and I won on points. My mother's censure when she found out I barely survived. I soon realised I wasn't big enough or tough enough to be a boxer so I foolishly determined to be a minder. However, weighing in fighters, towering over the ringside school medical doctor during examinations, and consoling a seemingly punch drunk loser as he stepped from the ring was not to be my future line of work. My face was too pretty to blend in with the swollen-faces of school friends and the cauliflower-eared boxing fraternity. More than that, my mother intended to keep it that way.

Later in life I once met a second who was an ace "cut man". He had legs like a pair of milk bottles and looked as if he'd fought in one of the supporting bouts before the Cain and Abel championship showdown. He was the original crossword puzzle boxer. He entered the ring vertical and left horizontal. In retirement he was the type of devotee who carried a 5 kilo medicine ball in his lunch box. My mother simply refused to meet him.

The major obstacle to my boxing advancement wasn't really my lack of skill or toughness, but my name. With the example of the Astoria Assassin, Homicide Hank, The Manassa Mauler and The Tipton Slasher before me, how could Gordon Lomax succeed? It was my mother who guided me away from seeking fame and glory as Gory Gordon.

I even told her George I was a great fan of boxing. Royal patronage and the consequent snob value made no impression whatsoever. I pleaded that I would adhere to the Marquis of Queensbury rules. She was equally unimpressed. I was bombarded with strong hints that words like tussle, clinch, close quarters and no holds barred were to be for later years and more romantic endeavours.

Lots of people do things that aren't good for them. They drink. They smoke. They have unprotected sex. They use drugs. My mother's contribution to family happiness was to ensure her son didn't box, so leaving his brains unscrambled for the rest of his life. Or so she thought.

ALGEBRA LURKS

Let me begin by saying I feel that $x+y+4y-3(x-y) = 11y+3x$. Don't you agree? You see algebra has influenced me all my life because all my life I've been wondering what possible use has it been to me.

When I was at school I could glibly chat about exponents and wax eloquent on coefficients. I could conjugate, diagram and throw cold water on anything. I could also hold my own in a debate about whether an 8 is just two 3's kissing. More than that, I could charm the girls with my etchings of the binomial theorem Q.E.D.

Now many years later I've proved that algebra doesn't exist in the real world. By the way, it slipped my mind. The above equation is the secret recipe for my wife's latest stir fry. Like all you readers I took algebra at school because I had to, and because of that sinister fact, I can honestly advise all children to be honoured to do the same. You need to take it because...because...well, because I did, that's why.

In the real world you need to be familiar with the four basic maths functions, plus proportions and percentages. But not much else. You need to be able to work out that if Bob Estupido is driving a lorry that's 5 meters high and he approaches a bridge with a clearance of 4.7 metres, then he should at least let .3 of a metre of air out of his tyres.

You also need to know how to measure cups and spoonfuls in metric and imperial quantities if it's your intention to be appreciated as worldly. You need to know how to balance a cheque book. You need to know that if your neighbour makes £95,000 a year and you make £9,500, then you're a complete failure. More importantly, you need to know that if you owe your demanding bookie £1.000 and you've only got £64, you've got to find £936 worth of blood.

How did algebra influence my career? Well, algebra had a great influence on me because I knew as a professional sportsman and businessman I would never have to do algebra. It has also never been of any help to me in dealing with life's myriad crises. You don't need it, for example, to work out that a hum bug is a bee. And if, after a difficult quadratic equation, you determine that you are six years older than your birth date, start all over again.

Algebra was certainly no help when I returned from holiday to find a gale had blown down two trees in the garden. Algebra didn't give me a jump start when my battery went flat. And algebra couldn't provide even the least bit of solace when my favourite football team was relegated to the Fourth Division. Nor did algebra save the day when two courts at my Spanish tennis club succumbed to a sink hole of vast proportions. Perhaps I couldn't repair them because my equation was faulty.

Still, algebra is great training. It trains you to do algebra, and algebra does have its defenders especially teachers of algebra. At this point they are sick to the stomach and their pupils, dangerously under the influence of juvenile hormones, are gleefully aware of this controversy. To assuage those who feel algebra has a place in this world, I'd like to report it's alive and well, and living in the minds of all people capable of logical thought.

    Deep down, what I object to are those irritating word problems like: Alice is 44 years old and her son Aubrey is 19. When will Alice be 3 times older than Aubrey? Who cares? Alice and Aubrey will both be dead!

    One last thought for those algebra deficients. Someday it will creep into your life, insidiously and without warning. When that day comes, you must be ready and involve yourself in reasoning about relationships and operations using symbols. No, that doesn't mean making a diagram of your girl friend's leg in plaster.

    In my view, you'll need algebra to determine the apex of gradual age disintegration. According to my calculations the degenerative process is stemmed with a five-speed convertible blessed with a CD player and 8 cylinders and 215-horse power under the bonnet plus extra large numerals on the dashboard displays.

GOOSE BUMPS A LA GRIPPE

    I'm coming down with flu. It's not quite death. My neighbour Tom says, "You don't want to get it. It will knock you out of commission for at least ten days. And, if it gets bad, it will make you hate your socks." Thanks Tom, you're a brick.

    At least my wife, my Florence Nightingale, is on my side. She functions like a symphony - every piece in its place, perfectly timed and tuned. Homemade chicken soup topped with fresh foliage from the garden served on a lap tray that has side pockets for newspapers and magazines. She negates the view that flu has few rivals among marital stress factors.

As I lie abed with a temperature topping the Fahrenheit ton, I wonder if the flu virus is A, B or C. Is it Asian, Bolivian or Columbian? My temperature rises even more when I read that the greatest pandemic was just after World War One when over 20 million infected souls died. I reach for a further dose of analgesics and sedatives hoping I won't need an antibiotic for an infected lung.

A phone call from a concerned friend doesn't help. "There's a lot of it about," she assures my wife. What she really means is that no one has a clue what it is or how to treat it, and its associated goose pimples, properly.

At one point I thought " I was gonna digh!" My vengeful spleen cheered me on as any appreciative audience kept out of my way. Was my flu caused by wind current, thermonuclear inversion, a continental grippe or an ever-irritating and mobile germ? I'll never know. Perhaps it was just my turn to suffer. "I don't want to hear such talk," says my wife, mistress of the light diet with the lightly boiled egg.

When sick I feel I've the right to be snide. The right to make a blithe reference to a suicide doctor. The right to feel sorry for myself. With swollen eyes, red nose, raspy voice and unfamiliar clutter surrounding me, I begin to hate the sight of small bottles, paper handkerchiefs and multi-stained teaspoons.

I'm at the point where I remember these words - "in sickness and health" - and wonder if they really mean - "as long as you're healthy, slim, fit and don't develop unsightly mutations." I should know better. My wife really cares. To prove it, she whips me round to see the doctor.

"Your numbers are excellent," he says. What on earth does that mean? Ten toes, two arms, one mouth? "The medical profession first used the word influenza in 1743," he says.

Really! That cheers me up a lot. By this time I'm convinced doctors don't like sick people. "Just keep doing what you're doing, and drink a lot of grapefruit juice," is the doctor's parting comment. What that means is my wife has been on the right track all along. I knew she cared.

Although my eyes are still glassy, the nose sniffy and the body weak, I forget the fever, chills and headache, rise in a totter and head for the shower. I immediately feel better, return to my bed and prop myself up on the cool side of the pillows, and await the return of my Florence Nightingale who has gone to the supermarket, on her way back from playing tennis, to purchase their entire supply of grapefruit juice.

A litre of grapefruit juice later I'm refreshed and feeling psychologically better. I feel even better and on the way to extremely good health when my next litre is laced with a liberally applied vodka additive.

Suddenly the world's a different place. I've won my battle with the dreaded lurgi. Germ warfare is at an end. My bed is one of roses. It's as though I'd checked into the Savoy. My cup runneth over when I'm treated to an aromatherapy back rub administered by loving hands.

Of course, being a kindly chap, I'll forward all the tips and advice to combat your flu on request. But please find your own Florence Nightingale, mine's just too precious to pass on.

WEDDING ENSEMBLE

Ladies Outfitter was the type of family business I was born into. The fact that my parents specialised in wedding outfits was a source of immense interest to a growing boy.

Strangely, even at a tender age, I was involved in more

ways than one. As my father was colour blind, I had to decide when red wasn't green, and brown wasn't grey. With my mother doing the paperwork and alterations, and my father doing the buying and ironing, I inherited more than a few so-called non-masculine tasks as to the manner born.

If there was amusement to be had, it was when a wedding group came to the shop to select their wedding ensemble. There's nothing like trying on numerous dresses to make a girl feel beautiful. The maid of honour, in her metal pointed bra which seemed more like a weapon than a piece of clothing, tended to be over zealous. The other bridesmaids, for whom marriage was still a distant threat, had to cross their fingers and hope for the best. With the bride in a white cloud of nervous anxiety, it only needed a bevy of doting mothers to bring farce to the proceedings.

Most customers looked for dresses that wouldn't be too expensive, would be re-wearable in later life and wouldn't make any of their bodies look hideous. It was almost as painful as finding a figure fitting bathing suit. Rail upon rail of bowed, sparkling and shiny dresses were combed through as taffeta vied with satin.

Appearances varied from too prissy, too glitzy and too severe, to sheer downright horrible. It takes quite a lot of imagination to find the perfect dress for such an important occasion. My father's secret was to let his customers eliminate the worst while, deep down, he knew definitely what was the best for them. As they deliberated, he was the archetype psilologist. His trivial talk emphasised his ability as a natural linker of conversations. There was no shame in silly and shallow talk as long as it didn't become a way of life, and the till rang up a sale as the end product.

My mother, to offset her spouse's deficiency, told me to

tell the truth at all times as then I wouldn't have to keep remembering what I had said previously. My father proved that this thought didn't apply to him. After all, how could you tell the truth? If he had, his source of living wouldn't have survived. How could he tell it as it was to a maid of honour whose favourite colour was putty; to a bridesmaid who was built when meat was cheap; and to a bride, who when she put her bra on backwards, it fitted better?

The wedding party hoisted the massive creations on to their bodies as my father discreetly withdrew from the fitting-room. With a cry of: "Are you on?" he reappeared to grab hold of the excess material in the back and squeeze, to prove a fit of doubtful quality. Everyone would stare while trying to work out what it would look like if it actually fit, and wasn't apple green or dusky pink.

One by one the garments were ruled out for having unflattering waistlines, unflattering skirts and unflattering necklines. Mothers, whose lives had momentarily slipped their working-class moorings, sat pew-like in a row as they drank their cups of tea and nibbled biscuits. They uttered pearls of doubtful wisdom which proved that people who can be so nice to your face, can be lethal behind your back.

Of the future husband to his friends: "They're a lovely match. Jenny's lucky to have found someone with such good prospects."

Of the future husband in title-tattle back-street gossip: "His hands are like silk. They haven't done a proper day's work in their life."

Of the future bride to her friends: "A wonderful girl with such a beautiful disposition. She's a fine catch for any man."

Of the future bride in tittle-tattle back-street gossip:

"They're well suited. As he's a sexual virtuoso, it's no wonder she's become the outlet for his energies."

If only teacups could talk.

Then, all of a sudden, the ideal choice for the bride. A dress in whispering flowing material with an understated elegance. Meanwhile the bridesmaids are gathering voluminous dresses into folds while they lift and pull. They bunch. They tug. They get stuck as size 16's try to become size 12, and size 10's attempt to be size 8 or even smaller.

My father is patient as he knows more than anyone that more diets begin in dress shops with rear view mirrors than anywhere else. He expertly controls the panic emanating from women wriggling and squirming like belly dancers. "It can always be let out," he advised with trepidation. With self-satisfied smiles they manage to unwedge themselves and jerk the dresses off their bodies without splitting the seams. Everyone seems out of breath and stunned from the ordeal. They wonder why their bodies have swelled so massively since they last told a lie about their hip and bust sizes.

Sanity returns. Choices are finally made. There is a saying that a man always feels so outnumbered by his wife and her sister. My father never seemed out of control no matter how many women confronted him.

As for me, my parents legacy was that I have always loved the femininity of women in dresses. And, I insist that the fact I always carry a small pair of scissors to snip out the size has nothing to do with the way my clothes fit.

A NATIVE BY DEGREES

Some people are never satisfied. Greater Mancunians

still hanker for the days when they were Lancastrians. The transfer of name in 1974 only a year after Britain's entry into the European Community still festers. Being a native of Greater Manchester has a far more cumbersome appeal than being a Red Rose Lancastrian.

I haven't figured out whether native is a boast or a warning. If it's a sign of great pride or massive insecurity or maybe both? Have you to be born in an area to be a native? If so, that leaves many good people clubless. They live in an area and pay their taxes and fully absorb into society, but what do you call them?

It's high time to end the confusion by establishing official categories so everyone knows exactly where they stand. Words like founder, partner, member, helper and freeloader don't exactly fit the bill, but you get the idea.

Here are my proposed sticker categories to help you through the maze of which type of native you really are, based on my area of birth.

TRUE NATIVE - Born in Manchester, grew up there, left the city once but not for long and couldn't wait to get back. Never mistakes a crumpet for a pikelet or an Eccles cake for a flat currant cake. Knows only one person from Cheshire. Does not go near the seaside until July or August. Instinctively has the perfect pitch for the rustle of money. Learned patience as a child waiting for the pools of water to dry up after heavy rain so he could play "footy" with his pals in the street. Believes if you don't know what "lobscouse" is, you shouldn't be living there in the first place.

HONORARY NATIVE - born elsewhere but moved to Salford when young and has maintained continuous residency for at least 30 years. Still does not dare to venture an opinion while watching a Manchester City v Manchester United football match. Has not the slightest appreciation of what "Get stuck in" and the game plan "Kick anything that moves" mean. Has however learned respect by watching a wall of rain move across the hills like a black curtain. Has cultivated a deep intensity of feeling for Lowry pictures and the culture emanating from those dark satanic mills.

LIGHTWEIGHT NATIVE - Born in the area but grew up somewhere else and returned to Oldham as an adult. Years of residence less than ten. Doesn't really care who wins the annual Roses cricket war between Lancashire and Yorkshire because he's a Worcestershire fan. Has learned humility by listening to Pennine thunder so loud it rattles his thinking process. Does not yet fully appreciate the culinary treats of Alice Nutter's Pudding, Boggart's Brew and Dad's Delight.

NOUVEAU NATIVE - Born in old Lancashire. Moved away at the age of 7, but has been back in Rochdale less than five years. Dons a sweater any time the temperature drops below 20°C. Rushes out to buy candles, torch batteries and distilled water every time the weatherperson on TV breathes heavily. Believes fervently the damp air can be cured with hot spiced milk. Succumbs to the temptations of Nellie Johnson's Cake and Annie Fanny Pancakes on his annual visit to Belle Vue.

ASPIRING NATIVE - Born somewhere else, grew up and went to school somewhere else. Moved to Bolton a year ago on a bet that she lost. Doesn't really care who wins the region's derby football matches because she's really a golf and squash fanatic. Loses sleep worrying that the rain will wash away her hillside home with a view of Blackpool tower, and the bad light will affect her eyesight. As a consequence, she spends her spare time teaching her parakeet to recite epic poetry. Has no comprehension at all what "powfagged" means while the thought of having "a reet good do" never enters her mind. Is also totally ignorant that The Guardian was once the pride of the north as The Manchester Guardian.

ALIEN NATIVE - Born on Mars, grew up in the USA and landed in Bury six months ago. Invariably gets "nowt" confused with "bowt". Actually phoned his parents in an outer galaxy to tell them about an exotic local delicacy called Black Puddings. Has heard of the Hallé Orchestra but believes Besses O'th Barn Brass Band to be a figment of the imagination. Settling in well, though. Has a NATIVE bumper sticker on his space shuttle which bears the motto: "We've never heard of you either."

Coupled with the fact that I was born in the middle of this area in a place called Radcliffe, and having lived in Spain and the United States for the past 16 years, I appreciate the feeling of being a native by degrees. I seem to have traversed the six stages from true alien and back again which proves "there's nowt so queer as folk."

A CUT ABOVE THE REST

As my wife will testify freely in open court, I'm not a lawn mower man. It's not that I hate lawns. I don't. It's just that I think lawns are quite boring green things and I believe that maintaining and cutting them are tasks beyond the roles of normal human beings.

What do people think about when they cut grass? I soon realised cutting grass can be a cosmic experience. Under the spell of the humming combustion engine I plotted fiendish schemes as I laid my swathes of wrath.

In my heyday of grass cutting in moorland Yorkshire, I

thought about things I don't even consider at any other time. Things like how lawn mowing is more than a weekend habit. It's a tribal dance to celebrate the subjugation of the wild. Those thoughts - many of them nasty - were released by the fumes and noise of the power mower. They were nonlinear, spontaneous and mystically satisfying. They came from the same region of the brain that likes to discuss carburation and fuel injection or various routes to reach the south of France.

I soon realised that for people like me, mowing the lawn can be a dangerous time. Thoughts become heretical. Like why poison daisies and dandelions? Aren't they actually quite pretty? Once you're on this slippery meditative slope, there's no telling how far things can go. You get into a state where daydreams seem to make perfect sense. And this was the case with my hand held mower fantasy.

Wouldn't life be better clipping the blades of grass with surgical precision rather than bludgeoning them with crude horizontal rpm's? Wouldn't life be better burning calories instead of petrol?

There must be a reason nobody's doing this. I advance two theories. One, yesterday's lawn mowers won't cut today's lawns fast enough so we can get to the golf course on time. Two, and far more subtle, there's a section of a man's brain that holds transcendental sweet communion with small petrol engines. Even the wimpiest person would rather do it with an engine than without.

Take my neighbour, the one who hunts bats with a letter opener. He discussed every aspect of buying a new lawn mower, European v Japanese, mulcher v bagger, two-stroke v four-stroke. Everything that is, except whether or not it should have a motor to cut his lush and rampant grass. He settled on one with a low-drag aerodynamic magnesium fuselage with two forward speeds and one reverse. I asked could I try it. He bit his tongue hard enough to require stitches. His wife said: "You mean you'd like to borrow the Other Woman."

After my rebuttal I decided not to plump for a crazy ecological experiment but regained my poise with a mower of humble virtue which proved to be ugly, functional and not too comfortable. It was a contraption designed to punish with the ergonomics of a brush handle. It was a machine any scrap dealer would love and the lady at the jumble sale was glad to see the back of it.

Yet it cut more than tentatively. It reminded me of an old cricket bat that demanded just one more inning. Was it the answer to my unspoken, unconscious prayer? I imagined myself striding across the lawn like a suburban peasant applying appropriate, sensible technology to an aspect of daily life that, for me, had got out of balance. Emotionally, I was back to the reality of true Nature.

My neighbour, the turfaholic from across the road, the one who specialises in using electric tools with cordless extension cords, came to scoff.

"Do bubbles come out when you push that?"

I soon appreciated that contemplation takes place on a different plane when you're behind a lawn mower. As there was no steady hypnotic vibration to numb my senses, I found myself thinking about the actual grass and surrounding terrain. My cutting patterns became different as angry red circles formed on the palms of my hands. There would be blisters. The gratifying meditation had come with a price. Two thick gloves later I'd decided. No more grass cutting for me. I've now coddled and spoiled myself by moving to a house with a lovely garden but no lawn.

Sorry Mr. Budding, I've forsaken further use of your

1830 invention, but worse still, I'll never make my road's precision lawn mower drill team for the upcoming County Fair. At least I now have time to play more lawn tennis - excuse me, tennis - in the growing season.

WHO NEEDS HAIR?

As tastes change and as the line between masculinity and femininity continues to blur, I have established a firm position. I have a head almost like a cue ball.

Having lost nearly all nature's foliage but not the virility that goes with it, I now present a far sharper silhouette with much improved performance. My testosterone having turned into dihydrotestosterone has converted my hair follicles to the "vellus" era or "yuk" stage of life. I know what happened, but not the evolutionary reasons for it. I also know that I'm at the cutting edge of life as three-quarters of men between the ages of 40 and 60 are trichologically challenged.

To be honest, when I started to lose my hair in my early thirties, I only accepted it because it seemed to be a family trait and therefore held no fear for me. Now no fringe, sideburns or fuzz offend the eye. To me baldness = maintenance free and the consolation of reiterating the legend of the bald libido.

Baldness is normal to hundreds of millions of men. Some are bare on top with a fringe on the side and back, which makes them the barber's 10-minute delight. And some shamelessly let the side fringe get long and comb those few sad strands across the bare top. But baldness is, along with your height, eye colour or the size of your feet, a matter of genetics. Unless of course you had a lush head of hair before an enraged girlfriend plucked out every wisp of hair in a fit of anger. You couldn't very well expect the man to say, "Well, I've no hair because my fabulous live-in lover and I disagreed over which TV film to watch, and she plucked my entire thatch."

As happened to me, it is far more likely a man's hair simply starts falling out. It either recedes at the forehead, which is the most graceful way to lose it, or on top, creating that empty round spot which is less desirable unless you are well over six feet tall and nobody can see it.

The arrival of baldness can be traumatic, especially for men who are young and have got used to equally young attractive women saying, "I really like men with hair like yours." Their minds are soon beset by stultifying melancholy, but as a great philosopher once put it, "Hey, doo-doo happens, man, dig? So be cool. Don't worry about your self-esteem, worry about your character." After all, since I became bald, I get lots of grudging appreciation. "Grass doesn't grow on a busy street, does it?" and the far more appealing, "Well, at least you've got a solar panel for a sex machine up there."

That's the way it is. Just as some people become nearsighted or farsighted, or have prominent noses, big ears or poor hand-eye coordination, others lose their hair. Some young man staring with terror at a dozen hairs in his sink might disagree, but there are outstanding benefits to baldness.

For one thing, it certainly speeds up life as it makes you more aerodynamic. For another, a young man who knows baldness is a family trait will know to get married before he looks like dear old Dad. If he's confident enough to wait until he's really bald he will know his partner is not a ninny concerned only with appearances, but is an intelligent, serious type who gives deep thought to a man's net worth.

One fact outweighs all other considerations. There is nothing more time- and cost-efficient than baldness. It takes me about 2 to 3 seconds to prepare my head in the morning. I haven't owned a comb for 20 years and spend nothing on sprays, lacquers, shampoo or a blow dryer. In contrast a good friend spends a minimum of 30 minutes a day at home and in the health club titivating his hair. I've added it up for him. It's about 182 hours a year. That's more than a week of preening! And if he keeps his hair for the next 20 years, he will have spent 150 days or more than 21 weeks using his hair dryer, brush and comb plus countless different "beautifiers" tending his thatch.

If you think of the zillions of hours that are worked each year by the millions of men who are over-haired, it's an awesome economic waste. As we are in a highly competitive global economy perhaps the government should introduce a law requiring all men to have their heads shaved each day. If modern sportsmen can accept being extravagantly tonsured, all you men out there can do it.

If the thought attracts you, the act of doing it might well induce pilomotor reaction. I've no worries. I've not many hairs to stand on end anyway.

DIETARY GRAPE RACING

I've been doing pretty well on my all consuming diet. I've eliminated the fats, ostracised the red meats, sentenced sugar to permanent exile and memorised what alcohol tastes like. I've also acquired a feeling of being semi-holy in the way the self-righteous dieter so often feels.

I'm a man serious about his diet. I'm committed to my whole wheat bread for breakfast, fruit for lunch and tuna for dinner. I'm totally beyond temptation. As a serious exerciser I do a six-mile-a-day run topped off with a couple of sets of tennis. I've totally left behind the need for a personal trainer to sculpt my body.

However, I do admit I've the inner desire to gorge myself. To feel guilt-ridden as I nibble! Oh, the joy! So, I can hear you say, how does he keep wicked desires at bay? Simply by following the famed Lomax approved dietary tips which will revolutionise your life.

1. Learn to push yourself away from the table by fixing fast-roll castors on every chair.
2. Store snacks out of reach, preferably in the attic or cellar. If possible get rid of the refrigerator to France.
3. Make mealtime overindulgence difficult by eating only in the shower or while standing halfway up a ladder.
4. Maintain an unshakeable mental image of why you are dieting. Stick a photo of the most obese person you know on the kitchen wall. Someone fat to the 10th power who is an ambulatory bucket of lard.
5. Learn to feel guilty as guilt burns off fat at the rate of 100 calories per hour.
6. Eat slowly. Nutritionists have found it takes the brain a full 30 minutes to appreciate the stomach is full. In reality, thighs and hips get the message in a millisecond.
7. Keep plenty of celery and carrots handy. The stalks can get into many places you can't reach with your tongue and the carrots will help you see the snacks you've hidden in the attic.
8. Use sports equipment to control your consumption of desserts. For instance eat that piece of death by chocolate with a snooker cue.
9. Put the most nourishing, least attractive food at the

front of the refrigerator. It will make it more difficult to get to that gateau at the back.
10. Men, whenever you can, wear a dinner jacket to the dinner table. You can hide a multitude of gluttonous sins simply by tightening the cummerbund.

My final tip demands a high ratio of intelligence and sporting knowledge. I'm referring to microwave grape racing. This will become so compulsive all thought of eating is banished from your besotted mind.

You put a film of sunflower oil on the bottom of your microwave oven. You then line up 6 grapes - 2 red, 2 green and 2 black (all seedless of course) - against one side, with the hole pointing at the wall. Turn the microwave on full power which heats the grape's interiors until steam shoots out of the holes. The grapes turn into little organic supercharged engines that rocket across the lubricated floor.

The most import facet of this form of racing is that the sport is performed under carefully controlled conditions, namely, when your spouse isn't at home! I assure you it's an all enveloping experience when the grapes begin to move and excitement reaches fever pitch as your favourite grape its the opposite wall first.

Occasionally, some of the grapes seem to lack the will to win - I blame the quality of soil in the vineyard - as they either spin in circles like helicoptric whales or explode on the starting line. The thrills of radiation induced entertainment can be addictive. The process of cleaning the microwave gives you even less time, in your spouse's absence, to overindulge, as the thought of food is totally banished from your mind. One cardinal rule of betting however. On no account bet that if the green grape number 2 wins for example, before the next race you can have a ten minute break attacking the de luxe ice cream languishing in solitary freezer confinement. Remember, if you don't take the first bite, your diet and figure will remain inviolate. You'll be a better person for it.

One last thing. Put your money on one of the black grapes, they seem to have more thrust.

FLOCKING FROM ALL DIRECTIONS

To become the most attractive woman in the world when you're away from home, all you have to say is: "I think there's something wrong with my car." Even as these words flow from my fingertips, I feel thousands of men salivating at the notion: "Something wrong with her car? Could it be the battery? Perhaps the ignition? Gawd, isn't she lovely!"

The very word "ignition" has overtones which render the average family newspaper into pornographic literature. The word makes otherwise respectable family men temporarily abandon their wives and do naughty, unregenerate things.

Now I appreciate sex should not be introduced into internal combustion problems but it's always there, latent and waiting. Sadly, I'll admit that if the woman is in her fresh salad days rather than laid up in lavender, the lack of horsepower turns more readily into a surfeit of manpower.

In life's pattern every woman's car is supposed to go into a mystery stall at least once in her driving career, especially on a wet and gloomy day in the middle of a narrow lane. As you slow down, lower the window and lean your head knowledgeably, you hear the most seductive words you've heard since you were married: "I think there's something wrong with my car." Immediately every male motorist within a radius of two miles hones in on the immobile vehicle addled by the alluring, musty smell of leaking oil and Chanel Number Five. Usually that leads to a serious convocation at a busy crossroads. The pulling power of a woman in a broken down anything is extraordinary and is the envy of Hollywood directors and Drury Lane theatre producers.

Once at the spot of inaction the beguiling helpless smile takes over. Strong men become as putty. The woman is surrounded by experts on the dynamics of interaction which results in a lot of waffling and little in the way of accomplishment. There are certainly more live wires outside the car than under the bonnet.

Words like thrust, compression and impulse plus phrases like: "May I make a suggestion?" and "I think your resistance is low," are studiously avoided as the imagery of these words can only jeopardise vehicular resuscitation. The centre of attraction should be the car, but it isn't. The theoretical male superiority in these matters is nullified by figments of the imagination and unverified suppositions. "It could be the coil," and "Well, there's definitely no spark." (except in his eyes of course). Inane remarks abound and smooth operators advance outrageous puns. "They don't make cars like they auto!" Platonic ideas are formulated and lead to the only situation I know in which a broken down car becomes a transport of delight. Friendships are kindled but don't progress into anything more when mechanical theories run riot. It's as well to realise that some, if not all men, need flirtation.

Entire fire services, on their way to a fire in progress, come to a halt to discuss the Mystery of the Faulty Ignition like erstwhile Perry Masons. To make matters worse, the police usually arrive late and lay out a series of phallic looking cones around the motionless car.

But men too can have a "breakdown" if confronted by a

real man-baiter. Beware the red or white immovable jalopy. The former colour signifies fieriness and devilment,, the latter innocence and purity. Before you know it, this driver is usually the enticing intermediary between two men who've become impaled on the totally irrelevant subject of which wax should be employed for maximum weather protection. Watching two male red deer locking antlers in the rutting season would have achieved the same effect upon this woman's fluttering girlish heart.

    I think I know what most of these "helpers" are after and it's definitely not marriage or even cohabitation. Let me be generous and advance the view that all and sundry are on an ego trip with dinner overtones. Don't forget that I'm from a generation where a double date meant that two men in a van were going fishing.

    One thought does cross my mind though. Why do hundreds of flattering women not appear at my door when I utter those sensuous words: "My computer screen has frozen, And what's that damn bomb sign mean?"

    Life is so unfair.

GUEST CONTROL

    It's great to get together with old friends to dine, gab, giggle, catch up and reminisce, but a steady stream of them can leave you frazzled. Central Florida, my home for several years, is an area everyone seems to want to visit and is definitely, according to the old adage, a location where fish and visitors go off after three days. An area which, if global warming continues and the polar ice caps continue to melt, will soon be under thirty fathoms of water.

The natural resources of this beautiful paradise are confined to sand, silt, flotsam, jetsam and the notorious amourite, a fossil derived from decayed squashed love bugs. This holiday melting pot encourages 36 per cent of its people to work in the hospitality industry while the other 64 per cent face the dangers of houseguests, mildew, air conditioning problems and insect repellents.

You can run yourself ragged trying to be the perfect host and mapping things out for your guests the whole time they are with you. As far as we are concerned .... when in Rome .... and that means when company comes, they adjust to OUR lifestyle and not the other way around. If guests can't do without their favourite brand of this or that for a week or so, they shouldn't have left their own shores in the first place.

My wife and I have two rules. We insist that "guests of guests may not bring guests" and, inconsiderate guests are NEVER invited again even if we have a real guilt trip by finding it difficult to say no. If they feel miffed, that's just too bad.

As living in Florida makes potential innkeepers of us all, here are the giveaway signs of the welcome and unwelcome guests. Readers of my column, the sophisticated and intelligent of the world, will instantly recognise which is which. First words: "Well, what time will you be getting up tomorrow to drive us to Disney World?" and "We've already made reservations for dinner tonight, our treat." Final words: "You must come and stay with us sometime." and "Here are the keys to our place in Bath, use it when you're in the UK."

The whole scenario is based on the premise that none of us is actually bold enough to tell guests that they are unwelcome. We are just too damn polite. However, for people in dire straits and in need of remedial guest-inhibiting tips may

I suggest the following.

One, sprinkle the guestroom with food particles a couple of days before the anticipated arrival. Marching cockroaches are not an attractive sight.

Two, serve native specialities at the dinner table such as Spanish moss soup, lovebug paté and water hyacinth salad.

Three, form a Neighbourhood Guest Watch group which can come to your assistance by feigning drunkenness, making passes at your guest's spouse and kidnapping their children if absolutely necessary.

I can also thoroughly recommend this three day itinerary.

Day One - a picnic in the Everglades especially between May and October when guests are likely to fall victim to heat prostration.

Day Two - go to the beach and while frolicking about half-naked tell your guests, because of Florida's unique climatic conditions, it's impossible to get sunburned.

Day Three - slap them on their toasted back, put them in a boat (especially if they can't swim) and encourage the catching of one of those shadowy floating logs in the nearby lake.

If all else fails, you can endorse a walking tour of Miami with passports, purses, wallets and handbags placed in prominent positions. Grasping these points is absolutely essential for guaranteeing your guest's visit is brief and altogether pitiful. Frazzledom will be avoided.

As I sit beneath vapour trails in a cobalt blue sky eating grilled quail wrapped in bacon with the barbecue sizzling invitingly, please don't be envious. With key lime pie hovering tantalisingly in the background you probably won't appreciate the joys of 100 per cent humidity anyway. Have a nice stay!

GIGG LANE

It was a cold grey November day exactly 58 years ago that my grandfather took me to wartime Gigg Lane, Bury to join 11,000 other hardy souls who anticipated rich entertainment for their price of admission. As always the local Silver (one up on Brass) band rendered warming Sousa-like marches before the doughty opponents took the field.

In spite of the war, association football continued on a geographical basis to save fuel and travel. Players varied from week to week with famous international players appearing for the lowliest of teams because they happened to be stationed near that town. On that marvellous, crisp afternoon, Stanley Matthews, the golden boy and the wizard of dribble, trod the finest playing surface in England on behalf of Blackpool, the visiting team and League North champions.

In those days, long before soccer hooligans, it was absolutely safe for an eight-year-old to stand on the spacious terraces and gaze adoringly at his heroes. The mixed friendly crowd looked older because of their sombre, wartime clothing, muffled appearance and a surfeit of fallen arches through standing for many years on the wet concrete. They were living proof of what loyalty to a cause meant.

My grandfather always watched Bury's games with his brother, known to me as Uncle Dick, in the enclosure which was directly in front of the main stand where the "big nobs" sat. As a kindness he took me to the Boys Only Stand, away from the drifting tobacco smoke, placed some lubricating toffees in my hand to ward off the icy wind and left me amongst those noisy enthusiasts, my eyes aglow with anticipation.

Ten players dressed in tangerine and white; ten Bury players in their traditional white shirts and navy blue shorts; both goalkeepers in woolly green. Three o'clock. The referee's whistle blows. The hairs standing up on my arms and legs betray my tingling anticipation. Only falling in love would later beat this experience!

The action was intense, the skill overwhelming.... trapping, heading, passing, shooting - all leading to reflex saves by the men in green. Players tackled like tractors, and I can clearly recall the blood on some of those white shirts. Yes, sport is war minus the ordinance. As the frenetic cheering of the local boys was diverting my riveted attention, at half-time with the score one all, I made my way to the enclosure through a forest of cloth caps, mufflers, steamy mugs of tea, mushy peas and Holland's meat pies, to cries of "make way for the little 'un!"

Indulgent smiles from the elderly brothers greeted my arrival. My grandfather, stolid, quiet and strongly opposed to alcohol, my Uncle Dick, wispy, more volatile and glad to take a surreptitious nip from his strategically placed hip flask on the blind side of my grandfather's seeking eye. How I worshipped them and the character world they represented.

As the players took the field for the second half, I was assured that Bury would win because they had a lion-hearted warrior, an Irish lad called Gorman, whose boundless enthusiasm inspired his team. More than that he played left-back and he stuck to Matthews like a leech with such verve that the maestro was reduced to ineffectiveness. A voice in the crowd, the owner of which couldn't stand players who didn't sweat blood, bellowed at a player who missed an easy ball, "You're as much use as a chocolate teapot!" Criticism can't get more derogatory than that.

Now it was two goals each with five minutes left to play and the crowd were urging their favourites forward for one final supreme effort. Then, after a bout of inter-passing, and a backheel of magical skill, the ball bulged the back of the Blackpool net. In a split second I turned to see the brothers stranded like ghosts in the middle of a conversation they'd forgotten before caps were joyously lifted to expose balding pates to that cold, but now warm, grey, but now bright, November day.

The walk home was full of sprightly chatter and going over the details in the evening paper was the cream on the cake. Much better than a press report which read like an obituary to a loved one after a defeat. Yes, Bury had really won. Life was golden and the war effort would be enhanced all through the following week.

In retrospect I learned two sporting truths that day. A winning team is its own marketing tool, and the greatest contribution Britain has made to the national life of countries all over the world was teaching people how to play football.

From that delicious, victorious moment at 4.45 p.m., whatever I did or wherever I roamed, I was a Bury - nay, a Shaker - supporter for life.

MASCULINE MOTION

Men who dance have always made me nervous. Even when they've got all their clothes on and they've got women for partners. It doesn't seem to me like the kind of thing somebody else ought to be watching.

So when I accidentally happened - that's another story -

on a male dance revue the other week, I approached the task with all the enthusiasm of someone who's been asked to identify a body.

As a writer, I convinced myself that it's my duty to be broad-minded, to cover a wide variety of events and to eat heartily from the buffet table of life. The Ultimate Male Revue featured the combined talents of Dr. Smooth, Kid Cholesterol, Agent XXXX and the Kool Fat Kat, a mere 1,000 kilos of sloppy fat dough.

These four mountains of flesh moved, if you can call it that, to catchy and effective tunes. In other words, boring, repetitive and loud music. The troupe, I believe a troop would be a better word, demanded wild women to encourage their complex, unexpected and sexually stimulating rhythms. It was not to be a plié on a tightrope type of evening.

Noise is an essential part of the inhibition numbing process. When it gets loud enough, people think other people can't see how silly they're acting. And, on these occasions, it's socially acceptable to do anything up to and including the silliest thing the drunkest person you've ever seen has already done.

The ladies became wilder, the lights went down, the music was turned up and the show shifted gear into weird. The heavyweight dancers were in sequined dinner shirts, bow ties and suspenders. Two of them attempted a pas de deux of questionable quality which, to a great roar from the assembled multitude, ended as a dramatic tumbling with adagio variations. Sustaining the lift had proved extremely difficult. The audience who would be normal rational women in daylight, went through all the stages of infection ranging from critical connoisseurship to advanced hysteria. At moments like these women seem oblivious to the fact that they should never revere a man whose belt buckle is bigger than his head.

The mood became more frenzied as the four dancers increased their gyrations into more pacy, suggestive invitations to dance. This was not a night you could hide in the corps de ballet. Everything was hanging loose. A clapping hands flamenco transformed into a fandango with castanets touching sexual organs in triple time. Truly a dance macabre with erotic gestures of mime.

As the music slowed the bumping and grinding between the dancers and the audience continued, but the overall effect was more like the appreciation you have for someone operating a bulldozer in a limited space.

Each dancer had a solo. One as a sailor, another as a caveman. The policeman actually fell over which caused the biggest laugh of the evening. The final dancer, Kool Fat Kat, with the strut of a phallic symbol, appeared dressed as a steel worker and undressed as a male nurse. His belly had a life of its own and it didn't look friendly. The women unbelievably stuffed tens and fivers into every available orifice and shrieked away happily as if they'd just won the Lottery.

It was not an inspiring night for a devotee of the English Folk Dance & Song Society. The smoke, the noise, the bawdiness was manna for the demented audience. How could their man at home compete with such rampant versatility? The ninety minute carnal escapade was beyond analysis. How to analyse next week's female blancmange wrestling, I'll leave to someone else.

At least the evening showed that this type of dancing is a locomotion that gets nowhere, rather like the progress of a parrot in a small cage. I know it's none of my business, but if I was asked for my opinion, all the dancers ought to get out of the business while still at the bottom. However, the tips seemed more than generous.

As for the women, they seemed to enjoy themselves with the compassion of exterminators on the prowl.

IN ONE EAR AND OUT THE OTHER

It happened when I wasn't looking. My attention wandered for just a moment, and, suddenly, to my horror, it had started.

The aging process!

Hastily, abruptly, instantly, call it what you will, the gentle character lines on my face had deepened into trenches leaving me looking like a very old prune. I consoled myself with the thought that men become distinguished as they age. Not being a woman, I don't need special instruments to apply make-up deeply into the furrows. I'm equally fortunate with clothes. As men are basically shaped like rectangles and require little variation in style, fabric or colour, it means that old men can wear the same clothes as younger men as body changes wrought by gravity are hidden. For the unlucky woman, it's a case of obscuring crêpey necks, drooping bust lines and thickening hips with orthopaedic, not gossamer silk, lingerie and subtler use of style and skirts.

Fortunately, as we get older, we all seem to laugh more easily, and we can indulge ourselves in ways we never could when all our energy was given to our families. Unless you're suffering from a vanity freefall, who cares how we look? "I care how I look!" says my wife as she reads this paragraph. I ignore the signs of rebellion as she's just brought me a cup of coffee and one single succulent (I'm on a diet) biscuit. I have my price. I can be bribed.

In my experience, the biggest aging problem is remembering.

"Her name is on the tip of my tongue. Didn't we meet her at the Fairbank's last Christmas?"

You must have used that expression or a variation of it many times as the years pass. There's no sure way to tell when I first heard the phrase, but from somewhere deep in memory's fog I seem to hear my grandma verbalising it, trying to recall the name of a neighbour long dead. This was back in the days when I was head high to the oilcloth on her kitchen table.

"It's on the tip of my tongue," grandma is saying, "it'll come to me when Nelson gets his eye back and our Jack washes his neck. I know it as well as I know my own name." Well, obviously she didn't, did she?

The phrase "tip of my tongue" is cleverly and poetically constructed to define a common shortcoming. Having had a high, formal education, why is it, at crucial moments, the bulk of my vast accumulated data deserts me? The information I need, instead of being at my fingertips, ends up on the tip of my tongue. At times it's downright embarrassing, like when I do finally come up with the answer, I forgot what I was talking about anyway!

What does bother me is not being able to remember the names of certain familiar items and people quickly. The name of every character actor I see on TV or the silver screen invariably escapes me, and I console myself with the thought that he probably doesn't know my name either.

This deficiency leads to serious fretting. How can I, at the snap of a finger, remember everything that will keep my mind as fit as a .... as a .... ? Gawd, it gets worse!

A small success is triumph indeed. We all need one to spruce up an aging day. To paraphrase Shakespeare: Ah, the tingle when at last the word rolls trippingly off the tip of the tongue. With me at all times as scant consolation are the words of that wonderful comedian George Burns ... "Aging isn't so bad when you consider the alternative."

IRREGULAR QUESTIONS AND QUESTIONABLE ANSWERS

My writing philosophy is quite simple. If you have good language skills, you will be respected and admired, whereas if you clearly have no clue about grammar or vocabulary, you could become President of the United States. So with the aid of questions posed by erudite readers and answered to the best of my limited ability, I hope to shed light on current thinking in the world of words.

Q: As I, am never sure, when, do you use ,commas?
A: The question of punctuation has always posed problems. By and, large you should use a comma, whenever you have a need, to pause for breath, in the middle of, a sentence (I've just, returned from, a cross-country, run.) Witness the example: "So me and Alice were out shopping and she ate three huge fatty fudge cakes which is why her backside is the side of an old Volvo."

Q: Why do doctors when they are around their patients always use the word "infarction" as often as possible?
A: I have often wondered that myself especially when my in-growing toenail was once described as an infarction. It has something to do with their long university training and similar unmanly practices.

Q: Have you any idea what is grammatically wrong with this sentence? "Walking down the street, the sun shone brightly."
A: This is a classical example of what grammarians call a pluperfect connubial imprecation, which, in simple terms, means that it violates government health-warning laws. The statement fails mainly on the grounds that if you live in Hartlepool the words do not apply. However should you live in Eastbourne the politically correct wording should be: "Walking down the street, the sun shone brightly, which can cause skin cancer."
Q: Where is Eastbourne?
A: It's a resort on the south coast where busloads of tourists go to enjoy the unique experience of meeting and mingling with other tourists, sometimes from completely different buses.
Q: Is this the correct spelling of the word "nomenclature"?
A: Who the hell cares as long as I don't forget my own name?
Q: What is the correct description for someone who talks too much?
A: He or she has tongue enough for ten rows of teeth.
Q: In the phrase "Pat-a-cake, pat-a-cake, baker's man." Does it mean the baker's man is actually back there patting the cakes?
A: Take it from me he simply loves his work. Any sign of affection must surely improve the product.
Q: What is the subtle way to describe a not-overly intelligent person?
A: He or she's got the engine running but there ain't nobody driving.
Q: Why is a refrigerator called a "re"-frigerator?

A: Because it should be used only for foods that have been frigerated previously.
Q: What if they have not?
A: Then you have a serious risk of infarction.
Q: How should you describe a stingy person?
A: As one who is tighter than bark on a tree.
Q: What is the difference between love and lust?
A: If two people on a Friday night date are still together at 4 a.m. on Saturday, that's lust. If they are still together at noon on Sunday, that's love. If they're still together at noon on Monday, call a dentist. Their braces are locked.
Q: What is the best way to describe a drought?
A: It's so dry the trees are bribing the dogs.
Q: Why do men prefer to eat with their fingers?
A: If you need a fork, you need a plate, so you need a table to put them on, then a chair to sit at the table. Before long, you're living in a house with a woman and a bunch of kids and a dog that demands you take it for walkies when you don't feel like it.
Q: What phrase best describes a lethargic person?
A: He or she was born lazy and reared tired.
Q: What is the difference between a lunch and a luncheon?
A: When you're invited to lunch you sit down, eat and talk to someone. At a luncheon, you sit down, eat and someone talks to you, usually from behind a lectern and usually with no polite concept of time.
Q: Can you flagrantly pad out the end of this column with real-life examples of thoughts which can help to throw light on life's quandaries?
A: Certainly. Padding is what I've been doing for years starting with my very first school exam. Four thoughts

come immediately to mind:
If you try to fail, and succeed, which have you done?
Why is the alphabet in that order?
Do infants enjoy infancy as much as adults enjoy adultery
If you spin an oriental man in a circle three times, does he become disoriented?

The writing tip of the day is for those with a potential for being arrested for showing lack of emotion and wish to adopt a more macho disposition: When writing a business letter or other professional communication, always conclude with a strong action statement that shows you mean business.

WRONG: "Sincerely."
RIGHT: "Looking forward to playing football with your spleen."

The conclusion of all conclusions surely belongs to an undertaker friend of mine. He always signs himself: "Eventually yours."

A COLD REALIST

Talking to a friend of mine a few weeks ago who was visiting relatives, I was struck by his attitude to low temperatures. Cold weather, in other words. Charlie was over with his wife from their home in Spain and the cold bothered them. The strange thing was, in my opinion, it wasn't cold. And having lived in Spain and Florida I have a valid judgement on the matter.

As a boy brought up in the heart of industrial Lancashire, that land of many cultures, mostly throat, I reckon my friend is just plain soft. In 1947 terms, a sissy of the first degree. All Charlie seemed to do was sit around in a huddle fighting to keep warm against sub-zero temperatures. Sub-zero? When I spoke to him it was 16°C and climbing! Charlie said that if it got any colder his eyes would begin to water and the tears would freeze to his face. Spoiled rotten I call it.

Charlie, born in Oldham on a grey cold November day suitable for cotton weaving, had obviously forgotten how he had once sat like a plump dumpling at Boundary Park watching his 'Latics snorting clouds of January steam like fire-breathing dragons. He seemed oblivious to having been raised in an area where you glove it or leave it, a region so cold that you had to jump start your children in the morning. Now all Charlie could do was talk in awe of the Spanish sunshine. Gone from his memory was the day as kids we took nearly one hour to eat a February ice cream because we were afraid our tongues would stick to it.

There was much to learn about the cold as children. Could it get so cold your fingers would fall off? How could you ensure hot tea retained its heat for a half-time warmer at the Saturday game? Charlie had conveniently forgotten the days when he wore thick gloves made out of material called wool. Slipped from his mind were the joys of clearing snow and making a path to the front gate for the grateful postman. Salting and sanding followed by murky, clinging, industrial stained slush had long gone from his memory.

We were children of pre-central heating days. Children who had no notion of the future merits of expedition weight thermal underwear. Boys who would never know until adulthood that duck-belly feathers were called down. In the North of England, a geographical area which protects the South of England from the vagaries of Scottish weather, and protects Scotland from the excesses of the South of England way of life, we accepted cold as the delight of winter and the herald of Spring. We thrived on it.

Later in the year my wife and I had the pleasure of visiting Charlie in Spain. There he was, still at 16°C, sitting in his long johns and M & S sweater while I lounged in T-shirt and shorts. His wife suffers from becoming chilly and going inside. Her sister in Liverpool suffers from Spanish phone calls extolling the virtues of the Iberian climate. Once you move abroad it has to be perfect to the folks back home or you look a complete prat for going in the first place.

Still warm, I sit outside reflecting.

"Charlie, do you remember as a kid when it was so cold, polar bears were in the majority on Oldham town council?"

"By 'eck I do," Charlie replied, "even in later years it was so cold we had to leave the fridge door open to keep warm."

Touché!

I will simply put Charlie's aversion to cold down to aging and thinning blood. He had a plus to his life however. On winter mornings in his part of Spain, you can at least wake up with the smell of orange blossom in the air.

PRESS SECRETARIES

I spent the better part of yesterday trying to get in touch with a politician and wound up instead talking with the politician's press secretary.

Let me put it this way. None of the questions I asked were answered directly, and the answers I got left me with so many other questions that I forgot my original questions.

The duty of press secretaries is to communicate. They do this by taking a simple yet exalted thought from a politician who couldn't make a profit on a charity stall where the goods are supplied free, and convert it to gibberish while delivering it to the media. It is then converted back to a simple thought that can be further misunderstood by the general public. The exalted yet simple politician and the press secretary then both claim everything was taken out of context. A good press secretary will teach their boss everything the boss will later deny knowing. It creates an impression of paralysis by analysis. In this art form words fit like oranges on an apple tree and are then fed to the public slaughterhouse by old fruits like me.

Aspiring press secretaries attend a special high altitude school where they learn the 4 -ates .... equivocate, vacillate, obfuscate and understate. They then have their active verbs surgically removed and are assigned to the various seats of government where they grasp any thread to spruce up the dingy image of their master's frayed dogma. Their "spin" is so deep and far reaching that it can even make earthworms dizzy.

Their curriculum has three main planks. Knowing how to save the ship when it's sinking. How to make hard fought delaying decisions against time. And finally, how to propagate the main formula of success which is - if A = success, then the formula $A = X + Y + Z$, where X is work, Y is play and Z is keep your mouth shut.

For a true appreciation of the craft I need only consider how press conferences in the past might have gone had the modern press secretary been around.

Monsieur Bidet, press secretary for the French Revolution, fielding this question from reporters in 1793.

"No one has seen Marie Antoinette for days. Rumour has it that she is dead. Would you comment on this?"

"She does not feel well. I can say with confidence that she has never rested more quietly. That is all I can say at this point in time."

A statement in 1912 from the press spokesman of the White Star shipping line.

"Early reports indicate that the Titanic on her maiden voyage has been negatively impacted by an unidentified mass of solidified water. Some 1,500 passengers have since failed to attend the captain's dinner party."

"Was that crushed or block ice?"

"Block, then crushed."

Captain Twaddle, the United States Army press officer conducting a briefing after the Battle of the Little Big Horn in 1876.

"General Custer and his men have just completed a heated debate with a minority group that has been trespassing on our land for nearly 1,000 years. The outcome has resulted in 226 job openings in the Seventh Cavalry."

And finally, Napoleon's press secretary in 1814.

"At the urging of England, Russia and their allies, the Emperor Napoleon has kindly consented to take a well-deserved island vacation."

As we all know politicians are the only people in the world who create problems and then campaign against them. This has to be explained away by press secretaries in an honest?, sincere?, charming?, adorable?, folksy? manner. They offer platitudes and placatory noises to the still gullible public.

Fully realising that the very first press secretary was a smooth-talking serpent, I'm now in full training for the highest ranking press secretary's job in Britain.

Would I mislead you over this?

ARE CROOKS BECOMING MORE INCOMPETENT?

I'm a worried man. According to the latest government statistics, evidence is growing of an alarming decline in the quality of the nation's criminals.

Apparently a robber in Chester-le-Street elected to wear a disguise, which was a good idea, since he was a regular customer at the Building Society he was about to rob. The problem was the particular disguise he picked.

An American style baseball cap on top of his normal unshaven face. For some reason the robber believed that this would make him unrecognisable. Despite the disguise, the staff instantly recognised the baseball-capped bandit who ran away and was later arrested by the police. Whether he tried to make himself invisible when the police arrived, by putting his hands over his eyes, I'm not sure but I would not be at all surprised.

Another example of a criminal not being the sharpest quill on the porcupine concerns a man who was arrested in Kings Lynn for robbing a restaurant and two banks. Do you think the police found fingerprints? Did detectives use ultra-modern cyber techniques to figure out who the culprit was? Or, do you think the bank's security videotape was analysed for clues? Wrong! The police knew immediately who the robber was because while he was waiting for a bank teller to hand over the money, he filled out a credit application form using his real name.

My point is that if this type of behaviour continues and the nation's criminals behave so incompetently, pretty soon they'll need some kind of government subsidy to stay in business.

For an excellent example of citizen vigilance, what about a crime report from Birmingham? This graphically describes the last act in a crime spree by a woman who tried to rob one of those new superstores by threatening everyone inside with an axe. She was foiled by the great presence of mind of one employee, known in modern retailing as a greeter, who, without regard for personal safety, walked up to the woman and put a sticker on the axe. This was to show that the woman had the axe in her possession when she entered the store. If not for this display of quick thinking, there could have been a major misunderstanding during the robbery.

Woman (with axe): "Hand over the money!"
Check out girl: "Wait a minute! Did you steal that axe here?"
Woman: "No! I had it when I came in!"
Check out girl: "Oh, really? Then where is your sticker?"
Woman: "Damn!"

With confidence totally evaporated, the woman lowers the axe and leaves empty-handed into the waiting arms of the law.

Even a resort like Bournemouth is not immune from criminal incompetence. An elderly retiree complained to the police that a bear on a bicycle had vandalised her bird feeder. She described the bear as big and that it probably came from a circus as it rode away on the bicycle in a wobbly fashion. Within the hour, a man in a bear costume went into a local pet shop complaining about the low levels of food in local bird feeders. He was detained while purchasing two packets of honey-coated canary seed.

I put this national criminal incompetence down to poor television and corporate business policy. It's alleged that TV contributes to more violence on our streets. However, if there were better programmes, criminals of doubtful quality would stay at home and watch them. The business world must shoulder some of the blame. Quite recently a large retail company planned a fire-walking on a corporate motivational retreat, supervised by a profusion of fire-walking consultants to whom the company paid thousands of actual sterling pounds. While at the retreat the employees bent spoons and steel bars, smashed bricks, split planks and walked over beds of sharp nails, which proves the senior management has cotton wool for brains and a surplus of cash which the average thief can't ignore.

In the future world highly qualified professionals will have their authority undermined as computer advancement will make it possible for influential experts, bred in motivational retreats, not to be qualified to do anything.

These activities are supposed to make the staff more self-confident and unafraid to make tough business decisions. If the soles of my feet were being punctured by a galaxy of nails, my first business decision would be to get the hell off the bed thereby enhancing my corporate status.

If there's a need to impress important clients, I'm sure subjecting employees to physical abuse isn't the answer. As study after study has proved, these standard corporate motivational techniques are a highly effective means of transferring large amounts of money to consultants.

But back to the fire-walking. It's surprising what happens to flesh when exposed to high temperatures on a 2-metre strip of white-hot coals. Two staff remain in hospital while several others will be wheelchair bound for many weeks. "The corporate gain," according to the obviously mad chairman, "is immense." My thought for the future would be for interviewers to snap the bottoms of feet with elastic bands to test employee suitability. To see if you have extra toughness, they could staple documents to your insoles and judge your corporate potential by your reaction.

On reflection, I think I still have what it takes to be an excellent motivational consultant for both criminal and normal minds.

First, I'd assume you and everyone else was gormless.

Second, I'd cut a small length of string, roll it in a ball, then push it up your left nostril and jam it in there as far as I could with a sharp pencil.

Third, I'd congratulate you on your perspicacity and send you a bill for £4,500 (or £4,000 for cash) with the date and time of the initial corporate outing.

I'm just kidding of course! Deep down I know you're not that stupid. But how do you explain that when I tried this approach two years ago at a much discounted price, a robber, who wished to improve his performance, stole exactly £2,000 in cash from a bank to send to me. And more worryingly, the chief executive of that very bank was the first to send me a cheque for £2,500 to launch their first corporate motivational experience.

My eyes flicker more brightly as my consumer base is such that only the addicted and afflicted remain. Perhaps spiking with drugs is more common than I think.

MAD HATTING

I was inducted into the family fashion business at an early age. Even as a crawling baby I became an expert on the hemlines of women's skirts as I played with the colourful remnants. Across the road from my parent's shop traded my Auntie Doris, a milliner of the deepest tradition who bridged the gap between art and fashion.

So it was that I learned that no woman, however impoverished, would be seen on a Sunday without matching hat and gloves. "In your Easter bonnet with all the frills upon it," was more than a song, it was a way of life. A way for every woman to celebrate the oncoming summer and the demise of a grey winter shielded by long dark dresses and clinging head shawls.

Now whether you believe fashion elevates the bad to the level of good or as George Bernard Shaw thought, "that fashions are only induced epidemics," hats fashioned by Auntie Doris had a certain influence on my life.

Early observation revealed that a new hat acted like a gin and tonic for the wearer and you never had trouble getting a taxi when you wore a hat. It also gave you the option to be demure or brazen at the merest turn of the head.

Auntie Doris was a precision artist, a maker of dream hats and wild creations, her only stipulation being that in a good design you must be able to see where you are going! She sought inspiration from the then centre of world millinery manufacture in Luton, and adapted her styling between the use of a block to hand-crafting with steam from a kettle. Her hats were amusing and witty but never ridiculous and she preferred flattering faces with fluid lines by using malleable materials she could push around. She would make the shape by pinning it, pinching and then wetting it, before finally putting it under heat in an adapted oven. Her speciality was using extravagant bows that resembled Sydney Opera House.

Her offerings, often belittled by her cynical husband Jack who was devoted to greasy engineering, ranged from sparkling diamantés on a delicious wisp of a hat that twinkled provocatively, to a gorgeous extravaganza of a sugar pink boater bedecked with fantasy flower buds. To make a customer look utterly wonderful was her object. She was not averse however to giving pungent advice. "Horrible hat, doesn't suit you at all." .... "Hats are about faces not bodies." .... and the ultimate advice, "If a short woman wants a broad-brimmed hat, she's going to look like a gnome sitting under a mushroom."

My own knowledge grew. At ten years of age I knew by rote that a sailor hat has a flat brim with a square crown, a hat that sticks up without a brim is a toque, if the brim turns down it's a cloche and if the brim turns up it's a breton. I also knew what it felt like spilling hat stiffener down the front of my trousers.

What are my views on hats today. My own wife looks devastatingly stunning in a wide brim style but like most women she's got out of the habit of wearing one. Now it's weddings only. Perhaps if men had hats to raise and caps to touch there would be a revival.

All these years later I still believe if you put on a hat you put on another persona especially if it's a black or a navy creation with a good crisp outline. If it makes a woman feel gorgeous and radiate confidence why shouldn't she rebel from the hatless norm occasionally?

While appreciating that a broad hat does not always cover a venerable head, the magic of millinery art remains. What with my parents selling dresses, coats and all things chic, and Auntie Doris topping them off with her creations, no wonder I grew up believing the women in my life were the smartest people around.

I'd tip my hat to that thought still, if ever I should wear one.

GENDER INTERPRETATION

If there's one thing that women find unsatisfactory about men, it's that men don't communicate enough. This theory is based on extensive scientific study of the piles of dog-eared magazines in my dentist's waiting room.

Take a normal home for instance. The husband will be reading the newspaper and the phone will ring. He'll answer it, listen for ten minutes, hang up and resume reading. Finally his wife will say: "Who was that?" And he'll say: "Terry Chandler's mother." And his wife will say: "Well?" And he'll say: "Well what?" And his wife will say: "What did she say?" And he'll say: "She said Terry's fine," making it clear by his tone of voice that, although he doesn't wish to be rude, he's trying to carry on with reading the sports page in detail. But his wife, ignoring this and knowing they haven't heard from Terry for 17 years, will say: "That's ALL she said?" And she won't let up. She will continue to ask detective style questions, forcing her beloved to recount the conversation until she's satisfied that she has the entire story. Which is that Terry just got out of prison after serving a sentence for a murder he committed when he became a drug addict because of the guilt he felt when his wife died in a freak shipping accident while Terry was having an affair with a nun, but now he's all straightened out and has a good job as a trapeze artist and is almost through with the surgical part of his sex change that has enabled him to become happily engaged to marry the lead singer of Devastation, the emerging group for people with very little taste. In other words he's fine which is exactly what he told his wife in the first place. But that wasn't enough. She wanted to hear EVERY single detail.

This scenario is quite normal and is fostered by the

more inquisitive need-to-know mentality of the female. Have you noticed when women phone each other they are glad they don't have video phones? One will have wet hair, the other is guaranteed to be eating, usually chocolates. They go over in infinite detail the flaws, the failings and shortcomings of persons east to west. You can hardly believe your ears. They laugh and talk using lots of exclamation points. Ex-boyfriends and former husbands would be amazed at the skewering they get. And, when women talk they get so .... so medical. Females bond so well on the phone as they listen sympathetically to each others tales of woe. Inevitably the conversation ends with life's favourite phrases like: "He's just not good enough for you." It's not surprising that behind every successful man is a truly amazed mother-in-law.

    Regardless of rumours to the contrary men are less verbose and they substitute sports for medical talk. They can spend a good hour reciting statistics from the first-class cricket averages, Premiership football or horse-racing from 156 B.C. to the present time. Most women, when listening to these fountains of irrelevance, would fall face down on their make-up in a boredom induced coma.

    By using many expletives men are far more efficient with words, consequently they have lower phone bills than women. Their farting, scratching, belching and grunting save superfluous comment. Sometimes they get quite emotional and even share their feelings. "That was not a penalty! Are you saying it was a penalty! Pull the other one! Where were you?" I don't mean to imply that all men talk about is sports. Men also discuss, openly and without shame, what kind of pizza to eat and which is the best beer to wash it down. Heavy conversations, except for women's body measurements, are not part of their sharing and it's not totally surprising to hear from your wife that your best friend has had a new artificial leg for at least six weeks. No, men are not Neanderthals, they're just different. Some don't even use words at all, they just share bait.

Occasionally men and women talk about the same thing .... usually the same man .... or woman. I find that comforting in a weird sort of way.

CONVERTIBLE CONVERT

Driving an open convertible at speed is one of the most exciting experiences I've had with my clothes on. My first open car was a green Triumph Herald, my latest a blood red Mercedes, in between a swoosh of others too numerous to mention. The sun out in a blue denim sky, the hood down and the open road for the taking is the ultimate thrill especially if there's room for some zippy overtaking. 'Tis music for the eyes and ears.

No need to go full pelt, that's for the foolish. Simply enjoy the rush of air and the smart pace of progress. In my younger days if you had a nimble convertible you headed off for a weekend in the country to drive along winding prehistoric motorway lanes, roof down, wearing scratched sunglasses and a flat cap. Your aim was a place where nobody passes through on the way to anywhere else. The suspension was so tight and hard that you felt every crack and bump as you bowled along close to the ground. The main interest on the journey was hoping a wandering pheasant would step out of line so the brakes could be tested dramatically. Ignoring rude gestures and bad lane manoeuvres was par for the course. On arrival the local misautomists would stare and mouth "lucky bastard" at the driver of the only sports car they'd ever truly lusted after. The village girls would smile encouragingly in the hope they would be "taken for a ride" and at the very least receive a proposal of marriage within the day from the pacy visitor.

Without a super strong jaw and rippling muscles, I was not a gorgeous example of guydom, but I did fit my clothes well and possessed a charming gangling vulnerability. The pub meals in those days might have been better had the food not arrived. If the soup had been as hot as the wine, the wine as old as the chicken, and the chicken as fat as the waiter, they might have proved palatable.

Today, in my sleek red missile, I've zoomed along in a car that feels much safer doing 70 than 30 as the faster you go, the more it grips the tarmac and squeals for more. I park outside the village hostelry, push my Prada shades onto my head and await the girls clambering all over the fiery object before them as they ask me to sign their bras. The onlooking Japanese tourists surround this English poser and insist on intense smiles to satisfy their Fuji lenses. Food becomes of secondary consideration in the realisation that a passionate French kiss uses up 35 calories while eating a chocolate kiss puts on 26. Alfresco consumption appears to be the one way of avoiding commitment which would be a tragedy for someone wearing a flat cap.

I am now more Versace than Armani whereas I used to be more Dunns than Burtons. As part of the orgasm hotline I drive the right car for young women not getting what they want from their local man. Although everything in life is now sadly bumper to bumper the nation's convertible drivers have a need for passengers in skimpy skirts and barely there dresses which offer lots of flesh available for ogling. If you refrain from driving your hunk of metal over the speed limit you are indeed in control. With 6 gears, a top speed of 250 k.p.h. and an acceleration from 0 - 62 in 5.9 seconds, spinning the 42 cm. alloy wheels furiously is not a difficult thing to do to test your lusty bravado. On a scale of 1 to 10, with 10 being the most stupid choice, testing your bravado in this way is a 14!

Driving convertibles can yield a distorted belief that only members of the Safety Council and elderly people obey speed limits. Most drivers don't see the copious speed limit signs because light doesn't travel fast enough to catch those rattling along at a spanking rate. If all else fails, I'm firmly of the opinion that should a police officer pull you over he should take into consideration what type of music you were listening to at the time of the alleged offence.

Calm prevails, the throttle is eased, the engine reluctantly slouches to a chug. Your adagio mood returns. You are simply content to watch the resentful drivers turn green at the traffic lights.

"In your dreams mate. Get a bloody move on!" I force my old Mini van into gear and lurch down the road. Who's been deceiving who?

HOBGOBLINS IN THE CELLAR

Once upon a time I thought it was my Grandma's mission in life to keep her grandchildren supplied with slices of sweet surprises.

On days when there was nothing in her oven except our snow-wet mittens drying out, you could count on being treated to something special from the pantry. But there was a catch. I would be despatched to the cellar for a jar of homemade jam.

In truth, I rather relished performing Herculean chores for my Grandma like laying in kindling wood for the stove, emptying ashes and carrying in a bucket of coal in each hand from the shed down the backyard. But I would rather have received and absorbed a cricket ball on the chin from the flagged streets, than be asked to take a solo trip down into that spooky, cool, unlit dirt cellar that served as Grandma's refrigerator.

You reached the cellar by a door under the stairs and as you pushed the creaking wood door with its noisy latch, you could feel the timeless arms of cold dark earth enveloping you. There was a strong impression of face paint, animal heads and nose bones ahead, all converging to scare off an invading army. You could sense the ghosts and gremlins like sharks and vultures after their prey.

For all I knew, evil lurked in the shadows below. And Grandma's proffered candle was of little use to a hesitant boy making the trip down and back with his eyes closed.

Now that I've returned from the world of sport and business, the horror treks into the cellars of my youth come flooding back. My Grandma would say, knowing of my fear: "What can happen to you? I'll be standing right up here!" Well, so be it, but how would that help if I came face to face with phantoms and zombies of mongrel origin or even a human burglar who'd slipped in through the leaky grid to the street.

Who knew what stirred below, skulking under the staircase or behind the old furnace? Spiders and the odd mouse I could cope with, but what if there was an uninvited bogeyman or worse, a doppelganger from foreign parts? If my tender age thoughts were released too vividly there was a guarantee that my breath would turn to sleet halfway down the stairs.

I countered this fear of the unknown all for the sake of the most delectable strawberry jam known to any Lancashire lad. Layered on a crackling crust of new bread straight from the oven, it was manna from heaven for a young boy. Quite inadvertently, or on reflection, quite deliberately, my Grandma taught me courage. There was no drawing the line in those days if you knew what was good for you. And Grandma's jams were certainly good for me and worth the scary descent.

Now, in my centrally heated modern home there's not a sign of a cellar. It's hard to convey to my grandchildren the nature and excitement of a dank and gloomy cellar in this age of electrical magic.

I wonder what happened to all those hobgoblins and flibbertigibbets of my youth that never jumped out to get me? They must lurk somewhere still, waiting to pounce but never, never on Grandma's jams. With Grandma in command, everything was kept at bay from the old coal hole of a cellar. She was an expert at keeping darkness and dirt away from her life. Her only complaint, which I heard many times before she died, was: "You know young man, you fight dirt all your life in this grimy part of the world, and then, when you die, they bury you in it. It doesn't seem fair somehow."

DANGEROUS WATERS

I have a friend, Simon, who lives in Exmouth and believes, despite what everybody thinks, water scooters are not noisy, obnoxious death machines driven by complete morons. "They are quite safe," he says, "as this type of watercraft don't have propellers. Therefore they don't chop up people."

Quite a theory. So, bearing Simon's words in mind I eye a water scooter with a monster 110-horsepower engine. "How fast will this little beauty go?" I ask. "About 60 m.p.h." I have to have it. From the moment I rode the bone-breaker, a sort of bonding developed.

I started out at idle speed, afraid to go any faster. That lasted about two minutes. Then I was hitting boat wakes at full throttle and making turns at 45 m.p.h. I was beginning to look like a complete moron.

The ridiculous urge to run over ducks, canoes and nude bathers came over me but I couldn't find any, so I made do with seagulls. The motorcycle-like creation propelled by an impeller device that sucks in water and also the driver's brains literally possessed me. As water shoots out of the back all you do is pull the throttle and steer. It's so simple anyone can kill themselves on one.

Simon, now up for the challenge of out-pacing me, uttered the understatement of the year. "Speed isn't the problem. The problem is close-proximity use." I soon discovered that "close-proximity use" is a euphemism for running into things. People on water scooters soon acquire the habit of running into docks, boats, swimmers, other water scooters and all sorts of stuff. If it's out there long enough, by crikey, they'll hit it.

One imbecile actually scooted right out of the water near the marina and ran over a woman sunbathing at the water's edge. "She had no business being there," as the defence solicitor put it. When will people learn to quit putting themselves in the paths of water scooters?

Simon is of the opinion that engines should be made to go faster for safety reasons. Ha! Ha! As far as I can see if you make a water scooter go faster, you make it louder. Naturally there are people who object to this, primarily folks with seafront homes. They need to move.

According to my calculations, adding 15 per cent to the power ensures that the beast could do about 70 m.p.h. If I hit a bather at 70, I wouldn't even need a propeller to transfer him from this life to the next.

The owner image is clear. Ideal riders are on the front of every brochure. Stud-like men, thick hair blown back in the wind, arms taut on the handlebars, beautiful young women who seem like genetic freaks sitting on the seat behind, all flushed with looks of excitement on their faces. These are people who love to spray because spraying involves zipping by someone close enough to soak him with the spray that shoots up from the side of the lethal weapon.

Rex, Simon's friend, appeared next day, cruising along at a mere 50 m.p.h. minus an orgasmic woman but plus his dog, Heathen the Rottweiler. "He loves it," I was assured, "can't keep him off it." A Rottweiler on a water scooter! There must be something about that in the Book of Revelations.

Later that day while swimming lazily, enjoying the peace and serenity, I heard this loud roar and the two of them, Simon and Rex, came zooming into the bay doing at least the speed of light. They barely missed me and almost swamped me with their wakes. I was angry but now realise I should have been more alert or better still, not been there in the first place.

If you see a water scooter on your neighbourhood water, be afraid. No, not of me, I've sold mine.

Be very afraid, especially if the passenger is a Rottweiler.

HOW TIME FLIES

The western world suffers a debilitating form of time distortion, a frantic state of mind that comes from speeding through life. We seem to be losing the ability to enjoy the present because we're too busy concentrating on the future and forfeiting the right to determine the pace of our own lives.

In reality we're running out of time because there's less and less of it to go around these days. You might as well try to control lightning as try to buy time. I swear time is slowly disappearing. I suspect time is leaking through that big gaping hole in the ozone layer.

Before the age of 10 even a trip to the shops seemed like going to Albania on foot. "Is it Christmas yet?" was the most uttered phrase after the other several times-a-week query of: "Is it my birthday soon?"

Between 11 and 20 life is still slow as school clocks actually move backwards before the bell rings, and the acquiring of a driving licence seems light years away.

Life in your 20's alternates fast and slow as weekends appear shorter and shorter, and the wages and salaries grow further and further apart. Time distortion is created by living in a culture geared to feeding millions of pieces of advertising and information to other people also running out of time.

From 30 to 39 time achieves warp speed. The type of speed when a billionth of a billionth of a second becomes an altosecond. "Is it Christmas already?" It seems impossible to schedule quality family time and get even one minute to yourself. A week barely registers a blip on the mental calendar. When I'm home by myself with the kids, it seems like 6 o'clock will never come. Then I look at the clock and not only is it 5.45, but it is Friday.

After 40 life's still fast, but approaching 50, does life slow down? Time obviously can't be trusted. That's why it's referred to as "Father Time" and not "Mother Time". Time is masculine and therefore sloppy. You begin to notice that time leaks faster from some places than it does from others. Time leaks away very slowly from games of cricket where two hours at the crease for 9 runs can seem like a week. Time also leaks very slowly when listening to political debates, going to the dentist or attending a funeral. Time however leaks very quickly when you're enjoying yourself, especially on a surreptitious weekend or on holiday in an exotic place.

What happened to the years 50 to 59? The drop in physical energy and the rise in emotional energy conserves such a lot of time. The kids have left home and with more disposable income you travel to boring countries which hoard time. To places like Finland where you can see all you want and still have lots of time left over. That's because the Finns are stockpiling time mostly at the bottom of their many lakes.

The decade of your 60's is devoted to performing tasks with the opposite hand to slow down time. Buttering bread becomes an art form in this way while attempting to saw wood or knocking in a nail in such fashion can brighten or bloody your day. Time is becoming faster because you can now see what's coming as you hum the opening bars of "As Time Goes By".

From 70 onwards, time goes unbelievably fast. Wars that used to last years are over in a couple of weeks. As people feel their bodies slow down internally, time appears faster by comparison. On the other hand, being housebound makes time crawl and if you're bored, time does go slowly.

Life's consolation is that you can't ever be on time despite Parliament ordering the whole country to set its clocks to Greenwich Mean Time in 1880. Being on time is like being on gravity. It's a metaphysical impossibility. Time gives the illusion of being orderly .... the sundial begat the clock which begat the pocket-watch which begat the wristwatch which begat the modern digitals .... in reality it's all camouflage. We've never really recovered from the fact that September 3rd, 1752, never happened. Nor did the ten days that should have followed it. For in that year Britain and American colonies adopted the Gregorian calendar, and to get back in step meant "losing" 11 days. The decision caused riots because people thought that the government had stolen 11 days of their short-lived meagre lives.

And you thought the government could only take your money!

Someday you'll understand. If there's time.

ANIMALS A-GO-GO

Anyone who knows me well, realises I'm not the world's most fervent animal lover. However, occasional happenings release a certain amount of sympathetic response to the plights of animals. Take the five cases concerning a squirrel, a pig, a monkey and a fox, plus my neighbour's attitude to bats.

What would you do if you had to extract a squirrel out of an upright piano? My Aunt Flo, a regally suburban woman, had the temerity to call the Exeter police after she saw a grey squirrel running around her living room instead of leaping from branch to branch like a normal squirrel. Whether the squirrel was tempted indoors by the expensive pecan nuts my aunt was consuming along with her nightly tipple of red wine, we shall never know. Suffice it to say, she said, "Shoo! Shoo!" with great vehemence but the frisky and most athletic squirrel decided to secrete itself inside the upright piano.

Most surprisingly, a young uniformed policeman arrived within minutes to deal with the "intruder" situation.

What astonished Aunt Flo was, not only had the officer the courage and determination to apprehend the nutty intruder, but he had the musical talent to go with them. In his spare time 6734 Police Constable Percy Talbot bashed the ivories with a local jazz ensemble.

After peering down the open top of the piano to no avail, the noble PC pulled the stool up close, sat down, stretched his fingers, before flowing with consummate ease into "Dancing In The Dark", which the squirrel probably was. In two minutes, the squirrel jumped out of the piano and on to Aunt Flo's curtains, damaging them. From there, the squirrel launched itself on to the officer's head, and from there to the couch where the officer was able to snatch it with a flying one-hundredth of a second (known as a jiffy) leap before landing softly on Aunt Flo's lap. In the firm grip of the law, the squirrel was released on the lawn with the dulcet tones of the piano ringing in its ears.

It's a moot point whether a more peaceful solution could have been obtained if Constable Talbot had played something from The Nutcracker Suite.

So, everything turned out for the best, but what, in the heat of the moment, would have happened if Percy Talbot, in his civilian guise, had played a composition by Barry Manilow? The mind boggles as the squirrel would surely have killed both the PC and Aunt Flo in defending its honour and integrity.

In an effort to learn more about the incident I made a phone call to Police Headquarters in Exeter, and spoke with spokesperson Cynthia Grunge. I asked her if the officer's tactics were based on those used by the SAS when our elite troops played loud rap and heavy-metal music to mentally disturb a group of Balkan rebels. She replied that Constable Talbot had simply made a spur-of-the-moment decision to play

"Dancing In The Dark" as he couldn't remember anything off-the-cuff from the Nutcracker.

The squirrel situation in East Devon appears now to be under control, but that does not mean we can afford to be sanguine, as, according to Ms. Grunge there have been three alarming "animal incidents" within the past two months in this area of Devon.

In the first, a pig "rumoured to be twice as big as normal" was "rearing on its hind legs while running and snapping at cars." In the second, "an escaped fruit throwing monkey" attacked a motorist in a supermarket car park. Apparently the monkey threw crab apples, not purchased at the local supermarket, in a violent manner before escaping. In the third, a fox charged at a woman in her garden as she was carrying a vastly overcooked chicken from the barbecue to the table.

These incidents are particularly disturbing because they're not random loner attacks by fugitive animals. Instead, they involve co-ordinated hostile wildlife displaying far more intelligence and planning ability than, for example, a House of Commons Select Committee. Should we as humans, be concerned about this? After all, Hitchcock's "The Birds" set wildlife a fine example. These are troubled times, especially when the bat situation is brought into the equation.

The bat is a much maligned creature and has a poor public image. An image cemented to Transylvania and Halloween plus the perception that they are things that go "whoosh in the night." This feeling caused my next door neighbour, Willy Olivant, to become sympathetic to the bat's cause. He maintains that bats play a vital role in the economy. Indeed, Willy respects bats, loves bats and on occasion has tasted bats with his colleagues in the European Cave and Bat

Society.

This society specialises in selling a wide array of bat-themed merchandise, including bat jewellery, bat candles, bat T-shirts, bat crockery, bat Christmas tree ornaments, bat tea towels and strangely, hot bat sauce.

Willy's wife, Hannah, has a different view which results from being the type of woman who hangs garlic on the front door to ward off vampires. She believes that bats are evil creepy demons from hell who bite and pass on rabies. The truth is that bats are generally flying mammals who form colonies, care for their young and take their families on outings. Statistically, the average bat is far less likely to be rabid that any member of the Conservative Party.

Willy responds by saying that sometimes a female vampire bat will return from a bloodsucking trip and share her good fortune by "regurgitating to her roost mates." He defends the eating of a tasty bat morsel by saying that it is quite the norm in South-East Asia and especially the island of Guam where bat soup and fried bat are considered treats.

In general, bats have really received a "raw deal" from us humans. They have the potential to become useful members of society or at least lawyers or architects. From now on, we should all remember that bats are our friends, and we should make every effort to be nice to them while remaining at a safe distance of at least, according to Hannah, ten miles.

I must confess I didn't ask Cynthia Grunge about bat attacks, which is a shame. I would have loved to know what music the estimable Constable Talbot would have played to a determined bat clinging to the wires inside a piano after it fled from embracing Aunt Flo's hair. Beating it to death with a 30-second rendering of the Minute Waltz would have been harsh justice in that most agricultural and peaceful part of Devon.

What is worse, we will never know if Willy Olivant would have tried to acquire it to sell as a bat necklace or deep fried it and offered it as "an oriental delicacy" to his unsuspecting neighbour.

GOLF ADDICT

His name is Joe and he's a friend. But he's also an addict. A golf addict. Joe looks like a golfer but doesn't sound like one. He has the right clubs, the right clothes but he doesn't talk the game well, and, ... his left hand twitches at the mere mention of the game.

Joe's scores hover in the 90's and he seems the perfect source of the old joke that if you can't break 90 you have no business on the golf course, but if you can break 90 you probably have no business.

Why does Joe, like many other golfers, spend so much money and time on perfecting a hideous swing, (the only one piece takeaway Joe knows is a pizza), and thinking badly around the course? Frankly his game has stunk longer than boiled red cabbage in spite of the millions of magazines, informercials, videos, golf academies, square grooves, hot balls, super drivers and remedial patter bombarding him at every opportunity.

Whenever Joe goes to his captive professional the word "hmmm" issues from the pro's lips. "Hmmm, you need more club head speed." .... "Hmmm, flex your knees." .... "Hmmm, your grip is weak," and so on. Thank goodness Joe's arms are not too short as I don't believe the National Health Service goes in for that type of surgery.

As I write, Joe is on his lawn proving that he needs to

keep his left arm straighter, his shoulder turn more pronounced and his follow through more cavalier. I can't resist chatting as one golfer to another.

"What's new Joe?"

"Just had a lesson Gordon, the best yet. Let me show you."

With that Joe launched into a check-list of theory relative to his own game.

"It's really quite simple. I was locking my right knee during my back swing and locking my left knee on my follow through, reverse pivot it's called. I was lifting my club, swaying, reaching out and up, hitching, looping, bending my left arm, standing up, looking away, pulling the club face across the ball, starting my hip movement too fast, not turning my shoulders enough and finishing with my hands in the wrong place." Joe paused for breath then continued.

"The pro moved my right thumb a fraction to the left on the grip, told me to touch my left shoulder to my left cheek on the follow through, told me to pivot, to take the club back low and slow, to close my club face and release, shift my weight slightly forward, keep my head down, stand closer to the ball, stand with a better body posture, try to swing in one fluid motion and .... oh, yes .... don't quit on it."

"That's amazing," I said.

"Oh, by the way, he also said relax," Joe offered with a bitter laugh as though describing an inner golf demon he can't control.

Undaunted, Joe went on to describe his latest weaponry for reducing his handicap.

"To improve my balance I've just bought a new pair of size 10 regular width, waterproof brown shoes with graphite in the sole, titanium in the spikes and toetanium in the toe."

Flush with enthusiasm, Joe was now unstoppable.

"Just as I took my shoes off I saw a Beefy Barbara driver, the chubbiest driver on the market, with a 1.18 metre iridescent Goofonium shaft and the new Finger Kisser grip."

Joe's wrists were now flexing and his left arm was on the twitch.

"But that's not the club," I said, looking at the swinging power before me.

"No," said Joe, "the pro put his hand on my shoulder and convinced me it had the wrong flex point for me. The next thing I knew, I was looking at the newest driver on offer, Whopping Wilma. It has a bigger head than my wife's. It's got a 1.28 metre, glowdark, vibration calibrated, resonance-resistant Loonite-Mornium blend shaft."

"Did you buy it?"

"No option. I couldn't help myself. I needed it. I craved it. I demanded it. I simply had to have it."

"You're a sick person, do you know that?" I murmured.

"But it's the best driver ever made. It will add at least 20 metres to my tee shots," Joe explained.

"That's what you expected from Mighty Martha and all the others. You ought to be driving the ball at least 400 metres but you're not past 200 yet are you?"

"Well, I'm getting better. Anyway, it's more exciting that getting a new putter and becoming an old wimp. I believe the driver is the greatest phallic symbol in sport," Joe concluded.

At this point I gave up and ventured to change the subject.

"How's Betty?" I enquired.

"Oh, didn't I mention it Gordon? She's left me and moved in with her boss over in Southampton."

"Sorry Joe, I didn't know."

"Not to worry, it'll mean I can get 36 holes in every Saturday and Sunday now."

I wonder if I'll ever turn into a swivel hips type of guy who can't hit the ball out of sight.

A LITTLE KNOWLEDGE IS A DANGEROUS THING

What is your science IQ? To find out, take this multiple choice quiz.
1. Tides are caused by:
    a) Gravity leaking out of the moon.
    b) Lobsters burping in unison.
    c) Over dumping of toxic waste.
2. What is magnetism?
    a) Invisible rays that shoot out of a compass.
    b) The molecular attraction that forms between refrigerators and ceramic fruit.
    c) The force that causes dogs to bark when you ring the doorbell.
3. The Earth rotates:
    a) Around the cosine.
    b) First one way and then the other.
    c) In a direction away from England.

As any intelligent reader must grasp, the correct answer to all three questions is .... d) No opinion.

If you did poorly on this quiz, don't feel bad. When it comes to scientific knowledge, many Europeans are as stupid as most Asians but less so than the majority of Americans. National surveys have shown time and again that Europeans have the same basic level of scientific literacy as gravel so you can tell the others are not up to much.

    This doesn't surprise me as I constantly see evidence that we don't understand the findings of that great, dead, gravity fed mathematician Sir Isaac Newton, who proved that no matter how hard you push, you can't fit an object into an aircraft overhead luggage compartment if the object is bigger than the compartment. Most people who travel don't understand this concept. That's why last month on a flight to Copenhagen, a man and a woman who, after taking 15 minutes to work out that row 19 was the one between 18 and 20, tried to stow a large, heavy cardboard box above my head. I can personally vouch for its weight because at one point during their struggle the couple dropped the box on my head after which they glared at me as though I was trying to harm the contents.

    These nitwits would benefit from better science training of the type I received from eight years old Teddy Foster when I was seven. It was then I learned that the Chinese Burn Torture would make the hairs on my arm stand up in alarm. It was the same boy who instructed me at a later age of the effect on dust of stroking the backs of girl's nylon covered legs. That was known as Advanced Science.

    Typically, many of my fellow Europeans didn't receive this calibre of science training, which is why they did poorly in the quiz. The occasional trick question caused a problem. "What is the difference between lightning and electricity?" lengthy dissertations were of no avail when the correct answer is: "From lightning you don't get bills."

    The question most people answered incorrectly was: "Which of these is the nearest living relative to the dinosaur, Tyrannosaurus Rex?" A) a chicken; B) a crocodile; C) a lizard; D) an elephant. As discerning readers of this column will know, the correct answer is: A chicken.

I forgive your first reaction which is: "Hold on a minute clever clogs. The giant fearsome creature that ate a car and a lawyer in Jurassic Park is related to a chicken?"

Yes. Tyrannosaurus Rex used to stride through the prehistoric jungle until it located its prey, and then, with a terrible cry of "cock-a-doodle-doo," it would lunge forward and administer the devastating Peck of Death to a piece of corn lying handily in the mouth of some unsuspecting creature.

The place to start improving our scientific literacy is with our young people who should be made to concentrate by whacking them over the head with antique slide rulers. Discipline and falling apples go together I feel. After all, when you attempt to drink at the fountain of knowledge, gargling is insufficient. Advances in science would be so dramatic that tiny children would be able to answer with complete confidence questions such as: "Do you have a Niantic Interface Equalizer modified with Psilocybermostics MCX-3P for a suppressed Diatonic Analyser in a solid state of despondency?"

The world would tremble at our expertise as they became totally despondent at their own lack of knowledge.

MORE MAGAZINES PLEASE

Have you noticed how specialised magazines have become these days? I can see by the show of hands that: 1. Some of you have noticed. 2. Some of you have not noticed. 3 Some of you couldn't care less but are in desperate need of a manicure.

There seems to be a magazine for every conceivable subject known to man ranging from "Chain Saw Age" to "The

Paint and Coatings Journal". But is there?

In my view there are still gaps on the shelves and specialisation could soon be breeding titles like:

YUK: For people who hate certain foods. There will be profiles of famous people and the food they despised. A lead article will follow on how Crippen had planned on becoming a librarian until his mother made him eat creamed parsnips. "Why Every Family Should Eat Kolocassi and Kohlrabi", plus "Fifty Ways of Dealing with a Guava", will be featured in the second issue. The cover charge will be £2.75 per monthly issue.

ANGST REVIEW: The magazine for worriers. Each edition will highlight a story on some new threat to life and what the stylish worrier is wearing this year. Featured will be gauze masks, knee pads and bullet-proof vests. Special pieces will follow on "How to Increase Your Fear of Rabid Dogs, Cancer, Acid Rain and Heart Disease". There will be no charge for this monthly as money exchange spreads germs.

TERRA FIRMA: The magazine for those people terrified of flying. Essential topics will be: "Is There a Bottom to an Air Pocket?" and "How To Make a Life Raft Out of Your Dinner Tray". A thirty minute, special offer CD will describe various engine noises and explain their deadly implication. All for the rock bottom basement price of 50 pence per week.

FIELD & SCREAM: The magazine for victims of hunting accidents. This import from America, the land of hunting idiots, will feature educational dissertations on "Chest Holes and How to Repair Them"; "Blood: How Not to Trail It" and the constantly demanded, "How to Differentiate a Grouse from a Hunting Jacket". Price will be one blood donation before the next monthly issue.

CELLS & PARDONS: The magazine for incarcerated people has helpful craft ideas on: "How to Turn a Bar of Soap

Into a Screwdriver" and "How to Bake a Hacksaw Cake". There will be culinary contributions on famous last meals. The third issue will concentrate on: "How To Tell Your Cellmate No Without Hurting His Feelings". The price will be just one packet of twenty every month.

TEDIUM: The magazine for bored teenagers. Early articles will concentrate on: "Indolent Lifestyles for Those Without Direction"; "Scowling as An Art Form" and "Will Putting Black Shoe Polish on Your Hair Improve Your Examination Results?" this publication can be traded in for "Angst Review", if you've a mind to!

WHERE AM I?: The magazine for men in their mid-life crisis. Penetrating contributions will hit the press on: "How to Make the Best of That Bald Patch"; "That Red Porsche .... Why Can't I?" and " Opening Lines to Feed Young Women". This quarterly issue will be priced at £25 because most men in mid-life crisis have lost all sense of reality.

SHOPLIFTER: The magazine for intending shoplifters. Riveting thoughts on: "How to Hide a Complete Home Entertainment System Down Your Trouser Leg" will be followed by: "How to Avoid Frostbite When Stealing Frozen Goods". Veteran shoplifters will be interviewed, both in prison and on location, and while under probation. There will be no charge for this weekly as it would seem pointless.

And finally, WIMP WORLD: The magazine that helps the meek cope with life. Essays of an inspirational nature in the weeks ahead will be: "Whining: Is It Art?"; "Cringe and Be Sexy" and "How to Give a Definite Maybe". Again no fixed cover charge for this monthly publication as you only pay what you think it's worth.

The potential list is endless, mindless and probably worthless. More will be revealed in "SQUIB", my own paltry publication for lampooning every magazine in sight. The only charge is your undivided attention.

HARNESS THE DREGS

When I have my blue and white striped butcher-type apron on, you know my wife's out and I'm directing kitchen productions. With my oven glove silk-screened with a large fish, and wearing one of those chef's hats that look like the paper frills fancy people put on turkey drumsticks, I cut a pretty picture.

With a single stick of parsley tucked behind my ear, I realise presentation isn't everything especially when you're alone. As a master of cooking dregs I know it's important to be seen to have a good table and be a master of improvisation.

Assembling dregs becomes the emotional focus of the whole day, as dregs are what you have to eat when your spouse is playing tennis in the next county and there's nothing of substance to eat. Dregs are what you have in the fridge or cupboard when you open up every door and say, "This is crazy. There's absolutely nothing to eat." Wrong! There are always dregs.

My favourite dregs are the contents of an old can of tuna which form the basis of a miracle meal which comes to be known as dinner - a hot entrée that miraculously materialises out of nowhere.

The key to successful tasty dregs meals means planning for those occasions when there is zilch to eat. That's right, zilch .... nada. So, you plan for nothing, by making sure you have these cheap staples on hand at all times: rice, pasta and olive oil. Rice and pasta make all things possible especially with more than a dash of curry, chilli or paprika. If you can back them up with a sprinkling of onions and olives, plus over-aged celery, carrots and frozen peas, the food gods are definitely on your side.

You now have the beginnings of Dregs Stir Fry. Start the rice first. Then throw some onions into a wok with olive oil. Chop the celery and carrots. Toss in the peas, olives and tuna plus whatever else comes to hand such as the odd nut or two extracted from down the sides of the sofa. It has been known for a wrinkled red pepper and few raisins to mysteriously appear out of some dark recess. Mix together with the rice or serve on a bed of rice whichever you prefer, and garnish with parsley and a sliced, vastly overripe banana. If tuna is unavailable you can no doubt conjure up a morsel or two of undercooked chicken or leftover meat crawling with potentially fatal bacteria.

This dish is not only good eating, it's healthy eating. I know, I know, I can hear you say, "Eating healthily is like driving a Ferrari with your gloves on." But remember, this is dregs eating, you have to make do with what you've got.

At this stage you have to relate to the kind of person whose favourite meal is fried chicken with mashed potatoes and gravy. Dregs cooking is not one of your more sophisticated friends who worships at the throne of vegetable bortsch followed by sole joinville and a '93 Chardonnay, with an apple mousse gâtinaise to clear the palate.

Like all talented cooks, I cheat a little. My favourite dregs meal of black beans and rice has a more than residual scrappy air about it. Let me explain. In this concoction you first boil then bake the rice in the oven. No soggy rice with my beans, please! From the nothings of the kitchen you dredge up olive oil, one leftover tomato, a bay leaf of crackly disposition, one tearful onion, a lonely stalk of celery, a wizened green pepper, one reeking garlic clove, dashes of crushed oregano, cumin, black pepper and salt, plus splashes of white wine vinegar and sherry. Simply mix with a can of black beans and pour over that bed of baked rice. You have a meal for eternity.

May your dregs never get mouldy, may your wok contents never get scorched, and may the devi of the fridge and cupboard smile upon you as you search for the scraps within. But a note of warning. Don't get too accomplished or you'll finish up doing all the cooking!

LADY BOUNTIFULS

The other day my friend's son Tom and I were talking and the subject of women came up, and I realised it was about time that he and I had a serious talk.

Far too often men avoid talking seriously about women to other men as it can lead to awkward and sometimes embarrassing lines of inquiry. Confining your discussion to the subject of buying gifts for women I deemed a less precarious but absolutely necessary subject for the furtherance of Tom's lifemanship education, especially as he was revelling in the first rush of hormonal love.

Buying gifts for women is an area where many men don't have a clue. Mind you his father, who is a very thoughtful man, is hardly one to follow. He gave Tom's mother, on their anniversary, the following token of his love, his commitment and probably his passion: An electric blanket. He honestly couldn't understand why, when she opened the box, she gave him that look .... the look that all veteran men know so well. After all, the electric blanket was the de-luxe model with an automatic thermostat. What more could any woman want?

Even my own uncle fell from grace when he gave my auntie for Christmas her first worthwhile electric gift: a multi-speed drill. As he explained for many weeks into the New Year .... "Well, we've needed one for a long time!"

The mistake that many men make is thinking that when they choose a gift for a woman, it should do something useful. Wrong! Wrong! Wrong! The golden rule of buying gifts for women is: The gift should not do anything, or, if it does, it should do it badly. Being pretty and colourful can yield many long-lasting bonus points.

For all those men who are still reading this advice garnered from years spent watching and listening to women chatting among themselves in my parents clothing business, let's consider two possible gifts, both of which, theoretically, perform the same function.

Gift A: A state-of-the-art gas-powered lantern with electronic ignition and dual mantles capable of generating 1,000 lumen of light for 12 hours on a single cylinder of fuel.

Gift B: A scented beeswax candle containing nefarious looking particles which provides roughly the same illumination as a faltering nightlight.

To a man, gift A is clearly superior because you could use it to see in the dark. Whereas, to a woman, gift B is much better because women (and my wife with her Scandinavian tendencies confirms this) love to sit around in the gloom with a smelly spluttering candle.

At this stage all I asked of Tom was .... don't ask me why! Just as I don't know why a woman's eyes would narrow if you gave her 12 bottles of the finest red Burgundy, yet her eyes would instantly reflect the thrill of receiving a tiny vial of liquid with a name like "L'Essence de Desir de Cologne d'Amour," which to the male nostril, doesn't smell any better than weak linseed oil.

All I'm saying is that this is the kind of thing women want backed up by very excited flowers thrusting their way into the bosom of her heart. Red or black lingerie is a poor third to the ultimate useless gift: jewellery.

Another factor about buying gifts for women is, you're never finished. For instance, if you have a girl friend, (at this point Tom was all ears), she will give you at the absolute minimum .... a birthday gift, an anniversary of our first meeting gift, a Christmas gift, a Valentine's Day gift and a miscellaneous gift to celebrate an occasion only she remembers. In addition, every one of those gifts will be beautifully wrapped and accompanied by an appropriate and most thoughtful card. (Tom's eyes were now wincing in anticipation of the troubles ahead caused by Life's Golden Rule.) When she gives you a gift you have to give her one back. If you simply put your hand in your pocket and proffer a £20 note you'll be giving it to a soon-to-be ex-girl friend.

And as I told Tom, it only gets worse. Looming before him, poor lad, are engagement, wedding, baby, anniversary and multi-birthday occasions plus Mothers Day (not financed by Dad), Fathers Day (not financed by Mum) and several Mandatory Gift occasions that would not even exist if men really ran the world. Women observe all those days and much more. Most women I know will buy gifts for no reason .... going on holidays, returning from holidays, moving in a flat, moving out of a flat .... even celebrating a divorce and, more bizarrely, the anniversary of buying Tiddles the Cat which finally replaced the departed husband.

In a gift store a woman will find something, maybe a tiny pretty box that won't hold anything larger than a molecule, and is therefore useless, and she'll buy it, plus a thoughtful card, and believe it Tom my boy .... she doesn't even know who the recipient is yet! You don't have to have a first-class honours degree to realise that millions of women, nay billions all over the world, are out improving the economy of nations while we men are at home watching instant replays and grumbling about the increase in the cost of living.

I made Tom realise that he had no chance of winning this conflict. Some truths in life have to be accepted as unpalatable. Someday when he's older and much stronger in mind and body I'll bring up a subject to which there's no really sound answer. It's when a woman asks her man: "Do these trousers make me look thin?" Unless he flees alone to a desert island Tom will have to leave my more advanced lifemanship answers to a later date.

RIDING A CHOPPER

Having spent my National Service flying Her Majesty's Royal Air Force planes, you'd think any attempt to become a helicopter pilot would prove a piece of cake. No such luck. Flying a plane, driving a car, hitting a golf ball 220 metres, what could be easier than moving a helicopter round the skies to my whim and fancy?

I soon appreciated that the first rule of piloting a helicopter is, always have somebody sitting next to you who knows how to fly the helicopter. The second rule is, maybe I should forget the whole thing.

My instructor, Eddie Fryer (Chips to his friends), is a pilot who flies radio reporters over big cities during rush hour so they can alert drivers to traffic problems. ("We have a ten-mile backup on the M6 due to a lorry depositing its load two hours ahead of schedule.")

Being used to military, well-prepared, awesome helicopters, my first look at Bessie, Chips' charge, made me feel I should insert £1 coins in a slot to make it go up and down. I knew that if we got airborne in a helicopter this size, some of our few remaining native dragon flies could attempt to mate with us to preserve the species. Also, this helicopter had no doors. This proves how modern life spoils people. Whenever I've flown on a normal aircraft the policy of having doors has been a plus for the booking system.

Over the static and the engine noise I hear Chips say something like, "I'll give you the controls when we're at 500 feet." In what seems a split second my stomach is left behind after the initial hover and Chips is yielding the controls to me.

This brings me to the third rule of helicopter flying. If anybody tries to hand over the main controls to you, refuse immediately.

Chips says: "You don't need much pressure to ...."

"That's way too much pressure," Chips says.

Now I'm flying the helicopter with cocooned concentration and not moving a single body part. I look like Nelson on top of his Column. Even my heart has stopped. I'm older than I think. Where has all my young flying daredevil gone?

"Make a right turn," Chips urges.

I move the control one millionth of a millimetre to the right and the helicopter leans over toward my side and that's when I realised there's still no door there. Mother Earth beckons and I instantly move the thing one millionth of a millimetre back.

I feel fully justified in thinking, "I'm not turning right

again. It's only left turns from now on - the person in the other seat can fall out first." I know my limitations even though my experience is short.

At this moment I realise that in my life I've witnessed a whole succession of technological revolutions, but none of them has done away with the need for character in the individual or the ability to think. You feel a dwindling sense of reality. Like rubbing two ball bearings together hoping they'll come up as two pound coins.

It becomes clear to Chips that if he continues to allow Nelson's Column to pilot Bessie, we're going to wind up flying in a straight line until we run out of fuel. Chips takes control. That's the good news. the bad news is, he's now saying something about demonstrating an "emergency procedure."

"It's for when your engine dies," Chips explains. "It's called auto-rotation, something like an amusement park ride."

Rule number four is logged firmly in my mind. Auto-rotation means dropping out of the sky at about the same speed and aerodynamic stability as an unleashed whirligig. Failure is not an option. As we near the ground Chips completes my training by having me hover the helicopter. Although the idea is to hang over one spot on the ground, I've got Bessie swooping and lurching all over the place like a demented bumble-bee. "Come, come you wally," I say to myself, "Nelson with one eye could have done better than this." Finally, overcoming the delicate balance between bravado and failure within my own mind and body, I become quite bold, even confident.

On landing Chips enthuses that I did fine and he'd be glad to take me up again. I tell him that sounds marvellous. These things grow on you by the minute. I'm convinced I was born to fly helicopters. Which brings me to rule number five.

I've always believed that taxi drivers are living proof that practice doesn't always make perfect.

FROM ASHES TO ASHES

As I ponder the start of another cricket season, my mind drifts to the summer of 1948 when I was at Bury Grammar School ("Where Leaders of Tomorrow Are Developing the Acne of Today.")

The big cricket story that year was the battle for the Ashes between England and Australia. In those days young people actually were interested in cricket unlike today's young people, who are much more interested in football during autumn, winter, spring AND summer, and of course, downloading dirty pictures from the Internet.

But in my youth, cricket ruled in summer. Almost every boy played the game, a character-building experience that helped some to develop a personal relationship of life-damaging quality with the "master in charge of cricket", otherwise known as God.

God used to put Clive on the deep long off boundary because it was against his religion to put him in Sweden, where he would have done less damage to the team .... "PLEASE don't let the ball come to me!"

But, of course, God enjoys a good prank as much as the next fallible deity, which is why he always made time in his busy schedule to make sure the next batter hit a towering stroke that would, upon entering the Earth's atmosphere, come down directly where Clive would have been standing, if he had stood still, which he never did. He staggered around cluelessly, so that the ball always landed a minimum of 40 feet from where

Clive wound up standing, thrusting his hands out in the no chance position.

Although I was one of God's chosen ones, we all stuck at improving our knowledge of the game "that cemented an Empire." My friends and I collected cricket cards like every junior male. I believe that at one time I had the original cards for Don Bradman, Len Hutton and Denis Compton, and that I'd be able to sell my collection for £100 million today, except my mother threw them out two years later.

My point is that we cared deeply about cricket back then, which meant we were passionate whenever England played Australia. My class was evenly divided between those who were England fans and those who were complete morons. Although I'd never met one, I never cared for Australian cricketers, and for very sound reasons: We had been indoctrinated to believe that bad weather and poor food after the war affected our ability and, Australian cricketers were much better than they had any right to be.

I followed nearly every ball of every over at the Lord's Test. It wasn't easy, because the game started in midweek when I was in school, which for some idiot reason was not called off for this important educational opportunity. This meant that certain students .... I'm not naming names, because even now, it could go on their School Leaving Report .... had to carry concealed radios to class. A major reason why the Russians got so far ahead of the West in the Cold War is that while Russian students were listening to their teachers explain cosines and tangents, we were listening to announcers explain how a missed chance had added another boundary to the Australian score.

I vividly remember how the Second Test ended. School had finished for the day, and I was heading home pushing my bike up the hill at Blackford Bridge, listening to my cheap heavy radio, my eyes staring vacantly ahead, my mind locked on the game. A delivery truck came by, and the driver stopped and asked what the score was.

The truck driver turned out to be a rabid Australian ex-serviceman who had stayed in England after the war. As we stood on opposite sides of my bike for the final minutes, rooting for opposite teams, I believed in my naivety that England might get the 596 runs to win. My rival was confidently chain-smoking full strength Capstan cigarettes and both of us were hanging on every word coming out of the tinny little speaker

And of course, if you were around back then and didn't live in Russia, you know what happened. Lindwall and Toshack ripped apart the best England could throw at them and Australia won by 409 runs to go two up in the series.

England had too many Clives at their disposal and was devastated beyond all measure. But, I will never forget what the Aussie said to me. He looked me square in the eye, one cricket fan to another after a tough but fair fight. "You Pommies could never play this bloody game!" With that the truck faded into the distance like my English hopes.

Australia had held the Ashes since the day I was born. I would be nineteen before English pride was restored.

WHITHER ROBOTS?

Sometimes during a period of S.E.X. (that is, when Science Expands Xceptionally), I wonder if scientific brains should be getting more sleep. Take the case of the new development with slugs of the slimy kind.

At this point I must explain that my wife, who treats slugs abominably in the garden, has a different opinion which so far has not caused too much friction in the Lomax household. But I digress.

The latest news comes from Bristol University where an inventive male mind has linked slugs to a new exciting robot concept. The problem, as the researcher saw it, was that today's robots need human help to function properly. When you or I run out of steam we are replenished with a cup of coffee, two digestives and a quick nod off. At the moment there is no such thing as a truly independent robot. The everlasting Terminator is not yet with us.

To produce a robot of that calibre, a scientific breakthrough is needed. That's where the agile mind from Bristol comes in. This truly advanced scientific brain has built a robot that when perfected, will power itself by catching "glistening semi-opaque slugs", and using them as fuel. I'm not kidding .... honest.

The idea came from the basic concept that the French have been converting snails and frogs into energy for centuries. Working on the assumption that these foods are not for the true humanoid, every available laboratory in Bristol has worked on developing a purely mechanical device that looks like a power mower with a long robot arm. When the arm detects a "glistening semi-opaque slug", the arm swoops down, grabs the unsuspecting slug and drops it into a "belly drawer." When the drawer is full, my wife is happy, but the bird population, according to the Bird Food Gazette, is largely disgruntled.

With the "belly drawer" full, the now fully operational robot converts the slugs into electric power via some chemical process that, quite frankly, I'm not scientific enough to understand. Apparently, slugs contain electricity which comes as a shock to those of us who thought they were basically little bags of slime that have worked out at slug gymnasia to develop their crawls. And who would have thought of filling a torch with slugs anyway?

If this slug robot concept works it could well be adopted in ways that would truly benefit humanity. Imagine the scene in a chic restaurant. You're enjoying a real food experience with convivial friends when, at the next table, a mobile phone rings, and some idiot speaks so loudly that every diner hears each boring word. Your evening is ruined, but no! With a silky smooth action, a silvery shape glides to the adjacent table. A second later, a robot arm snakes out and the offending mobile phone is plucked from the idiot's hand. Applause pours forth from every table. It grows louder when the robot arm reaches out again and .... yes, the idiot is snatched from his chair. Your hope is that the robot is short on slugs and needs to replenish its food system urgently by other means.

With this type of encouragement in mind, research continues apace on this new generation of robots. Developments are expected within the year on how "spandex-groined frogs" and "spangled-thighed snails" can improve robot longevity. Current experiments are confined to observing what happens when a female "spandex-groined frog" wishes to attract a male. They tried playing a recording of a frog call but this did not cause real frogs to respond in an attractive manner. It only caused them to ask for a Bud Light and drink more beer. The problem was solved by building a robot frog which sits on a false log in a pretend pool with a speaker inside its body. Scientists report that real frogs become attracted to this robotic device, apparently fooled by the fact that it has a realistic-looking inflatable throat sac made from a translucent condom.

So there's the present position. Scientists have, at long

last, found a way of using condoms to make "spandex-groined frogs" agitated. I know I speak for all humanity when I say to the scientific community by way of sincere appreciation: Please keep working with the "spangle-thighed snails" and any other erotic creature in order to satiate the appetites of energy deficient robots.

As an earthling, I await with great apprehension the next resplendent outcome from our Bristol seat of learning.

SILENCE IS GOLDEN

I read the other day that a man in Brighton totally fed up with the repetitive strains of "Pop Goes the Weasel" emanating from an ice cream vendor's vehicle, attacked the hapless driver with a half-eaten ice cream cone and - here's the worst - a stick of rock with the word "Blackpool" running through it.

In this day and age there's no excuse for this kind of incident. Just because a driver is operating a van that repeatedly blares an annoying song over a loudspeaker in a public place doesn't mean that we should attack him with sweet teeth impairing products, especially those promoting an alternative resort. We should use strike weapons of the latest kind.

Forgive me for sounding hostile (it's my age) but I'm getting sick and tired of loud intrusive noises in public, especially loud and tinny music. It's everywhere. All the shopping malls, restaurants and airports are riddled with low-fidelity loudspeakers, which apparently have developed the ability to reproduce themselves. These are all connected to a special programming service called Music That Nobody Really Likes, and you can't get away from it. When I'm in the gents at the mall, I'm not there to listen to a singing nun, I'm there to commune with nature and listen to gentle farting and belching like everyone else.

Likewise I don't go to the airport to listen to music. I go there for the same reason as millions of other travellers, which is to wait in queues, be hassled at security and find out that my flight has been delayed or cancelled.

And why, when you're in a restaurant, is the music so loud that you can't communicate with anyone at your own table or the fussing staff?

Waitress (shouting): "Good evening. Would you like anything to drink?"

Me (looking glazed): "Does that come with mustard sauce?"

It's just as bad when you go outside. One day I was on the beach at Bournemouth, along with hundreds of other people, all of us enjoying an afternoon listening to the barely audible "ping" of solar rays ricocheting off our SPF 45 sun block, when some men arrived with a boombox the size of my car, and of course it was playing the latest Rabid Dreadlocks release. It was tuned up so loud that the English Channel started to ebb with waves rushing out to sea to get away from the noise. Finally, I'd had enough. I stood up, brushed off the clinging sand, flexed my hips like a gunslinger, adjusted my hat, steeled my eyes, spat on the beach, adopted my John Wayne walk, and decided that no matter what the risk, I was going to write about it.

The solution for this ticklish and potentially dangerous problem came to me in the dentist's chair which is the ideal place to have wicked and vicious thoughts. It involves a transmitter that's easily carried around. When a person starts playing loud music in your vicinity or drives a car with one of those sound systems emitting base notes so low and powerful that they cause big cracks to open up on the M4, you'll simply press a button, and the transmitter would send out a signal which explodes the offending appliance.

As innocent people could be hurt by flying debris that might only be a short term solution, but at least a signal that would cause annoying static to loud music perpetrators might solve the problem. On reflection, they probably wouldn't notice the difference.

Anyway, I think somebody should produce a transmitter like this and send me one. I think a feature, whereby, when you're driving, you could point it anywhere and reduce noise would enhance sales. Just think what you could do to barking dogs, lawn mowers, screaming children and Members of Parliament.

FOIBLES OF THE MOTHER TONGUE

Feeling in a fusty literary mode my mind flashes to linguistic oddities and idiocies of the English language that need to be cleared out regularly like a filter in a washing machine.

The other day on Radio 4 I heard someone talking about the quality of life and the quantity of life. "Quantity of life?" I get the meaning, but it grates on the ear. Life is a journey, not a bulk item. We don't measure it out in quantities like a kilo bag of flour.

The more I thought about this wonderful language of ours, the more peculiarities I began to compile. For example, "A coffee" as in "Would you like a coffee?" Whatever happened to just plain "You want coffee?" There was no "a" in front of coffee when I started drinking it 40 years ago. Western heroes never had "a coffee" with the guys around the campfire.

It must surely be an affectation engendered by asking for "a cappuccino" to go with "a baguette".
What's next? "Do you need a pliers to tighten a nut?" or even "a scissors"? I might ask you for "scissors" or "a pair of scissors" but never "a scissors". That's as bad as "a binoculars".

"I have to *take* a meeting at noon." This is just a self-important way of saying, "I have a noon meeting." I was taught that you *take* a break, *take* a nap, *take* a friend .... you can even *take* tea. But you don't *take* meetings. You have a meeting, go to a meeting, chair a meeting or perhaps skip a meeting. I also have a problem with "*take* a decision" which is often used instead of "make a decision" by the same people who "have a coffee" and "*take* a meeting" instead of just showing up like the rest of us.

You have to marvel at a language in which your house can burn up as it burns down, in which you fill in a form by filling it out and in which an alarm goes off by going on. Pursuing it further, why is it that grocers don't groce and hammers don't ham? And why is it that you can have one goose and two geese but never one moose and two meese? And isn't it strange that you can make amends but not one amend; that you can comb through the annals of history but never through a single annal?

"Brings to the table" has nothing to do with food or dinner tables. It's a term chic among journalists. A powerful politician "brings a lot to the table in the budget negotiations." The irony is that powerful figures who "bring a lot to the table" in the metaphorical sense never bring anything in the physical sense. They leave the heavy lifting to their aides, who bring nothing to the table.

"At the end of the day" also drives me mad. This is

another political phrase that has seeped out of Westminster to pollute discourse across Britain. As used by politicians, "at the end of the day" really means "when we and the upstarts on the other side are finished posturing and wasting the taxpayers' money." We don't know exactly when that might be, but we know for sure when it won't be: At the end of the day. Fat chance, or I could have said slim chance which means exactly the same. All these words spoken by a wise man, not a wise guy which means exactly the opposite.

Bubble .... bubble .... bubble .... my mind is now in torment. How can overlook and oversee be opposites, while quite a lot and quite a few are alike? How can weather be as hot as hell one day and cold as hell another? If teachers have taught, why haven't preachers praught? If a vegetarian eats vegetables, what does a humanitarian eat? And so on. Why is there no egg in eggplant, no pine in pineapple and no ham in hamburger? If you're out shopping don't forget that sweetmeats are confectionery and sweetbreads are meat. As a further thought it makes logical sense to talk about a "rainbrella" and to realise that the modern plural of adult must surely be adultery.

A few years ago, after "borrowing" some Kleenex from a friend, I realised that she probably didn't want it back. That's when the unsavoury connotation of "borrowing" Kleenex hit home, and I resolved not to use the phrase. You might borrow a shovel or a ladder, but not Kleenex. I now make a point of asking if I can have some Kleenex. It means I owe that person Kleenex, but it's a much neater transaction. Come to think of it: Is it some Kleenex or a Kleenex?

It's amazing the things we can't do in English. Have you ever run into someone who was gruntled, combobulated, ruly or peccable? Have you ever seen a horseful carriage or a strapful evening gown? Have you met a sung hero or experienced requited love? English becomes really creative as you appreciate that when the stars are out, they are visible, but when lights are out, they are invisible.

And finally, why when I wind up my watch, do I start it, but when I wind up this column, I end it?

INCONTESTABLE TRUTHS

It's surprising how many times in later life you tap the cerebral filing cabinet in which are stored the great truths learned in childhood. You know the kind I'm talking about.. Truths such as Queen Victoria ascended the throne in 1837, Paris is the capital of France and always wear clean underwear because you never know when you'll be knocked down crossing the road.

Oh, the things we learn at our parents knees. I grew up imagining a doctor consoling my heartbroken Mum and Dad: "I'm very sorry, there was nothing we could do. His underwear was dirty."

The baggage of growing up between the Corporation bus depot and the Crown Brewery was heavy and loaded with discipline. "Eat it, it's good for you." This maternal entreaty was drilled into me because it applied to ALL foods at EVERY meal. How burned kippers and dried up rice pudding was good for me was beyond my tender years, and I was only too happy for Popeye to consume all my spinach. A clean plate signified a pure mind and a frugal attitude especially when you were brought up in a Primitive Methodist tradition.

"Eat it. It will put hairs on your chest." This was a masculine riposte to a child's poor appetite. I'm still not sure whether I owe the hair on my chest to genetics or stewed liver. All I know is the little girl next door, who had a similar diet, has not been the same since. And why was it that just as my Auntie Millie asked me a question or I wished to protest at her dog using my leg as its favourite sexual toy, my mother would invariably spurt out: "Don't speak with your mouth full!"

"There are millions of children in the world who would give anything to eat those mashed turnips." Name one of those children. Go on, name one. That's all want. Just a name. No one in England for sure, they've more sense, "Eat up your porridge, it will make you a big strong man." At that early age I had no pretensions or desire to be another Charles Atlas or budding Tarzan. And, if that were the case, why weren't all the kids in my area big and strong? More than a few were plump and stumpy with bandy legs.

"If I see you chewing gum again you'll deserve having your insides stick together." Such talk from my Uncle Jack gave me a pathological fear of chewing gum and certainly blowing bubbles with it. What if the bubble burst and the house walls came together and squashed me like an errant bluebottle?

"Never put your knife in your mouth, you'll cut your tongue out." Why, if this was a rule of life, did the gabby woman next door, I observed doing this dastardly deed on more than one occasion, still blabber on? My overzealous Aunt Eliza had a good line. "Say grace before you eat or you'll choke on your food." My surly reply of: "Whatever did atheists do and why aren't they all dead?" was deemed too clever by half and could lead me to purgatory. Of course, not all the advice was restricted to the meal table.

"You'll put your eye out." My mother thought that any object with edges harder or sharper than a marshmallow would obviously blind you for life. I'm certain those turnips were mashed out of fear I would one day miss my mouth with my fork and hit my eye. "You'll break your neck!" and "You'll scramble your brains!" were the standard responses to riding a bike with no hands and heading wet, heavy footballs. Hanging sloth-like from high oak tree branches was beyond words. My favourite ploy was to get caught leapfrogging over dustbins to see if my mother would amend the admonition to fit the true anatomical risk. The nearest she got was: "You'll ruin yourself for life."

"Don't spend it all at once." When my father extracted these words from his font of dubious wisdom as he parted with the traditional minute spending money, he probably never imagined his advice would be followed by boring a hole through the sixpenny coin, attaching a piece of piano wire, and using it again and again on certain vending machines. I never spent it all in one place.

Looking back, I can't condemn my parents for passing on such faulty advice. They were helpless in the matter, conditioned and brainwashed in Lancashire manners, just as I am. As far as I know, no one ever died of acute kale deficiency and the lack of mashed turnips.

OVER THE HILL? DEFINITELY NOT!

Lucky? Well, yes, I think it's a rather fortunate situation being alive in this day and age when men and women are living longer than ever before. There's a line of thinking that the more birthdays you have, the more of them you're apt to amass. I'll go along with that.

To ensure my amassing large quantities of birthdays I stay active mentally, I refrain from becoming a couch potato and I try to look as old as I am by keeping up appearances. It was George Eliot who wrote, "It's never too late to be what you might have been." I know I can be alive and happy at any age. But does my body?

Physically I feel good, but my mind plays tricks especially in relation to the age I want to be. I'm now at the age when I wonder why they've started printing everything in smaller type. And why is everyone beginning to mumble? Stopping for a chat I seem to start every sentence with "Nowadays" as the conversation lapses into segments of "duelling ailments."

Worse still, I keep repeating myself.

Health topics loom large in every exchange of views at a party where regularity of bowel movement is now considered a reasonable topic of conversation. Things are so bad my chemist and all his staff call me by my first name. I've convinced myself I'm not over the hill in spite of my back going out more than I do. My mouth has developed the sad habit of making promises my body can't keep, and I've come to the conclusion that my worst enemy in life is gravity. Which brings me to the subject of sex.

Worse still, I keep repeating myself.

Which brings me to the subject of sex. (I simply like the word sex. It comforts me to realise I still know what the word demands of me.) It was only a few years ago my mind began to wander as I thought libido was a new form of Italian pasta. I'm now at that vulnerable age when it takes me an hour to undress and another hour to remember why. And when I've remembered, it takes me all night to do what I used to do all night. As sex assumes the mantle of a job, I know I may soon be unemployed. My venerable interpretation of a "quickie" is having a nap at the traffic lights.

Worse still, I keep repeating myself.

Things aren't much better at breakfast. I hear the "snap, crackle and pop" and am totally aware I haven't yet poured milk on my cereal. All my favourite foods now seem to be "soft", and I seem to be cultivating an abnormal taste for milkshakes of magnesia. Even when watching TV my ears prick up when a laxative commercial leaps before my eyes. I try desperately to be good and not complain too much, but I find myself frequently telling people I can remember what a loaf of bread used to cost when I was a lad. The fact that a postage stamp today costs more than going to the cinema did when I was growing up seems to have great social significance to no one else but me.

Worse still, I keep repeating myself.

So, as the years begin to add up and everyone else seems to be getting taller, I have to visit a museum to see my childhood toys in their prime. The two ultimate chagrins to my life happened this morning. My insurance broker has begun to send his free advertising calendar one month at a time And, to cap that, while out for a stroll in the park I decided to rest on a bench and a sprightly Boy Scout approached and helped me cross my legs.

Worse still, I keep repeating myself.

As it stands, there's a multitude of people out there simply tickled with my situation. My sociological fears are being addressed.

Worse still, I keep repeating myself.

By the way, if I've repeated myself lately, do let me know as it's quite an annoying habit .... to keep repeating yourself.

MORE JUICE AND LESS GLUE?

When I experience a power cut abroad, I complain about living in a third world country. After all, what else can you expect? However, when the electricity goes off in Leeds, it can cause so much havoc it makes the possibility of moving to Mozambique appealing.

But be warned. What can happen to Leeds can happen to the rest of Britain. So it is vital that I analyse the Leeds electricity shortage and see if I can develop a workable solution before I become bored and change the subject to its connection with tiling.

The first question that must be asked is: What exactly is electricity? As any schoolchild knows, electricity is actually a fast-moving herd of electrons which are extremely tiny uni-celled animals that can survive in almost any environment except towns in Yorkshire and inside double-A batteries, where they die within minutes of purchase.

Electrons are formed when clouds rub together and become excited thus creating electricity. Once there, it forms into lightning which is attracted to earth by golfers taking a backswing. Then, after entering the ground usually down the golfer's right leg, the electricity hardens into coal which, when mined and burned in big ovens called generators, turns back into electricity, which is sent in the form of volts and watts through special wires with birds sitting on them to consumer's homes.. Once there it is transformed by TV sets into commercials for beer which passes through the consumers and back into the ground, thus completing what is known as the circuit.

Who is responsible for the Leeds outages? The electric company first comes to mind but it could well be the entertainment industry which uses over 750 billion watts of electricity per day just to blow-dry the TV news presenters. But I fear the real culprits are college students. I base this allegation on widespread observation of the genre who in Leeds alone consume more electricity than the whole of Denmark. If a student is in a room, every electrical device within 200 metres of that room .... every light, television, computer, stereo, microwave, mini-oven, coffee machine etc. will be running. Students don't normally have to turn the devices on; they activate themselves spontaneously in response to the student's presence. The meters located in student's halls of residence are notorious for bursting into flames generated by the mechanism rotating at a speed beyond the ability of the naked eye to see it.

So what's that to do with tiling, I hear you say?

According to a Leeds friend of mine, a friend of hers who wants to be identified only as "Paula" for reasons that will become clear, decided to surprise her husband by tiling the kitchen floor herself. Most people think laying tiles is a job for a professional tiler. After all, any home decorator will tell you that there is nothing like a tile floor for transforming an ordinary room into an ordinary room that has tiles on the floor.

Paula was of the opinion that all tiling takes is a little planning and the right materials. What she didn't contemplate was a power cut and the essential intervention of the esteemed Leeds Fire Services.

Step One, of course, was for Paula to spread powerful glue on the floor in order to bond the tiles firmly in place. Paula was about to instigate Step Two, when .... you've guessed it .... the lights went out! At this point, totally disorientated, Paula slipped and fell face-first into the glue she had spread in Step One, thus bonding herself to the floor.

Fortunately, Paula was not alone. Also in the house,

thank goodness, was one of the most useful companions a person can ever hope to have - a low bellied Dachshund. Paula's dog, called Sophie, saw that her owner was in trouble, so she did what all dogs do when their owners are in trouble: lick the owner's face. Dogs fervently believe this is the correct response to every emergency.

When Sophie, ill-fatedly, decided to help out, she naturally also became stuck in the glue, stomach and all. But again, luck was on Paula's side, because also at home was her 8 years-old daughter, Gabriella, who, realising that the situation was no joking matter immediately began laughing hysterically. As the laughter subsided, the glue sniffing and barking increased. But Gabriella had the great presence of mind to dial 999 for the fire rescue team.

Paula meanwhile was trying to solve her personal glue problem. Her right foot was stuck to the floor, her legs were stuck together; on rising, her bottom stuck to the wall (becoming stuck to a wall while tiling is quite an art form in itself), and her hand became stuck to Sophie.

Perhaps this is the time to relate the fact that Paula had been working in, and was still wearing, only her underwear. Fortunately, the firemen were serious, competent, highly trained professionals who only laughed until they cried. Once the firemen recovered, they freed Paula and Sophie with solvents, and everything turned out fine.

Paula ultimately got her new tiled floor and saved herself a lot of money which I'm sure more than made up for suffering enough humiliation to last three or four lifetimes. So, what has the nation learned from this episode?

One, be sure to lay tiles only with a dog and a child handy.

Two, any tile layer should wear clean underwear,

preferably sponsored by Paula's Secret.

Three, only lay tiles in a university town when the students are on holiday and the electricity supply can be guaranteed.

TWO DON'TS FOR MEN

Having had over 50 years experience of doing the wrong things as a male adult, there are definitely two activities not to be recommended for those of the male persuasion.

The first: Don't attend morning wine tastings.

Even if you do spit out the great majority of the wine intake, the membranes of the mouth and tongue absorb enough alcohol to make everyone a chattily intelligent but in reality a gibberishly-oriented lunch companion.

It doesn't take you long to realise that if you swilled down the 17 different glasses they poured at 9 o'clock in the initial morning session, you'd never make it up the escalator to lunch after the second session, even if the steps did move by themselves.

When you've had Beaujolais for breakfast; when you've swirled, sniffed and sipped a varied assortment of wines at such an early hour, there are occupational hazards to be dealt with, like walking to lunch on your knees. And, if you taste them all again to confirm your appreciation, the rest of the day becomes something of a blur.

One ardent taster insisted it was all about the occasion, the location and the companionship. After deep contemplation and excessive lingering, the occasion, location and companionship blended into a fuzzy haze. With my taste buds by now exhausted, my nominations for the top ten wines had the certainty of being unreliable.

The tenth and worst was Pipi du Chat, a white wine that smelled exactly like cat urine.

Ninth place went to another inconspicuous white wine I christened Stale Brie.

Eighth, and more sophisticated, was a blush wine I called Mothballs as my eyes watered after the second spit.

Seventh came a savage Italian red that reminded me of fiery Red Peppers.

Sixth was a pleasant white tipple that had the aura of vintage Klebestift (solvent free Glue Stick) to be called anything else.

In fifth place I chose Smoke, a Burgundy of smooth yet cloudy proportions.

Fourth I nominated a jolly red of mixed parentage I could only identify as Barnyard.

In third place for the bronze medal I selected a Chardonnay that truly reminded me of rather pleasant Rust Remover.

For the silver medal in second place I picked a leathery Cabernet Sauvignon that could not be mistaken for anything else but Pommel of Saddle.

In prime and gold position, I plumped for a true Burgundy of outstanding merit that brought back memories of Forest Floor. The taster next to me agreed. She referred to the unique aroma as "boxwood with a hint of carbon." As I had never licked boxwood or tasted carbon I could but nod my head in sage approval.

As for the other seven wines, suffice it to say I couldn't separate the sheep from the goats. And that was purely on bouquet.

The problem of morning wine tastings is that you are

not really fit enough to travel home alone after lunch, or for that matter, wrap bottles of wine for family gifts before leaving. Which brings me to the second thing a man shouldn't do. Keep away from gift-wrapping when wine has control of your senses.

When the Three Wise men brought gifts of gold, frankincense and myrrh there was no mention of wrapping paper or beverages. The people giving these gifts had two important characteristics: 1. They were wise.
2. They were men.

Although today nothing can be given without it being gift-wrapped, men are not big gift wrappers. Men don't understand the point of putting paper on a gift just so somebody else can tear it off. There are two good manly reasons for this opinion. First, if you're giving a poor gift, you don't want to be there when the recipient rips the paper off. Second, a maximum effort of 20 seconds is sufficient time for wrapping under any circumstances.

Usually, I'm as good as the next man at wrapping gifts, but a wine tasting lunch after 34 samplings plus an excess of the winning Forest Floor is not the best preparation for wrapping a few bottles of wine for those dear to me. I couldn't have wrapped even one bottle in a parachute without the neck of the bottle protruding. On the other hand, if my wife had been there, she could have taken a 12-inch square of wrapping paper and neatly covered a Jumbo Jet immaculately. My wife, like most women, actually likes wrapping things. If she gives you a gift that requires batteries, she wraps the batteries separately which to me is very close to being a symptom of mental illness. If it were possible, my beloved would wrap each individual volt as an extra act of kindness.

My point is that gift-wrapping is one of those skills - like having babies - that comes more naturally to women than

to men. As a consequence, there are three golden rules to be observed in gift-wrapping for men.
1. Whenever possible buy gifts that are already wrapped.
2. If you're giving a hard-to-wrap gift, ignore the wrapping. Just put it inside a bag and stick one of those little adhesive bows on it.
3. Do not attempt to wrap anything with too much alcohol inside you.

In relation to the second golden rule, a problem arises when you're giving your wife a petrol operated leaf blower for her birthday. You need a large black rubbish bag and an exceedingly large adhesive bow. If this situation should lead to a request for a divorce, remember your mother's wise words. "It's not the gift, it's the thought that counts."

The modern situation however, leads me to two conclusions. First, it's not what you give, but how you wrap it that matters. And second, when you've no intention of wrapping a gift, the only reasonable alternative is to give a present of gold, frankincense or myrrh, which will enable you to go to morning wine tastings.

UNMENTIONABLES

As I was raised in a Ladies Outfitting business, seeing women in the nearly altogether was part of everyday life. From a tender age, the sight of corsets and underslips left me totally unphased. Everything in those days was muted, discreet and white or beige. Today, unmentionables are mentioned and revealed in multi-colour splendour with no reserve at all.

Underwear has come a long way from the frozen loins

of a 5,300-years-old Tyrolean iceman to the modern-day revelations of exciting colours and intimate versatile lingerie. The loincloth or schenti is the universal antecedent of underwear, and Pharoah Tutankhamen was buried with 145 of them, which seemed more than an ample supply for the afterlife. As in the ancient world, the higher you stood on the social scale, the more you wore, it wasn't surprising that female slaves in Ancient Egypt wore scanty cachessexe, much like a strip-teaser's G-string.

The modern woman now has a choice beyond the comprehension of her grandmother and possibly, her mother. While underwear has always been associated with modesty or the lack of it, what women have worn next to their skin over the centuries is full of contradictions and gritty realism.

In the 16th and 17th centuries, under multiple petticoats and complex costumes, women at court wore little or nothing. The bulky crinoline had to be hung from the outside of their conveyance in order for the wearer to get aboard. In a high wind the crinoline was difficult to manoeuvre so drawers and pantaloons became necessary lingerie in the early 19th century.

Corsets have immobilised women longer than any other article of underwear, and for nearly four centuries, tight stays made of whalebone, reed, metal or double stitched cording were items of restriction. Fortunately, the first elastic "easing" insert appeared in 1885.

The idea that the ungirdled might be wanton or loose led to women being confined "in a cage" below the waist, which the chastity belt carried to an extreme. By the 19th century there was little time wasted on modesty, and the vanities of fashion ensured that a "straight-laced" woman would be hard put to dress herself. The fabled 19-inch waist was not easily achieved. By the prudish Victorian era, the sight of women in their underwear became quite titillating. It was at this time that the fetish and voyeurism into getting dressed and undressed became well established.

When the austerities of the early 29th century had faded, underwear revolutionised itself after World War II. A new language developed with a tendency to refer to underwear in a form of baby talk: undies, panties, scanties, snuggies, teddies, scivvies and smalls. Lingerie designers celebrated their liberation from wartime restrictions with a lavish use of colour, sheer fabrics and lace, as they believed lacy lingerie maintained feminine (and masculine) morale. The pointed bra and zippered panties of the late 1940's seemed a great escape from the rougher materials and cami-knickers of wartime restrictions. The arrival of the panty girdle ensured a slimming task was performed relatively painlessly.

Lingerie was soon to hit the headlines. It was America's Gussie Moran who, in 1949, became the first player to wear lace panties at Wimbledon. A theme carried on by Italian Lea Pericoli who loved showing off her lace panties in the 1955 Wimbledon. In even more liberated form, Pat Stewart, another American tennis player, then became in 1961 the first woman to embroider her phone number on her panties. The wide publicity created by these torchbearers ensured lingerie was never again to be hidden from the gaze of men.

The Sixties saw the beginning of the greatest lingerie revolution. Legs were put into perspective with the introduction of panty hose and mesh-enhanced stockings. Underwear became arty and more seductive with ranges of lingerie being specifically designed for evening wear. Black became known as the colour for a woman of many loves, while the mini skirt launched a decade of crotch watchers. Designers kept in tune with fabrics suitable for "skin as soft as a hamster's underbelly."

The one-piece exercise suit inspired by a dancer's leotard and tights in the mid-1960's was enhanced by the invention of spandex in the 1970's which made possible even better lightweight body shapes. Still evolving, lingerie redesigned the body with the strapless bra, the push-up bra and the no-bra bra. Madonna in 1990 became the signature for underwear becoming an outerwear costume when she wore her corselette with cone-shaped cups.

Today, women may jog in sports bras and cut off shorts but they still retain satin, lace and cologne in their vocabularies. Designer underwear for the liberated body in ever developing stretch fabrics has created unprecedented freedom of movement for the modern woman.

Call it what you will .... underbodice, waist cincher, camisole, shapesuit, secret hug, undershaper, body-briefer, bellyband, or even a butt booster, and regardless of what men think or wish for, there will be no turning back as fashions invariably do. Intimate apparel will remain attractive, easy to wear and affordable in an industry generating billions.

VIVA LAS VEGAS

As I've never been one for betting or the bright lights, seeing Las Vegas didn't have much appeal. However, by courtesy of a few free air miles, I made myself overcome my innermost feelings and dropped in for a two-night stay on my way back from San Francisco.

You can play slots at the airport, field bets in craps, hit a hard 17 at blackjack, play your birth date at roulette and bet extravagantly on any sport.

I expected things to be larger than life. I wasn't disappointed. Las Vegas offers a stylish gaming experience, a galaxy of restaurants and huge bedrooms with wall-to-wall marble in the bathrooms. The Flamingo Hotel is one of the last bastions of Las Vegas' greatest art form. Its neon sign is one of the last great neon whirls in Nevada. It offers a large black-light-illuminated jellyfish tank and a gang of entertainers who never repeat a song during a week-long engagement.

Caesars Palace is now a garish mishmash of classical silliness that makes the place look like Caesars Townhouse. A place where, if you're feeling flush, you can get a $10 concoction of Muy Generosa Margarita. If you have the "green" you can get wild yet outstanding food in Las Vegas while watching topless jiggle until you sleep from eye exhaustion. The town has an entertainment scene fermenting with sexuality that seems plucked from an alternate universe. From one end of the "strip" to the other, you come across women, tightly sheathed in transparent fabrics, slung in enigmatic postures on low sofas. It doesn't require too much imagination to understand they might have a wish to engage in explicit acts with anyone ranging from teenage gymnasts, live game hens or Amish lesbians.

The Palms Hotel oozes chic and its Little Buffalo Bar is the hippest spot in the hippest hotel in town. It seems like the little sister to the famous supermodel hangout in Paris. Waiters fly about on wire pulleys to fetch bottles of genuine Bordeaux, Burgundy and Champagne from the four-storey-tall glass wine bin. They also extract from unseen parts, strange wines varying from Grape Expectations, Chateau d'Horrible and Nasti Spumante. It's a cross between Mission Impossible and Wine Extravaganza. It appears to be an endless "Battle of the Bars" which leads expensively to a wrath of grapes hangover.

A massive 106 lanes of bowling exist under one roof. When the place is cranking, the sound of rolling balls on lanes and the crash of pins is deafening. Soaring 1,149 feet into the desert sky is the Stratosphere, the tallest free-standing observation tower in the USA. Non-acrophobes can try out the Big Shot roller coaster which runs 100 floors above the town. Nearby is a water-park version of drag racing which drops 76 feet at a 70-degree angle that will leave your swimming trunks waistband around your Adam's apple.

When your eyes are saturated with neon (it doesn't take long), your nostrils are filled with cigarette smoke (much too much), and your ears are ringing with the clang-clang-clang (never less than incessant) of slot machines, you can at least head out in your hired luxury sedan to a silent, still spot - Red Rock Canyon National Conservation Area. Here, you can find out that Las Vegas wouldn't exist if it weren't for the water and energy supplied by the massive Hoover Dam on the Colorado river. The dam completed in 1936 after 5 years of work is 726 feet tall with walls that are 660 feet thick at its base. Big, mighty big.

Garish flamboyance and seduction predominate. It's a town in which you feel you can never have enough money. Even the mysterious and ultra-wealthy Howard Hughes had to negotiate hard to buy out the Silver Slipper across from the hotel where he lived. The owners didn't respond kindly to his request to turn down the neon lights so he could sleep - so, he bought the place!

Was my fleeting visit worthwhile? If you like meeting people thickly coated in influential connections; people who seem more than a little tipsy and keep repeating themselves like functioning drunks, and women who look sort of orgasmic, real touchy feely types, Las Vegas is the place to be. As for the restaurants, they offer themselves as temples of indulgence, but in many cases their chefs are false gods.

I'm glad I discovered why I didn't want to go to Las Vegas in the first place.

Most emphatically, my wife agrees with me.

CHANGING A WOMAN'S MIND

It's the time of year when we put the holiday season behind us, a time when we suck in our stomachs, leave the cosy confines of our homes, purchase some liquid refreshment, return to our homes, slump down in front of our TV sets and watch the beginning of a new football season.

I love to watch football on television, and I will tell you why. I have no idea. Perhaps the appeal of this boisterous game stems from some basic biological urge that men have, dating back millions of years to when primitive spear-carrying men would go into the forest to hunt game for their families, and their very survival depended on their ability to operate a remote control.

Whatever the attractions, a lot of women seem to be immune to it. I've seen women walk right past a TV with a football match on and - this always amazes me - not stop to watch, even if the television is showing replays of what is called "a disgraceful incident", which is a tackle so fierce that it causes at least one major internal organ to actually fly out of a player's body. The average man can't ignore something of this importance. He's going to stop and watch, even if he's supposed to be doing something else, such as visiting his sick wife in hospital. The average man might not be able to name the Foreign Secretary, but he can tell you who crunched

Arsenal's midfield star in an instant. A crunch so horrible that the TV people basically cancelled the rest of the season so they could show replays of the incident in slow motion.

As is usual at family gatherings, the women congregate in one room and talk about relationships, children, make-up and clothes, while the men gravitate towards the television and stare, cowlike, at a rerun of the most hideous tackle ever perpetuated in the name of soccer. The men only talk to analyse the details of the ferocious acts in slo-mo detail.

> Geoff: "Look at that! What's that on the end of his boot?"
> Tony: "I think it's his spleen."
> Ben: "No, a spleen that far out is going to rupture. That has to be a kidney."
> Sam: "That's not a kidney, it's a sod .... a dirty sod!"

If someone strapped these men's wives to a table and attached electrodes to their feet, not one of them would ever watch a game of football. However, after 36 years of fierce indifference, I detect Geoff's wife, Sally, is revealing an interest, albeit of the mildest kind. What prevents Sally from taking an even keener interest in the manly game is her lack of an answer to the following questions.

1. Will I grow chest hair and stop painting my nails?
2. Will I lose all interest in sewing, cooking, home decorating and shopping for cute footwear?
3. Will I always be looking over the shoulder of the person I'm talking to, in order to see a replay of that vitally important goal?

Sally did briefly discuss midfield players with me the other day. I felt quite honoured. She is gradually succumbing, I sense, to the relentless, driving force in our lives .... the defence splitting through ball. Her own friends think she is betraying a sacred trust. "When your Geoff turns on the Saturday Premiership matches, you should get up and leave the country, Sally, I don't know what's got into you."

Sally refuses to answer. It has to do with a certain core belief that if huge numbers of people (even if they are men) are interested in a particular subject, then there's got to be something meritorious and good embedded in the subject. After all, a woman gets to the point in life where she realises that every May the F.A. Cup Final will demand her attention. An event so full of statistics which are repeated 162 times, that a certain amount of football knowledge just sort of sinks into Sally by osmosis.

At some point, I decided that if Sally was going to acquire the knowledge, it was going to be quality knowledge. I encouraged her brain to care about whether the teams we were watching had "depth" and "vision". Quite soon she was uttering pithy comments, words of discernment and understandings the disconnects of press coverage. "Well, everyone used to write off Liverpool, but not now. They're strong all round but especially in central defence now that they've bought ...."

Sally is now at the time of life where she stops men dead in their tracks. By far the more surprising reason is her accumulated knowledge of the people's game. Husband Geoff now has different priorities. "Geoff, can I come round and watch the big game tonight?" I said hopefully. "Well, you can, but I might be back a bit late from shopping. You can watch it with Sally if you like."

What a turn up for the books. Could be an interesting couple of hours getting to grips over 4-2-3 or 3-5-2 with Sally. With a bit of luck crunching tackles could be a feature of the evening. We grouped in front of the television like birds with a

similarity of marking.
    Who says a man can't change a woman?

ONE OF LIFE'S GOTCHAS

    A week last Tuesday morning I excused myself from the breakfast table, collected the unread sections of the newspaper and stepped innocently into the bathroom. And, oh boy, do I wish I could do that scene over again, warily this time or at least watch it on tape to find out what went haywire. At any rate, I bent down to pick up a foreign object, and let out a yelp and a fart at the same time.

    Most readers will know what I'm talking about in this regard. Not a surreptitious breaking of wind but one that could be heard in Vladivostock. The yelp was emitted because some little known part of my spinal bone structure seemed to have slipped into the vacuum created by the ejection of wind. No friends, I don't need sympathy like, "I know, I get the same thing. Why, only last week ...."

    I sought solace in knowing that breaking wind is healthy and shouldn't cause embarrassment. Indeed an ejection 15 times a day helps to expel digestive gas that would otherwise cause discomfort. the authority for such thoughts emanates from the Netherlands Liver and Intestine Foundation which launched a taboo-breaking publicity campaign on the problem to try to clear the air.

    So you've got the picture. I behaved like an old fart as I placed my hands on my lower back and slowly straightened up. Like many individuals I'm sporadically stricken with mean lower back spasms, although, thank goodness, mostly of the minor variety. The kind that can be self-treated or wife-manipulated with kneading, manoeuvring and loving hands if caught early enough.

We back sufferers can't bank on case histories. Backs and fate are fickle friends. And what doctor dispenses guarantees? One remark I definitely don't want to hear is some misguided but well-intentioned individual advising that I must not despair because a) it takes older people much longer to heal, or b) there's always someone worse off than you.

I know that. I fully realise my age. I also fully acknowledge that I'm better off than George Mills who was nearly electrocuted at work and was left in a coma for weeks. He hired two solicitors and a QC. One was disbarred, one died and the other ran off with George's wife. His landlord wants to evict him. The insurance company wants to reduce his compensation. His heart and liver ailments require him to take 56 pills a day and to use a cylinder of oxygen. Recently he was in a car crash and after the police left the scene, he was held up and robbed. That's why the newspapers collectively chose him as the world's unluckiest man. The worst part, as I see it, is that George is only 31. How much more can he take?

My back is as nothing compared with George's problems. On the positive side, affliction is just one more stringent reminder of how splendid life was, is and can be.

Still, it's all awfully embarrassing, especially when not being able to perform as a normal, loving husband. I can't make the bed, clean the windows and put out the rubbish, assignments at which I come highly recommended. It hurts to have to watch my woman play substitute in these matters. It also makes me realise I've reached the age when sex is nice, but a warm toilet seat and the sports pages come greatly recommended.

Laughter has been tried as a remedy. Over the years I've

read that it relaxes the muscles and works all kinds of mysterious wonders for one's system. Only this morning my wife came in to find out why I was standing in the kitchen chortling.

I said, "I was just thinking, wouldn't it be funny if someone gave me a gift certificate to use in a massage parlour?"

She gave me the usual quick, remonstrative look. It was the same look I received a few weeks back when I said, "Did you know that women sneak me into the bedroom while their husbands read the sports pages?"

"Don't laugh," she said, "you'll pay for that!"

I still laughed. Doubled up, the process that began in the bathroom started all over again.

THINGS THAT MOVE

I'm standing with my wife in the kitchen of our new home. Having cut through several layers of tape, prised back thousands of box flaps and pulled out objects that had been laboriously cosseted inside roughly 1,000 square metres of white paper, we discovered numerous items we couldn't even find in our previous home. One of them was a tea cup. With tea in it.

If you're wondering why we packed a cup with tea still in it, the answer is, we aren't that stupid. We are much stupider than that. What we did was pay somebody to do this, I am, of course, referring to the professional removing company whose numbers on the estimate had to be specially trucked in.

Unpacking and mislaying things seemingly at will, nothing surprises me anymore. But I'm surprised by those who are surprised that something could get lost in a home that is normally very tidy. Buckingham Palace with all those rooms? Yes. But in our modest abode? Definitely not. Yet it happens all the time.

The scene is played out at least once every few days. I know from personal experience that two people can conduct a daylong search for a remote control and come up with nothing. Then have said remote appear - miraculously - the next day. In plain view. This is just one example of a lost-and-found habit that bedevils our home like some landlocked version of the Bermuda Triangle.

I once had a cheque book disappear for weeks, resulting in repeated room-to-room, drawer-to-drawer searches with the help of cheque book sniffing adults. Only after officially calling off the search did the cheque book incredibly appear under a folder on a study shelf.

My wife and I looked at each other. That shelf? Under that folder? Impossible! We'd looked there ten times at least!

Just the other night when we were preparing for our big moving day to a larger house in which mislaying things will multiply, my wife stood between me and a football match on TV and said, "Have you seen my new pale green slacks?"

"Have you tried the closet?"

"No, they're not in there," she said. "I just looked."

Although a penalty shoot-out was in progress I rose, and within 15 seconds, found the slacks on a hanger, in full view, on her side of the walk-in closet.

I should add, my loved one has returned the favour many, many more times than I care to remember. It so happens my car keys have a way of hiding from me while hanging in full view on the key holder in the utility room, exactly where they should be.

Anyone who lives in a home with inanimate objects and animate people knows we're dealing with the immutable Law of Lost Objects which operates under the jurisdiction of the Laws of Natural Cussedness. These laws spring from the Watched Pot Never Boils syndrome, which I disproved years ago on a wet Sunday afternoon when I had nothing better to do.

In case you missed that particular lecture, the Law of Lost Objects states that a lost object cannot be found by anyone who is actually looking for it - only by an unwitting bystander.

In our home the law applies to a wide array of objects starting with anything you need quickly, matching clothing and favourite food allegedly in the fridge. Other lost-and-unbelievably-found items include the umbrella, the shopping list, the TV guide and the "best cutting knife". "I just don't understand it. It was there the last time I saw it. I came in and put it down right there! Surely you saw it?"

Our current mystery involves a large pack of premium cashew nuts which disappeared, unopened, around Easter and remains at large to this very day despite many repeated and in depth searches. There just aren't many places for a pack of quality nuts to hide, and we've searched them all - or so it seems.

Foul play had not been ruled out. But all family members and close friends have sworn under oath that they didn't squirrel away the nuts for personal consumption. Our failure to come up with these nuts proves that we've been looking much too hard in all the right places. I should be asking myself: Where wouldn't I look?

Can you imagine what lies ahead? In about three weeks, the new owners of our old home will be buried in boxes and white paper when one spouse will say to the other: "What on earth do you think they were thinking about leaving a packet of nuts behind the bath panel in the guest bathroom?" We can't wait to finish unpacking so that we can resume our life of looking in vain for things. We're looking forward to many happy years here, during which time we hope to eventually locate the box containing our son.

SPRING ASPIRATIONS

My late March birthday signals a time when memory meets desire. A thirst that is quenched again each Spring. When a clear blue sky means cricket.

It's time once again to gaze upon outfields so deep, so lush and so manicured. Even at this early stage the wicket looks so bare, so brown and so contrasting. Hope and exuberance bubble into an elixir of anticipation, a heady tonic for a devoted fan of the game. A fan who can eat, drink, clap and groan his way through a sultry day toward the distant horizon of evening.

Cricket, despite its sagging popularity, still remains, at all levels, a magnet for devotees who can recite specific moments in a player's career that perhaps the player himself has forgotten. Cricket trivia and statistics dance in their heads.

As kids don't bat and bowl in back streets anymore, the national game has been replaced by football. Where kids are able to play in open spaces they kick black and white balls now. Fortunately, the allure of watching long-trousered combat after a long winter of short-shorts confrontations seems a gentle relief.

Players will soon be warming up near the pavilion rails, leisurely throwing leather from hand to hand with no game-time tension lining their faces. They'll banter with nothing at stake except getting their eyes and reflexes in tune.

I'd pay them if they'd let me play at county level. What could be better than chasing your dreams in what to most people is the never-never land of professional cricket? Imagine playing in front of a knowledgeable crowd as I attempted to become Mr. Impact, the player who hefts the team on his shoulders and carries it to the championship. If I won an England cap, I'd be accepted, then accosted, by young adoring fans jockeying around the boundary edge looking to snag my autograph. Up close and personal, as it should be. My teammates seem in good mood. There's a sense of optimism and hope in the air.

As years go by somehow the fans look older and greyer. They are thicker around the middle, their waistlines straining tight below T-shirts emblazoned with cricketing slogans.

The devoted season ticket-holders look forward to their squat frame opening batsman being at least 4 kilos lighter than last year. They anticipate their flamboyant top order batsman changing his attitude from self-pity to self-criticism, so that he can gracefully stroke the ball into the pigeoned distance. They expect, nay demand, their opening gangly bowler to have smoothed his herky-jerky style. They wonder if the one newly contracted foreign player will realise he won't get a second chance to make a first impression.

As for the rest of the team, three so-called professional cricketers of modest pretensions are stuck in the twilight of their careers and are the kind of men you dread your sister meeting. The medium pace trundler is a player who loves himself so much he gives pet names to his teeth, while the main support bowler is alleged to have doctored so many cricket balls he's been inducted in to the British Medical Association. The fans hope the wicket-keeper batsman will at long last score more runs than the number of extras he gives away, and the principal spinner, a man of many callings, will desist from the Kentish habit of long-hopping and concentrate on at least spinning the ball and bowling a length this season.

As for the captain, suffice it to say, many of his decisions leave the majority among us bewitched, bothered and bewildered. As my grandfather used to say, "Wouldn't pay 'im in washers. Ee'd have to go if I 'ad anything to do wi' it."

Camaraderie around the ground sprouts quickly. Young women in tank tops - their pre-melanoma skin bathed in baby oil should the sun come out - spend more time looking at other fans than the action on the field. Last season a female fan was shushed for shouting by an older fan because her shrill voice played havoc with his hearing aid. In no time the woman and deaf man were like old friends as they chattered non-stop. This season they reserved seats together.

A lot rides on the first match. Will it be the veteran's last season? Will the newcomer's hopes be dashed? Will the fans retain their enthusiasm should the team get off to a bad start? The players in early season good form will be hoping to catch the eyes of the Test match selectors especially as the Australians won't be here to destroy English hopes yet again. As a nation we never appear to tire of the Aussies dancing on the ashes of our demise, and the games being so one-sided that if the Aussies win the toss, the game is over before it starts

Spring is when the action begins. Both players and spectators will, by strong tradition, attempt to cull its rhythms and realise its promise. I know I'm ready for vernal combats which will blossom in summer then fade into a victorious or failed autumn. Although a bit faded and ragged round the edges, the poetic game remains magical.

WAR CHILD

Recent conflicts ensured my mind flicked back to those days when I was nearly five years old and first taken to school the day before World War Two began. At dinner time (words like "lunch", "courgette" and "kiwi fruit" were words of the future) I went home raving about school. Then my mother said it was time to go back. "I've already been," I implored. "Yes," she said "and you've got to go for the next ten years at least." For some moments life seemed excruciatingly hard but partly because I was an only child, school days glowed forever.

Until the age of ten I attended East Ward Infant and Junior schools in that most diversified of cotton towns, Bury. I grew to love arithmetic, history, geography, singing and games. Apparently everyone thought I had a good voice which benefited the school choir but not the composer of "Nymphs and Shepherds".

The pupils, mostly inadequately clad from hotbeds of socialist thought, respected authority and learning. The teachers were all powerful; they were always well dressed and at 9 a.m. they called for silence in the main hall. At 10 seconds past the atmosphere was like that in a church. It was strict. If you were late, you were caned...if you bullied, you were caned...if you were cheeky, you were caned. The bottom took the stronger punishment, the hand the lighter chastisement. No one ever complained to their mother (father was in the desert fighting Rommel) and fortunately for my generation, litigation was still years ahead. In spite of the occasional justifiably administered striped bruise my life was happy.

At 10.30 a.m. there was a 10 minutes break for milk and a quick exchange of cigarette cards. With food being rationed meagre school dinners were a treat. There was no choice of menu, we simply ate what we were given and dutifully emptied our plate with relish. Seconds were as rare as bananas getting through the U-boat cordon around Britain

Fond memories persist of every teacher. Mrs. Smith was an absolute gem. Her eyes radiated kindness from behind her tortoiseshell glasses. It was entirely due to her and my mother that I became a juvenile expert on the Canadian salmon industry. Mrs. Smith, later a war widow, supplied the knowledge, my mother the tin of salmon complete with label. From the moment I brought that red salmon creation to school my prestige went up. It created a sort of affluence in my classmates minds and hence respect.

Mr. Fargher, the headmaster, benign, blinking and bald was at his best when leading the school down to the air-raid shelters for the weekly gas mask drill. Our little brown cardboard boxes were the carriers not only of life saving equipment but sticky morasses of biscuits and toffees. The atmosphere of those underground havens was a mixture of dank rot, stale air and body odour - a putrid concoction. Little did Hitler know of our plight although he did try his best to ventilate the area by dropping a bomb a few hundred feet sway.

The emergency water supply tank was a source of great worry to the teachers because in spite of it being covered with a wire mesh, everyday it was feared a drowned child would be pulled from its murky depths. A grass playing area circumnavigated this tank and timing became an art form as you fell down in the boy/girl three-legged race to grab a furtive kiss behind those sheltering gallons.

Although everyone was well-scrubbed, literate and numerate, there was seldom any suggestion that you should better yourself. Most of my friends ended up in the local factories and dutifully married a local spouse as anyone living more than 5 miles away was regarded with the suspicion reserved for Nazi saboteurs.

The final line on my leaving report read ...."He is bright, hard-working, dependable and good at games. Has a great deal of potential." For what? If only Mr. Fargher and Mrs. Smith had known what the next 50 years had in store for me they would be amazed beyond belief. Looking back on those war-ravaged days, whatever I have achieved in life, I owe in substantial measure to that halcyon time of strict discipline, kindness and rich learning.

FOLLOW YOUR BENT

Having recently spent some time visiting friends in North Yorkshire it was unusual to come across two former neighbours from Surrey, Mark and Jocelyn, who, we had forgotten this in our travels, have two obsessive traits. They grow sweet peas and change the shapes of rooms.

That's one thing my wife and I noticed when we moved to Yorkshire some twenty years ago. No one in that part of England sits around saying, "I think my room is the wrong shape." In the south-east of England they do that all the time.

In Surrey you would have dinner parties featuring attractive tableware, candles in unusual holders and fabulous topiary centrepieces made by the hostess herself with loving and pruning care. As soon as she got up from the table and left the room to usher in the apple and hazelnut galette while the host was replenishing the glasses, someone would say, "I wonder if she knows this room is the wrong shape?"

Someone else would say, "She could change it with paint."

"Really? How so?"

And the first person would say, "Well, you know, a trompe l'oeil panel can enlarge a too-small window by visually linking all the segments, then banding them with a closely related hue."

The return of the hostess would then fortunately silence the gathering.

In West Yorkshire, where I live, if we had words like trompe l'oeil hanging around, we would probably name a lake after it.

There's been a lot of talk recently about closing some county borders to prevent the encroachment of enforced gentility. Every time a large truck containing issues of "Living Style" tries to penetrate a county line, it would be turned back at the Culture roadblocks.

There are those who tell me, "Gordon, don't be too worried. If the magazine penetrates into West Yorkshire, nobody intelligent would ever take it seriously." Quite true. In the Spring issue there's actually an article titled, "How To Cook A Fish." It begins, "Even if we know that we should cook fish more often, there's something daunting about it." ("Put it in a pan" would be the choice of any northern infant.) This article was obviously written by a man used to hailing a cab in a rainstorm while wearing a natural-fibre suit, which unfortunately shows water spots.

The full colour centrefold shows a "Salmon Roasted on Chardonnay Twigs." Nowhere is there a mention of where one might find "chardonnay twigs" growing in the wild, or for that matter, in captivity.

I do concede that there's some useful information in the magazine for those of us inhabiting the less sophisticated areas of the country. Take amateur bookbinding for example.

There's a section on "What to do" if you happen to have an edition of "The Life and Works of William Cowper" published in 1836 lying around in the house in a battered state. To prevent rot attacking the delicate pages, "Spread wheat starch on a piece of glass ...."

"Living Style" should probably be banned in many impressionable areas of Britain to avoid seeing photographs of magnificently dressed women smiling like hostages in a war zone about to partake of "navarin of lamb with spring vegetables; consommé with herb dumplings; dauphinoise potatoes with laver; and pansy layer cake."

When we lived in the north, and I'm sure it's still true today, we served actual food. Obviously, we're 20 years behind the times in so-called poised and polished fashion, but way ahead in common sense.

If we want to change a room's shape where I come from, we knock a damn wall out!

DON'T GET YOUR KNICKERS IN A STEW

I have alarming news from Scotland that a woman named Flora McTavish was pouring her favourite brand of porridge oats into a mixing bowl when - please try to remain calm - out fell a fist-sized clump of porridge oats all welded together. Was a mutant porridge on the rampage?

Here in England, a consumer confronted with this situation would probably just take it in full stride, don a neck brace and sue the offending company for £2 million. But Scotland has its own legal system and over the border things are much different. What Flora McTavish did was contact her local newspaper which provided a story headlined: "Woman

Surprised to Find Lump the Size of a Haggis in Her Porridge Oats Packet." This tactic was not surprising for a woman of the tartan who always lost more men than she found every New Year's Eve.

Like most writers and so-called journalists who know little about a variety of topics (that's how we stay objective by the way), I investigate any case of breakfast foods spontaneously welding together. Appreciating that Scotland, as the southern part of the Icelandic empire, now has mobile telephones, I phoned Miss McTavish on her travels and asked her for an update. She told me that she had received "several compliments" on the press article, and that a number of people had already paid to view her prized lump, which she is keeping for posterity in a re-usable plastic bag. The £5 viewing fee had certainly not put off one hardy visitor from London. "Whatever butters your croissant", as they say south of the Thames.

Flora (now becoming more friendly with every long distance conversation as she was not paying for the calls) also reported that a company representative had come to her home and examined the offending clump, and had wanted to take it away, but she refused. "I'm going to have it analysed," she said. The company had given her an overabundance of free products in spite of their suspicions about a woman who wears Spandex, the Wonder Bra, pours hot wax on her legs and gets sexually aroused when her boyfriend carries her groceries. "They're going to bend over backwards to kiss my ...." At that precise moment the line went dead as is usual on these important international and emotional occasions.

In a subsequent conversation I gathered from the friendly Flora that another product of this particular company had burst into flames within 5 minutes of boiling. Her consolation on this occasion was five sorts of crustless sandwiches and a highly destructive chocolate cake.

Can Scotland be a land of danger?

Speaking of threatening consumer items, I've also received news from the Isle of Man that somewhere on that green and pleasant Irish Sea paradise, a story of equal import awaits page one. It seems that a pair of branded athletic shoes being worn by a ten-year-old boy exploded. The boy's mother alleges that her son had jumped to catch a ball in the playground when his shoes "exploded on impact with the ground making his socks and jeans catch fire." The local fire department are investigating but are not prepared to commit themselves at the moment except to say, "anything can happen when you purchase over-priced products for children." Perhaps the relentless multimillion pounds advertising campaigns will now be supplemented with a boost for athletic shoe sprinkler systems.

My secretary, Scary Mary, keeps reminding me that these examples of product sensitivity aren't unusual in a nation in which one-sixth of the population eats custard at least once a day, and chocolate éclairs add over a trillion calories to the national diet. All these revelations sadly sprout from that old English proverb, "Life is short and unpredictable, eat the dessert first."

At this stage, as you recover in hospital from an excess of exploding tartanic foods, all I can do is recommend for your perusal my two recent publications, "How To Handle Touch Hungry Women " and "The Gordon Lomax Post-Mortem Workout for Small Islands."

LET'S DRINK TO THAT!

Having been on both the giving and receiving end of after-dinner speaking for many years, I have great sympathy for the bored and afflicted at these functions. Before my first venture into boring people I received advice that I've never forgotten, "Stick to the 3 B's of speech making and you won't go far wrong," said a wise friend. "Be introduced, be brief, be seated." These words reinforce my own feelings on the matter. A good speech should have a strong beginning and a great end, preferably close together.

This advice has prevented me feeling like a fourth husband. I know what I'm supposed to do, but I'm at a loss as to how to make it different. On a smaller scale the best after-dinner speech you'll ever hear is - "Waiter, I'll take the check, please." May you never be the rooted victim of overlong speeches too often. When I was on the receiving end of a marathon offering, the woman sitting next to me whispered, "I've just got a new theory of eternity."

In many cases the speech ends with a toast, and as I cast my mind back through the years, the fiery starts, the memorable lines and the punchy conclusions come readily to mind. Male speakers carry a rougher edge than their female counterparts and "get away" with far more humbling remarks.

"What can you say about Gerald that hasn't been said about hazardous waste?"

"I'm proud to be here to honour Charles. I love him. I have no taste, but I love him."

"Tony's wife is delighted that he's here today. While he's away she's having his cage cleaned."

Women about women are far more gentle.

"Every day you look lovelier and lovelier - and today

you look like tomorrow."

Men talking about women have to bring sex into the equation.

"To women and wine. May our lips meet both."

I remember a toast from the RSPCA dinner which lingers still.

"To the animals who know all our faults, and never tell a soul."

Plucked from my memory are three sporting lines.

"Here's to Walter who just missed a hole-in-one by four strokes."

"To tennis, the only excuse that some women get for wearing white."

"Here's to our coach. A man who's willing to lay down our lives for his team."

Health and environment gatherings have produced the occasional gem.

"To the new 3 R's - reduce, reuse and recycle."

"I drink to your health when I'm with you
I drink to your health when I'm alone
I drink to your health so often
I'm beginning to worry about my own."

The future and retirement are not to be forgotten.

"May Dame Fortune ever smile on you, but never her daughter, Miss Fortune."

"Here's to your holidays - all 365 of them."

The occasional quandary thrown in the middle of a speech can be quite thought provoking.

"If you ate pasta and antipasta, would you still be hungry?"

"Why is there an expiry date on sour cream?"

Several odd assortments spring to mind.

"Those who can, do. Those who can't do, become critics."

"Here's to the best nation of all: Donation."

"To all those who have graduated. May you now go on to become educated."

"To the professor. A man who talks in his student's sleep."

"To harmony, and those who produce it."

"To those who glide through life, rather than chunter."

Two subtle doubles are worthy of mention. As the speaker twirled his spectacles in his hand, he concluded, "To absent friends. Although they are out of sight we recognise them with our glasses." At a recent wedding the best man's last sentence before the toast to the bride and groom was, "May your wedding days be few, and your anniversaries many."

Male to male aggression however has the last few words.

"Here's to Howard, our local MP, a man who stands for what he thinks others will fall for."

And to an overweight host. "May your shadow never grow less."

As the polar bear said to his mate, "I just love eating those igloos. They're crunchy on the outside and the chewy centre is a pure delight." And that's what a short speech should be. Crunchy all round with a delightful middle.

I could share many, many more with you, but suddenly I see the wall opposite about to fall on me ....

MEN v WOMEN

Today I want to talk about housework and the

importance of helping wives with .... HOLD IT RIGHT THERE MEN, DON'T YOU DARE STOP READING.

The fact that most women think we're doing a splendid job on the housework front is a joke of course. What women actually said was that in terms of sharing the housework burden, having a man around is like having a 90 kilos ball of wool permanently bonded to the settee flicking through TV sport while consuming vast quantities of beer. As all we men know, those thoughts constitute a gross libel. They're nothing more than a totally inaccurate, insensitive, crude, stupid, soporific, tasteless and flagrantly sleazy excuse to cash in on the truth.

Just once I'd like to see a survey with questions that would tend to put men in a more positive light, such as: In the event of a family emergency which gender is most likely to be able to remember - coolly, calmly and without panic - what position Nobby Stiles played for England in the 1966 World Cup Final.

Surveys unfortunately always ask about female-type qualities like maturity, sensitivity, communication and the ability to remember names and dates - as if those were the only issues that mattered. Men have unique problems of their own - ask any man with a crotch itch!

Just recently my wife and I were in Bolton sitting with a lovely view of the Town Hall and directly in front of us, the length of a cricket pitch away, was a man clearly experiencing a life-threatening need to scratch himself. He was about to attempt the impossible. He was going to try and make contact with himself while still keeping a safe distance from his hands. Trying hard to look casual he glanced (or wurped in Red Rose Lancastrian) around to see if anybody was watching, then .... GROPE, he made a fast move to hide his discomfort, and then his eyes cast around again, and then .... GROPE, and then another look and then .... GROPE, GROPE, GROPE. He totally lost control of himself and plunged frantically at the speed of fear with both hands to the offending area. He was too absorbed in his task to realise that he'd now surpassed Crompton's Mule as the main local tourist attraction with a large crowd watching him and small banner-towing aircraft making U-turns to come back for a second look. The lively disposition of this poor fellow ensured it wasn't to be a gloomy afternoon.

You know, I really felt for the demented man - and all my wife did was laugh.

Do surveys think about these sensitive male issues? No! All they think about is housework where women establish a lot of picky rules leading to male exasperation. At that stage you can only stomp off and calm yourself down by gripping your putter tightly as you practice on the carpet.

Another problem is that TV commercials for housework-type products are always aimed at women. What about one where a man opens his fridge and sees a Swedish Bikini team trapped in tomato sauce and is rescued by an exclusive grease-cutting formula? As a thank you, the Bikini team members express their gratitude by leaning over a lot and giving the impression they'd like to have tomato-smeared sex with you.

Yes, it's up to us men to make more of an effort to help around the house. At the same time, you women out there need to become more aware of an important fact. The only time a woman really succeeds in changing a man is when he's a baby.

Oh, I nearly forgot. Nobby Stiles was a darn good tackling wing-half with a toothy grin.

I HAVE TO HAVE IT

Like most men I'm a big fan of technology. Although it wasn't all that long ago that I thought semi-conductors were part-time London Symphony Orchestra leaders, and microchips were very small snack foods. It should be no surprise therefore when I state my favourite TV programme is "Tomorrow's World", and yet, my wife gives me a hard time when I have a desire for "the latest gadget".

For example, as a man, I feel I need another computer every time a new model comes out, which is about every 20 minutes. This baffles my wife, who has had the same computer since 1984 and refuses to get a new one because - believe it or not - the one she has works fine. Virtual shopping to her mind is for those with no grip on reality. While we have a remote controlled telly, our neighbours have remote controlled houses.

I try to explain that when you get a new computer, you get exciting new features. My current super new computer has a truly fascinating feature. Whenever I try to turn it off, the following message appears on the screen: "Error. Failure to comply. An exception has occurred at 643872:D 404 x 468 in N x R. It may be possible to continue normally after a reallocated time."

Clearly the message is not of human origin and confirms two thoughts. One, my state-of-the-art computer is receiving messages from aliens in outer space. And two, if computer manufacturers ever go in for making cars I'm not going to buy one - they would crash too often.

What concerns me is the last sentence, because if the aliens are telling me that "it may be possible to continue normally", they're clearly implying that it may not be possible to continue normally. In other words, the earth may be doomed, and the aliens have chosen me to receive the message. I might be on the point of saving humanity if I could figure "after a reallocated time."

Unfortunately I don't have any time to squander because I'm busy using my new GPS device. This is an extremely important gadget that every man in the world needs. It receives signals from orbiting satellites, and somehow it works out exactly where on the Earth you are.

Let's say you're in Scunthorpe (goodness knows why), but for some reason you don't realise this. You turn on your GPS, and, after seeking for a few minutes, it informs you that you are in .... Scunthorpe. My wife reasonably argues that it's easier to just ask somebody, but of course you can't do that if you're a man.

I became aware of how useful a GPS can be when I was on a plane trip with a sports club called the Rock Bottom Activists, which has been hailed by critics as having one of the world's highest ratios of incompetence to talent. On this trip were two players whom I will identify only as "Slugger" and "Beefy", so that you'll not know they're actually Charles Cartwright Tel: 06488 227432 and Benjamin Howell Tel: 04737 886012.

We were flying from Manchester to London, and while everybody else was reading, sleeping or eating their meagre allotment of dry roasted peanuts, Slugger and Beefy, who are both fully grown men, were riveted by their GPS devices and periodically informed each other how far they were from Heathrow. Slugger would say, "I'm showing 79 miles," and Beefy would say, "I'm showing 81 miles."

The figures flowed to and fro between Slugger and Beefy. My wife, her nuts now eaten and in full possession of her wits, thought this was the silliest thing she had ever seen.

Whereas I thought: I MUST have one of those.

So I got a GPS for my birthday and I spent the entire day sitting in our living-room putting the device to good use. I worked out exactly where our house is. I also used my GPS to work out precisely how far (to the single millimetre) our kitchen is from the Eiffel Tower. There's simply no end to the usefulness of this invention. Any man worth his salt needs to get one now, so you can locate where exactly you are on the planet.

By the amount of time men devote to these new and fascinating mechanical gadgets, my wife thinks they're a substitute for arousing sexual desire. She's on the right track, but doesn't appreciate that it's an Audi TT Coupe Quattro that does the trick for me.

SNOWSPORTING

When you've reached that wise and respected over sixty period of your life, you somehow hear a voice inside you that says: "Just because you're over sixty doesn't mean you shouldn't seek new adventures. You get only one ride on this wild wonderland we call life, and you should make the most of it."

Thus is the voice of Lucifer.

Recently in the Alps, I listened to this voice, and as a result my body feels as if a team of Clydesdales has trampolined all over it. My current breakfast is black coffee and 250 anti-inflammation tablets.

All because I went snowboarding and played snowplough hockey, Snowboarding (a so-called sport) is an activity that's popular with people who don't feel that skiing is lethal enough. On the ski slopes my method is purely IJCMB - "I'm just catching my breath." On a snowboard you reach a maximum of 80 k.p.h. as you knock down trees with your face. In skiing you wear two skis and hold two poles with which you can stab people as you pass. With snowboarding, all you get is one board shaped like a doctor's tongue depressor. Your feet are strapped to this board and the only way to separate yourself from the board is to smash at high speed into a solid object.

Skiers hate snowboarders because these crazies are really rebels wearing pre-ski clothing voluminous enough to cover the snowboarder and four passing skiers. Skiers like to glide down mountains. Snowboarders like to attack a mountain, spinning, gyrating and blasting the snow as they go. Snowboarders specialise in denting crisp, icy and concrete-like snow with the back of their heads.

All the time you're entreated to "Keep your knees bent!" Have you noticed that whatever sport you're trying to learn, some earnest person is always telling you to keep your knees bent!

Not to labour the point, I spent most of a so-called idyllic holiday flat on my back, groaning. My only observable method was NDTTCMB - "No damned time to catch my breath." It posed the question: "What goes up, other than golden handshakes and executive compensation, when everything else is going down?" My brain was now a whimpering wad of useless pummelled tissue and I was forced to conclude that the trouble with over sixty ideas is that they started out just being for fun.

My troubles didn't end there. The tension in the air was so electric and still that when I unzipped a much frequented zip, I caused an avalanche. When the white shroud settled I turned to snowplough hockey as an alternative lifestyle. I was determined to consolidate my position as Prince of Wince.

The problem with this form of hockey is that you could end up being trapped in a snow bank and being eaten by wolves. For those readers who insist on leading an active lifestyle year-round, I can recommend this new winter sport that keeps you warm and yet, at the same time, enables you to have the potential to be arrested.

Rather than pass the time in some unproductive manner, such as nurturing friendships and exploring your latest girl friend's innermost feelings, take up snowplough hockey. Three ingredients will suffice.

1. Each of the two players should have a snowplough.

2. Both sides of the street should be lined by steep hard snow banks.

3. Purchase one red ten-pin bowling ball.

The rules are simple. The object is for your snowplough to force the ball by direct or indirect means to the opposite end of the street from whence you started. The major skill is to angle the ball off the snow banks like a billiard player. Sadly, referees are hard to come by. A major penalty is that you retreat 50 metres when a ball rockets past a defender into the intersection where it knocks down an elderly woman who just happens to be the mother of your opponent. If unrelated in any way there is only a retreat of 20 metres. I'm glad to say, the police were unable to confiscate our ball as they seemed unable to keep on their feet while behaving like stick-waving Canadian ice hockey players.

This pastime has immediate appeal for the wealthy businessman seeking lucrative product endorsements and demolition contracts.

I'm glad to report that the protected snowplough cabin saved my body from further heavy punishment but the jarring did revive bitter memories.

Reluctantly I returned from my winter triste on the piste realising that my best option is intensive therapy and coffee, lots more black coffee and the tablets of course.

REAL WORLD EDUCATION

Despite recent advances in the range of courses our universities and colleges offer, what you find are mostly academic and devoid of stimulus and challenge. In general they attract those with the brainpower of a walnut and those who are senselessly and conclusively complacent.

For potential students of the real world what about bringing a little exotica into your life by attending the more dynamic and practical courses of the Lomax Conservatoire for Enterprising Education. Motto: Spiritus Asper .... Cough it up, it's well worth it. The proffered curriculum isn't for those who feared parsing sentences at school and who had to undergo three years of therapy before they could enter a room with a prepositional phrase.

As the self-appointed Dean, allow me to illustrate what this new invigorating style has to offer.

DOMESTIC FINANCE - Features what to do when your credit card balance is larger than your annual income and how to cope with a bank balance lower than your IQ. Special emphasis is placed in midnight flits as a means of debt management.

EVERYDAY DEBATE - Dwells mainly on how to use persuasion to get your own way with ancillary seminars on pouting and whining. You learn how to argue effectively with small children including how to say, "Because I said no, that's why!" in 11 languages. Already overbooked is the series of lectures on explaining how to deal with anguished cries of relatives who now have to go to work because you're studying at the Conservatoire.

EVERYDAY ETHICS - Students learn to refer to tools as more than just "that thingamajig over there". They learn how to replace a fuse without plunging East Anglia into darkness. First-year students will develop the technique of choosing a tool which doesn't fit the hand so ensuring the "yourself" in "do-it-yourself" becomes obsolete.

MODERN BUSINESS SKILLS - Special attention is given to holding one's own with the complexities of office equipment and at what stage do you call an engineer or an exorcist. There'll be special lectures on "The Memo As An Art Form", "How To Send Death Threats Through Inter-Office Mail" and "Faxing Your Favourite Body Parts". Emphasis will be placed on how to survive an endless staff meeting and how to use words like "maximise", "annualise", "prioritise" and "input", while mastering that hallmark of good manners, the ability to yawn without opening your mouth.

PHILOSOPHY FOR OAFS - This course of study answers the three most perplexing questions of the age:
1. Why are we here?
2. How can we reconcile out ontological preconceptions with empirical arguments for determinism?
3. What the hell is that all about?

For the completely bereft, demonstrations proving that ignorance is salvageable but stupid is forever will be compulsory.

RELIGION FOR FOOLS - The set books address such questions as: "Is there a hereafter?" And if so, can I meet Napoleon? The main haranguer, evangelist and de-frocked professor, Billy Avidity, will heal the affliction of your choice and guarantee an A-grade pass for a £2,000 donation.

SOCIOLOGY FOR THE MASSES - The course for people who like people. Students take field trips in which they learn where to find people and why some people are nice and quiet but others become your next door neighbours. Verb declination in relation to people will be a feature, for example, fail, failed, bankrupt. Extracurricular subjects will be "How to get in Touch with Yourself" and "Expand the Notion that Joan of Arc is a French Descendant of Noah."

For the final exam every student must call their local Gas Company and persuade the service department to send out a fitter immediately because you think you smell gas. If the student fails, a grade report will be forwarded to the next of kin. For those who survive, I recommend booking early for the inaugural course which will result in you graduating in Eyebrow Maintenance.

This facility of breezy subversiveness is at your service. Regard sending your offspring to the Lomax Conservatoire as a home improvement loan. However, if application forms are received asking: "Were do I sine up for the touturin in math and readin?", it will be assumed that like most handicaps, yours is from the neck up and you're planning to fail in life. We cannot drop our standards to the level of those who believe that Hannukah is a duck call.

CRAZY LANGUAGE

English is the most widely spoken language in the history of our planet and has acquired the largest vocabulary of all the world's languages with perhaps as many as two million words. English is also a crazy language.

There is no butter in buttermilk and no sign of a goose in gooseberry. Quicksand works very slowly, boxing rings are square and how is it that a king rules a kingdom but a queen doesn't rule a queendom? Fingers don't fing and humdingers don't hum. And why can I tread water and then tread on soil?

If we conceive a conception and receive at a reception, why don't we grieve a greption and believe a beleption? You can meet people who are great shakes and some who you would never touch with a ten-foot pole. If you choose to wear only your left shoe, then your left one is right and your right one is left. Right?

And then there are phrases. "I really miss not seeing you" which means "I really miss seeing you." "The film kept me glued to my seat," doesn't mean you are bonded permanently to your cinema seat. "A hot cup of coffee" should be " a cup of hot coffee." "Watch your head" is impossible, it's like trying to bite your teeth.

English has weird rigid expressions. Beck can appear only with call, cranny with nook, hue with cry and spic with span. Why are we allowed to vent our spleen but never our kidneys or livers? Why must it be only our minds that are boggled and never our eyes or our hearts? Why can't eyes and jars be ajar, as well as doors? And why must aspersions always be cast and never hurled or thrown?

As language is invented it reflects human creativity. That's why six, seven, eight and nine change to sixty, seventy, eighty and ninety, but two, three, four and five don't become twoty, threety, fourty and fivety. That's why we can open up the floor, raise the roof, bring down the house and chop a tree down before we chop it up.

Oxymora abound. Even odds ... good grief ... inside out

... mandatory option ... military intelligence ... original copy ... pretty ugly ... tight slacks ... working vacation and so on. My favourite is the double oxymoron ... fresh frozen jumbo shrimp.

Heteronyms are a pure delight. "After the slaver had sold his slaves, he would slaver over the money he made." .... "The storm began to buffet the outdoor buffet." .... "The sewer threw her sewing into the sewer." and "She is now resorting to resorting to the mail."

Food expressions mushroom constantly and season our tongue. We chew the fat about food filled phrases that are packed like sardines and sandwiched into our everyday conversation. I know what's eating you. I've heard via the grapevine that you don't give a fig because you think I'm as nutty as a fruitcake. Beware however, I can feed you a bunch of baloney, rub salt into your wounds, upset your apple cart and rehash an old chestnut that's just pie in the sky. But nuts to all that. That's the way the cookie crumbles. You might be the greatest thing since sliced bread but I'm going to put all my eggs in one basket and spill the beans, for as you know the proof of the pudding is in the eating. Every day while using the English language, we truly eat our words.

It's also a language zoo out there, quite an unbridled rat race. You can take a gander, you can fight like cats and dogs until the cows come home, and you can become a lame duck, a sitting duck or a dead duck. You can preen yourself like a strutting peacock while you fish for compliments. You can have a whale of a party that compels you to eat like a pig and hog the lion's share until you're as plump as a partridge. As I continue to separate the sheep from the goats and pigeonhole the human race, I doggedly think at a snail's pace like a big fish in a small pond who never works for chicken feed.

English is also violent, frozen in the expressions of

everyday life. "I'll be hanged!" we are likely to exclaim. "I believe that I've hit the nail right on the head." The world of business is a veritable jungle of cutthroat competition. No wonder that business executives are often recruited by headhunters! In sport, we can't get within striking distance of a Cup Final with bumping into a ticket tout who is out to rip us off and get away with murder. It's like using a double-edged sword to cut off your nose to spite your face.

Verb tenses in English are fraught with a fearful asymmetry and puzzling unpredictability. You can add -d, -ed or -t; you can have an internal vowel change like begin, began; you can have a combination of both like buy, bought, while some don't change at all ... set, set. The pulse must surely quicken when you have to form the past tense of verbs like baby-sit, dive, shine, sneak and weave.

It's impossible not to have stumbled into the potholes and booby traps of spelling English words. I can't remember who said, "It's a damn poor mind that can think of only one way to spell a word!" In what other language can you find pairs like float and flotation, led and read, harass and embarrass, deceit and receipt? How is it that manslaughter and man's laughter can be spelled with exactly the same order of letters?

In effect, we have two languages, one spoken and one written. The four letters "ough" can produce ten distinct sounds, as in bough, bought, cough, dough, hiccough, lough, rough, thoroughbred, through and trough. And don't forget the silent letters in answer, debris, doubt, people, racquet, would and wrist.

Alliteration abounds. From Jack and Jill to Donald Duck; from dry as dust to prim and proper, from rough-and-ready to wishy-washy. This leads to what I believe is the most difficult tongue twister in the English language ... the sixth sick sheikh's sixth sheep's sick!

English words are always moving, they seldom sit still and remain the same forever. Some expand and some narrow. Words have expansion joints and are not shrinkproof. Some words come up in the world while others slide downhill. English words are wonderfully serviceable, maddeningly random, frenetically creative, and, of course, completely crazy.

In that we should rejoice.

MEN! YOU'RE OLDER THAN YOU THINK

I'm at that age so I'm told, when age is in the mind. Unfortunately, age is also in the legs, the arms. the neck, the shoulders, the arches and most definitely, the back. I feel it, I know it, but my mind says ignore it. Growing old seems such a bad habit to fall into and I convince myself that I'm somewhere near a structural crisis.

For certain I've left adolescence, that age between puberty and adultery, behind. I know I'm long gone from the wedding age of aisle, altar, hymn. I also recognise my sporting prowess isn't what it was. I appear to be too young to take up lawn bowls and too old to ski race downhill. The years between 50 and 70 are the hardest, because you're always being asked to do physical things, and, you haven't the sense to turn them down. Sport is now confined to running around in circles, flying off the handle, throwing your weight around, jumping to conclusions and jogging the memory!

Fighting a bulging waistline with foods you never previously liked, and wondering whether to use 133 calories on a round of golf or 151 making love, declines into a mere 20 while standing at a cocktail party. Years are shed as that fabulous looking woman across the room eyes you in a lascivious manner that will ensure your wife seeks revenge throughout the rest of the year. Your only reward is, you discern your mind and your organs are still functioning.

However, you've reached the age when you need glasses to find your glasses, your arms are never the right length for your eyes, and your hair deserts the head and flourishes elsewhere, and more copiously. The skin droops and takes six seconds to go back in place as everything sags and seems to get nearer the feet. Late nights ensure you'll become a bear with a sore head although it's impossible to lose your footing when you're already on your knees.

You betray your age by opening presents carefully to save wrapping paper and by reading job adverts with envy and depression. You even have the temerity to believe buying a sports car might cheer you up. In fact you settle for a reproduction of a Roman legionnaire's helmet and continue to worry that women will find you boring, and worst of all, women do find you boring.

If you're not careful, grudges can become your only companion and you compensate by trying to be trendy. Wearing purple lurex tracksuits with rainbow coloured dreadlocks and designer shoelaces isn't a wise move. It looks hideous, and worse, it repels women.

Aging is when a man falls into his anecdotage; when the thought you're dignified and distinguished betrays you're antiquated and ponderous, and the belief that you're intellectual means other people think you're a gullible dispirited nitwit. Your sparkling personality bursts forth only when you're as high as a kite. You wonder which part of you will be preserved for posterity; you worry if you're turning into a weird gerontophile; you puzzle why the golden age of life was never the age you were at.

The good life is fading fast. No more illicit week-ends, high stake gambling and general debauchery. Your interest in the Kama Sutra, Ananga-Ranga and Ching Ping Mei has waned. Your sole bedtime reading of Human Sexual Inadequacy eliminates thoughts of massive mammaries. The knowledge that Attila the Hun and Pope Leo VIII died having sex doesn't inspire you, neither does the fact that Samuel Pepys was so raunchy it was a wonder the pages of his diary didn't catch fire. Even worse, you find no mutual bond with Napoleon who liked his sex fast and furious. "Like a fireman tackling a fire," said Josephine.

You're concerned that many a man owes his success to his first wife and his second wife to his success, and you worry if your wife wished she'd married an archaeologist because the older she gets, the more interested he would be in her. Deep down however, you're most grateful for a loving and caring relationship because your slowing brain cells are aware that good health and a good wife are a man's best wealth.

WHERE HAS THE SWIRL, TWIRL AND WHIRL GONE?

I consider myself a very lucky man. I've seen every Fred Astaire film. During all those hours of gazing in awe at Fred and his gliding partners, not once did he grab his crotch. It's possible of course that he did so in the privacy of his dressing room, but in full view of the public, never!

I mention this because modern dancers like Michael Jackson and Madonna, never seem to leave the bifurcation of the human anatomy alone. While appreciating that the dance styles of Fred Astaire, Gene Kelly and Bill "Bojangles"

Robinson were nothing like the modern interpretations, I feel the sexual explicit part of dance is overdone.

When you looked at Fred you were in no doubt that he was of the male persuasion. A quick glance at the modern dancers moving at disordered speed leaves you in doubt of their true gender. That, in my view, is why the crotch is touched so often. They have to reassure themselves.

Sadly, when the current crop come to a halt after releasing their greased contortions, they look like aging female movie stars who have had too many face lifts.

As I said, Astaire never did touch himself in this way. And from what I've read about him, he wouldn't have grabbed his crotch even if the film director had given him a direct order. He was not that kind of man.

"Why did he do that?" said Tom, my next door neighbour, as we watched a young Michael Jackson on TV. "Surely if he had to go to the bathroom he would cross his legs and spin a bit more!" My wife simplified matters. "He's making sure it's still there." "What's still there?" was Tom's naive response. "You know!" my wife urged. "Oh, that! .... He should damn well know that shouldn't he?" concluded Tom. We all nodded sagely.

"It doesn't make much sense to me," Tom continued. "A crotch is not something you misplace or lose like your car keys. If his crotch had gone he would certainly know it."

I tried to explain. "Look Tom, just like Madonna, this Jackson fella has a worldwide audience and he's making a social statement. In philosophical terms: I grab, therefore it is."

Tom's response was swift and to the point. "Like hell it is. As far as I can see it's just dirty dancing." We all paused to reflect on this wisdom as we continued to gaze at the gyrations in front of us in the full realisation that the only thing Tom does when he's naked is play the ukulele.

Like a lawyer coming to the defence of a wronged victim, my wife offered .... "Perhaps he's rebelling against traditional sexual inhibitions by saying, through that gesture, that it's OK to grab your crotch in public."

"If you did that in the supermarket or on the street corner you'd get arrested," said Tom. "if you did it in front of the barmaid at the Red Lion, she'd have you thrown out, and, if you did it in front of my wife, I'd have a go at you myself."

Now in trim fighting mood Tom was unrelenting. "I know these days girls are anything but demure, but what was that in the paper about a teenager who won two free tickets to Jackson's concert by displaying her nipple rings in the street? Disgusting, that's what it is."

"I didn't hear about that," I lied. "Things have changed a bit since Fred was in his heyday." "Aye," drooled Tom, "things were smooth back in those days, none of your shakin', jerkin' and twitchin'. Gawd, he was smooth, especially with Ginger." We all nodded eagerly in agreement, readily forgiving Tom his views, as we knew Tom's earliest moment of sexual arousal was when he realised only late in life that every woman is naked under her clothes.

Tom was now too far gone for men to suggest that rock performers had been crotch grabbing for a long time. In spite of our own archaic reservations modern audiences seem thrilled by this art form variation.

"I suppose that's show business," conceded Tom, "they'll be sticking their fingers up every orifice next."

"That's on Channel Five," observed my wife.

TRIPLE WHAMMY

Within one month, three events have displayed the problems with which humans have to deal in order to pass peacefully to the next.

First, the huge Enron company ran out of money.

Second, an asteroid from outer space could, at the very least, have made a huge dent in our planet.

Third, the Winter Olympics nearly caused a second Cold War.

The scandal surrounding the collapse of Enron, the seventh-largest corporation in America, came hard after the September 11 New York terrorist disaster which had already adversely affected world stock markets. Enron was supposedly in the energy business but nobody knew quite how it made money. Using a financial technique called "leveraging" (a word substitute for "telling lies"), Enron executives turned their original assets into a huge enterprise whose stock was valued at billions of dollars. Once they'd achieved this worthy aim, the directors ensured that their own interests were fuelled before Enron became bankrupt.

Stock market analysts had consistently recommended investors to buy the stock, rating it "a great buy opportunity." These analysts, to prove their minds were filled with jelly, are still recommending shares in Taliban of Afghanistan Ltd.

How could this deception go on? One good reason was that the board of directors were paid over £200,000 each per year. The second good reason was that Enron employed a well-established firm of auditors who didn't discover and report the firm's problems. "Stupid" and "totally negligent" are words that come to mind as the auditors fell for accounting tricks initiated by the board.

Auditor: "You say you made a £410 million profit?"
Director: "Yes."
Auditor: "Can I see the accounts?"
Director: "I'd love to show you but Sandra, my personal assistant, is on sick leave and they're locked in her desk."
Auditor: "OK then, I'll take your word. By the way, how is Sandra? I know she's been sick at this time for the last four years."

So with the company in trouble, the directors cashed in their investments in Enron and at the same time cheated thousands of small investors and hundreds of the company's employees.

From one real Earth disaster to a space near one. Did you realise that an asteroid over 300 metres across has just missed the Earth? The asteroid travelling at 108,000 kilometres per hour came within 640,000 kilometres which, to me, is a hell of a long way, but in astrological terms, is ranked as a very near miss. If such an object had struck the Earth "it could literally wipe out a medium-sized country," as one learned astronomer put it. That's why residents of Russia, Canada, China and Australia carried on as normal, but citizens of Italy, Colombia, Japan and New Zealand were in a great state of anxiety.

As it's believed that 65 million years ago, a large asteroid struck Earth and wiped out the dinosaurs, astronomers, casual to the 'nth degree, were totally unimpressed by the nearness of this latest asteroid, and insisted that the discovery of a soft cheese-looking object on the moon was far more important. If that's their attitude, you and I will have to combat any future intrusion by taking the matter into our own hands. The next threatening asteroid will have to be blown up with several hydrogen bombs directed by someone with courage, skill and proven ability to perform in the face of grave danger. Only Arnold Schwarzenegger comes to mind. Sadly, his fee and percentage of the take would be more than the world could afford.

If all else fails, I'm prepared to have a go. Perhaps as the damn thing is about to strike I could engineer a direct hit on Colombia. In an instant a major drug problem would be solved, and who cares about Colombia anyway?

I know for the Winter Olympics it's supposed to be cold, but they got extremely frigid in Salt Lake City when the Canadian Pairs ice-skating team were elevated, after an appeal, to the gold medal position alongside the Russian pair. Quite frankly, this solution ticked off the Russians back home especially after drug tests had eliminated some of their Nordic skiers.

Cards on the table. I'm not a fan of any sport in which music is an integral element. I go further. I don't consider them a sport at all. What compounds the problem is that musical sports are judged by people just below politicians and lawyers on the scale of international menaces. My analytical expertise, refined every four years, demanded the Canadians won the gold but the Russian parliament voted they should return home. Fortunately Mr. Putin encouraged them to stay and another Cold War was avoided.

What with the moguls, ski-jumping and half-pipe snow-boarding events, judges were constantly on trial. We know the Olympic Games are never going to be perfect, indeed it was rumoured a Spartan judge cut a deal with an Athenian judge way back in the first Olympics, but we humans never learned from that. You can never eliminate bias and opinion, so perhaps it's better for the major events to do without sports that require judges.

So after a triad of ills, I can now relax and smile.

I didn't own any Enron shares; I wasn't given a 4.2 for my artistic presentation, and the Earth is still in the same shape it was over a month ago.

UNBECOMING BEHAVIOUR

I was just about to enter my local supermarket when the woman in front of me skidded to a halt amidst a gooey substance on the floor. The object of our investigation proved to be a dropping of chocolate ice cream which had escaped from a nearby cone, held at a precarious angle by an otherwise engaged small child.

The habits of small (and not so small) children are quite bizarre, funny or simply outrageous. My own sister-in-law, as a child, was traumatised by her first sight of a yellow banana after a food depleted World War II. We work so hard "to raise them right" but kids seem to have a sixth sense empowering them to know just how to drive us crazy, especially when eating. Food seems to taste better when it's been squashed, thrown about and mangled beyond belief. To a child, eating without making a mess seems to be as useful as a square tennis ball.

I appreciate adults have wilted a parlour aspidistra by surreptitiously pouring on it the contents of a foul drink, and that many a cushion has hidden a galaxy of inedibles, but, children are the masters.

They have a Rule Book all their own.

PEAS & BEANS. Mash them into a paste on plate. Press back of fork into offending vegetable. Hold fork

vertically, prongs up, and lick off.
Alternate method - Push as many of them as you can up your nose, into your ear or any other convenient orifice.

ASPARAGUS, BROCCOLI, CAULIFLOWER & SPINACH. First of all, look as if you've found something of intense interest on your plate. Divide into little piles. Rearrange into new piles. After five or six manoeuvres, sit back and say you are full. Transfer as many as you can to other plates while eyes are looking elsewhere. Feed to dog under table or put into pocket for later disposal.

MASHED POTATOES. Pat mashed potatoes flat on top. Dig several little depressions like ponds. Fill ponds with gravy. With your fork, sculpt between them. Decorate with peas or beans. Do not eat.
Alternate method - Make a large hole in centre of mashed potatoes. Pour in tomato sauce. Stir violently until potatoes turn pink. Eat as you would peas and beans.

SANDWICHES. Leave crusts especially if your mother says you have to eat them because that's the best part. Stuff crusts into pocket or down sides of nearest upholstered chair.

WATER MELON & CORN ON THE COB. Your eyes light up as you know the adult world has made the huge mistake of selecting these "missile" foods, especially when there are two or more children around the table. You are deeply envious of your grandparents who were initiated on grapes with pips as opposed to the modern, harmless seedless offerings. If you can't spit corn or seeds a decent distance, throw them at timely intervals. Feel a sense of satisfaction that these tactics are simply improving your cricket or netball arm.

Alternate method - Use fork as long range launcher for flicking accuracy. Learn how to duck without splattering your brains on the edge of the table.

SPAGHETTI. Wind too many strands on fork and make sure at least two strands dangle down. Open mouth wide and stuff in spaghetti; suck noisily to inhale dangling strands. Clean plate. Ask for seconds, and eat only half. When reluctantly carrying plate to kitchen, hold tilted so that remaining spaghetti slides onto floor.

CHOCOLATE CHIP & CHOCOLATE BISCUITS. Half-sit, half-lie on bed, propped up by a pillow. Read a book. Place biscuit next to you on sheet so that crumbs get into bed. As you eat biscuit, remove each chocolate chip and place it on your stomach. When all biscuits are consumed, eat chips one by one, allowing two per page.
Alternate method - Lick chocolate off biscuit slowly, then place biscuit sticky side down on sheet, making pretty diarrhoea-like patterns that mother will find irresistibly puzzling and nauseating. For an encore, and to prove that kids like foods that are "mighty chocolaty", you may leave "chocy-laden sticky fingers" on any pale unwashable surface.

FRUIT CONTAINING STONES. As for Water Melon & Corn on the Cob. Please note the missiles are heavier, but are much more fun as they can hurt on contact. Parents normally regard severe missile launching as attractive as eating a bucket of sour plums soaked in vinegar. When under the full glare of behaving properly, you can always put the stones around the edge of your plate and recite a sickly, merry rhyme for luck.

ICE CREAM CONE. Ask for a double scoop. Knock the top off while walking out of the door. Cry. Lick remaining scoop slowly so that the ice cream melts down outside of cone and over your hand. Stop licking when ice cream is level with top of cone. Bite a hole in bottom of cone and suck rest of ice cream out of bottom. When only cone remains, throw on floor for older person to slip on.

MILK SHAKE. Bite off one end of paper covering straw. Blow through straw to shoot paper across table. Place straw in shake and suck. When shake just reaches your mouth, place finger over top of straw - the pressure will keep the shake in straw. Lift straw out of shake, put bottom end in mouth, release finger, and swallow. Do this until straw is squashed so you can't suck through it. Ask for another. This time shoot paper at someone who isn't looking. Sip your shake casually until there's only a fraction remaining. Then blow through straw as hard as you can until bubbles rise noisily to top of glass. When your mother says she's had "just about enough", get a stomach ache.

BUBBLE GUM. Parents and gum are not a natural mix. "Does Your Chewing Gum Lose It's Flavour On The Bedpost Overnight?" isn't a question many mothers ask. Being confronted by a child whose face is totally hidden by a huge bubble of gum can be quite off-putting.
Alternate method - When flavour has vanished, spit out on floor at a place where you are absolutely sure an adult will step on it.

Of course we adults love kids although some of the things they get up to are as unbelievable as having a pregnancy test in the Vatican. We breed kids who, in later years, will proudly state in history classes that Hitler's instrument of terror was the Gazpacho, and Roman senators wore purple tubas, but who can precisely target a spot on the wall with a spoonful of jelly from any distance.

We are repeatedly assured by child psychologists that, in the end, a child will choose a balanced diet. Don't worry about it. If your children pay no attention to you when discussing good eating habits, they will probably grow up to be waiters.

IN VOGUE

It's surprising how ones attitude to clothes changes as you go through life. Born to well-tailored parents, my mode of dress was always considered far too casual for their taste. I was encouraged to be smart so I wouldn't let down the family clothing business I innocently represented.

Yet looking back, I have no pangs of guilt. I was spruce both in school and on the playing field. It all boiled down to a suit and a tie. My recently departed father, even at the age of 90, wore suits, ties and leather soled shoes, and, until the day she died, my mother was chic and never to be seen without a hat, adorning matching gloves and handbag. My problem was being sporty, as sporty people aren't known for their haute couture.

In Shakespeare's "As You Like It" there is a line .... "Thou art not for the fashion of these times." These words quite accurately describe my attitude to clothes. Frankly, some people must believe I don't change at all. The way I dress is very simple. Casual shirt of the tennis genre, casual shorts (in all except freezing weather) and casual comfortable footwear. I do admit however to owning many items in my wardrobe which I don't enjoy wearing.

Basically I've trouble keeping up with the modern obsession for style and its application from underwear to politics. There swells within me a blatant defiance of all fashion diktats. Deep down I consider that contemporary style worship is deeply unstylish as it becomes as obsolete as last year's cycling shorts and sushi bars. Whether I should stamp my authority and achieve a vein of elegance, restrained good taste is all that is demanded. The problem is, should I cut a dash, be in the rage, follow the fad or simply be the last word?

When you decree that fashion has gone out of fashion, you've really arrived.

Fashion descriptions amuse me. My early days soon taught me that elegant meant expensive, and audacious was the plain man's absurd. Fashion for the young at heart pursued a desire for mutton dressed as lamb. Simple uncluttered line was a long-winded way of saying sacklike. A revival item was an admission that the designer had run out of ideas. and anything casual always took at least three hours for the buyer to achieve the desired image.

When faded jeans were in, I wasn't in vogue and now I'm not in vogue with anything. I wonder if I'm turning into an old fuddy-duddy? Perhaps my fashion conscience could be resurrected if I worked in an office with young women. Now there's a thought! On reflection, I would probably be out of place there as a friend of mine told me the only time they had a middle-aged person in their office was when someone called to repair the fax machine.

Only a few months ago it was said that style mania was over and the rest of this decade onwards would be a caring period. But so far, nothing has changed. Sadly, I'm not even in fashion with words. I always seem to be too early or too late. I've missed being a "yuppy", a "dinky", a "lager lout" and a "soccer hooligan", and I've never experienced "yomping", "niche marketing" or the "big bang". Perhaps if I pull myself together I'll have time to become a "crappie" - no, not a fish, but a "caring right-wing, aspiring, perceptive professional interested in the environment." But if I do, as founder I want it all, the warehouse apartment overlooking the harbour, the designer clothes, the flashy but expensive jewellery, and the ability to lie in the sun soaking up the good life while thinking of taking my favourite girl to a far-off Pacific island.

Becoming anti-style could be the most stylish thing to do. I could even become the smartest person in these parts. It's a pity my parents aren't around to discipline the tormented thoughts and actions of their renegade son.

THE TWO FACES OF WOMEN

There's a quiet revolution happening that some of you may have missed. Call it the feminisation of electronics. Women of all ages are turning into the sort of people you call when the lights go out.

It's a far cry from the women of former years who were burdened by over-domestication and seemingly outlawed from their surrounding culture. Today's woman is an expert on chain reactions and surface tensions and hold valid opinions on the Ettinghausen effect and corpuscular theory.

My next door neighbour's wife shows this all-round capacity. In her house the VCR never flashes 12:00. She brilliantly navigates through the electronic maze in which most of us are hopelessly lost. Paula not only sets the time on the VCR, she tapes the programmes. She's a wizard of a technician long removed from the fatigued, frail, depressed, confused, muzzled, unaroused, shame-bearing, uncreative, chronically apologising wife of yore. And as a bonus, Paula with a seamless body full of curves, is the type of woman who scrubs up rather well.

Paula is motivated to tackle any of life's problems. She has long exceeded the old norm of being good and decent, married to a worthy man, having children, and, if you can't have children, losing yourself in giving. Being neat and tidy, a good cook and cleaner, and attending only to others are a mere trifle of Paula's new feminine virtues. She has worked hard to overcome her anti-romantic image when foreplay meant stripping down an AK47 machine gun. Paula has long surpassed the maxim, if you can grease the car with it, don't eat it.

I know my own limitations. I know I can figure out VCR's, camcorders and pentium computers if I really wanted to. I don't. I've enough things to work out like trying to find out if there's a word in the English language that rhymes with "bulb". By the time I get home in the late afternoon, I barely have enough juice left to compute the microwave. Let's face it, the only people with enough time are super women like Paula who squeeze the last ounce out of life and know all the answers,

Women being subjected to subliminal domestication happened imperceptibly over the years. It was a clever male ruse, one which has taken centuries to reveal. Song lyrics perpetuated the condition .... "Run, comb your hair, fix your make-up, time to get ready for love. For wives should always be lovers too. Run to his arms as long as he comes home to you." Yuk!

While I admit my mechanical dexterity extends to opening a new can of tennis balls, Paula's husband, Clive, is a man who, to my knowledge, has never changed a fuse. He's certainly never switched on the water heater and the thought of programming the dishwasher never crosses his mind. Putting soiled clothes in the washing machine is also totally beyond his wildest dreams because he wouldn't know which knob to turn to set the machine in motion. If a light mysteriously goes out, he simply abandons the room and uses another one. Clive is simply the type of man who could easily mess up a one car funeral.

Paula's versatility leads to stunning demonstrations of her expertise. When their sprinkler system was watering my garden instead of their own, and I suggested Clive turn it off, his reply was a weak, "I don't know how." Granted it was hard to reach, and you did have to use a special spanner while on bended knees getting soaked, but the Daedalian Paula not only rectified the situation but greatly improved it.

I have two thoughts about the historically held conception of gender differences. One, in recent years women have been conned into believing that if they're not accomplished in every aspect of life for 24 hours a day, they're not fulfilling their true selves. And two, for goodness sake, don't tell Paula that her garage workshop is a boon for her bumble-puppy next door neighbour.

I'VE NEVER BEEN SO COLD

The recent cold spell reminded me of the time I visited my wife's country, Denmark, in a severe winter not all that long ago. I knew it was cold when I saw white dunes in the distance and asked what they were. "The sea," my wife said casually, "it's frozen. Isn't it pretty?"

Wow!

When you get to the east coast on the middle island of Funen in winter, the Danes are incredibly nice to you, treating you with such warmth and hospitality that before long they invite you to accompany them to the nearest branch of Ikea to watch couples argue and then split up.

We English often make fun of other countries, but I assure you in that Danish winter between where the earth and sky were supposed to meet, there was a layer of really hard ice and a helluva lot of snow.

I've never been so cold in my life. And that was inside several layers of thermal clothing and Eskimo worthy boots. I wouldn't have been surprised if polar bears were stalking me. I can certify that the wind-whipped area where I parked my car in Svendborg left me wondering if there was a colder place on the planet. It was a place you needed 20 hours of sleep under a winter duvet with a warm consort to restore your glow.

Even inside the car it was cold. By the time I had scraped the windscreen both inside and out, and de-iced the steering wheel for an encore, I was too exhausted to drive. The trick, I later learned, is to leave the engine of the car running which explains two things:

> One: Denmark's fuel-economy average is 2 kilometres per litre.
>
> Two: At that rate of consumption plus the exorbitant price of petrol, no wonder every Dane is in a state of permanent overdraft.

It's rumoured that the Danes start their cars with remote-control devices but I don't believe that to be exactly true. I believe that Danish cars, being more intelligent and better educated than their European counterparts, start themselves to keep warm. Indeed, the Danes are so considerate that every car has an external boot warmer to keep your hands warm should you have to push start it. In winter their noisy diesel engines seem to be powered by dozens of sweating bodies under the bonnet, furiously shovelling coal.

The Danes in Svendborg are so peaceful and law-abiding. Nobody seems to steal anything even though tractors and lots of machinery are left casually lying about. The population is quite diverse, ranging all the way from people whose ancestors immigrated from within the Arctic Circle, to people whose ancestors immigrated from a different part of the Arctic Circle.

When you drive around at this time of year, you can see breathtaking spectacular vistas ranging from frozen sea, thick crisp snow and severe ice slopes, before your eyes return to the magnetic shapes of the frozen sea. The sight of frozen fish on the docks makes you feel quite normal and warm.

Svendborg itself is dotted with pretty houses, shops and restaurants with the occasional car running outside. Its main virtue as a tourist area is that there's plenty of parking especially when the temperature is a 100 degrees below zero. The white landscape looks to be littered with tens, perhaps hundreds of phallic symbols worthy of a pornographic contribution to any Museum of Modern Art.

A family celebration in this singular part of Denmark has many traditional virtues. A warming schnapps to repel the cold being the main one, closely followed by marinated herring on rye. I appreciate that the herring is one of the most widely eaten foods in the world, but here, the locals eat so many of them, their stomachs rise and fall with the tides. I even managed to endure one of those long-winded Danish speeches cultivated over the years to allow hot food to grow cold gracefully. It was nice to hear the speech enthusiastically applauded by the sound of heavy gloves meeting in unison. It cemented the image that strip poker would not be all that revealing because everyone wears too many clothes.

As the cold gripped me, I wasn't surprised to learn that one of the guests had just returned from ice-fishing, which is irrefutable proof that prolonged exposure to cold causes brain damage. Apparently, ice-fishing is the only alternative to long drinking bouts for the rugged outdoorsy types. While sheltering under a rickety fish house, men of doubtful sanity drop lines into holes in the ice and wait. And sometimes within two hours nothing has happened. It appears the fish have far more sense. They are not under the ice at all as they've all gone to the warmer waters of the Mediterranean. But at least the fishermen return with a warm glow after imbibing litres of schnapps, Denmark's cheaper alternative for petrol.

My own glow returned with two bowls of hot chicken broth with dumplings - hønsekødsuppe med bolle. "No, no!" said my wife agitatedly, "bolle has an "r" on the end. Bolle means sex. It's boller for dumplings." Well, I don't know about you, but when it's bitterly cold, a bowl with boller and then another with bolle, suits me just fine.

BRAVE HUNTER OF DUCKS

Let me say at the outset I don't like guns and I'm a keen environmentalist so, you might well ask, how come I went on a duck hunt in Norway? Notice I said duck hunt and not duck shoot.

At 3.30 a.m. I slipped out of bed hoping not to waken my wife, but no such luck. "You're not actually going are you?" said my deprived beloved in a tone usually reserved for people who arrive late for tennis matches and over-bearing telesales people. "You're crazy!"

I call it going into the unknown, another of life's experiences - after all, sitting in a swamp at 4.45 on a miserable morning while it's raining so hard the fiords are bulging, is not to be sneezed at.

Deep down I was hoping Thorval, my guide and mentor, wouldn't show up but he has the patience and guile for early morning ventures and he was not to be deprived. In sporting terms he's always trying to make something happen with his dedication and persistence. He certainly made it rain. We were both drenched before we even stepped in his boat and, worse, demented insects surrounded us and attacked at every opportunity. Worse still, the coffee in the thermos soon went cold. I was beginning to realise that good intelligence cannot compensate for a bad policy.

I sat all crunched up in the bow, a bag of decoys where my feet should be. I couldn't even feel my toes. It was a long paddle to where we set up the blind. The water was thick with weeds which caught our oars and made for tough going. My shoulders cramped in the damp and rampant Nordic exposure.

We were in duck land and dozens of beady eyes furtively looked at us. We set out the decoys and adjusted the blind as best we could. As soon as we did that, the wind shifted and we had to adjust it again as we squelched.

"Now we're sitting wrong," says Thorval. So we took down the blind and reset the decoys. The wind switched yet again, rendering our efforts useless. So we took down the blind and reset the decoys - AGAIN.

"I love duck hunting," says Thorval. "Yes, I can see why," I reply reflectively. The thought did cross my mind that people who pay good money to suffer sleep deprivation and be so miserable must be mad.

We spent the next hour just sitting there getting colder and wetter, waiting for sunrise and legal hunting time. Finally, the ducks began to fly. To prove our humaneness as hunters all the ducks continued flying. Not one shot from Thorval, or from another hide across the lake, found its intended target. Thorval appeared as in a dream - brimful of irrepressible hope, a stranger to despair. It was a miracle how he endured the boredom between the all to brief periods of sedate activity.

As for me, I constantly found my thoughts drifting to lunch and a hot shower. I can't possibly be a proper duck hunter when I long for a morning cuddle with my duvet wrapped wife. My dream turns to reality as I worry about falling in the water and becoming a feed for all those slimy creatures beneath. I think of it as the duck's revenge. The state of finely tuned alertness is beginning to fade. It was a morning in which I was now searching for a few quality moments too save the day. The wish to return home had become more than a simple desire.

As for Thorval, he'll always be trying to make something happen in his fastidious and passionate way. The spirit of a duck hunter doesn't reside in moments that lack devotion. He'll be at it for years while I'm hopefully still abed.

Thorval's final view on the morning? "Not bad Gordon, if you like 'em perfect."

As for me, if anyone asks me to go fishing next week, I'll kill them.

WOE IS ME

The problem with people who worry is that as soon as one worry is resolved another creeps into the mind and chips away at the worry cells. All of us worry about dangers to our well-being: serious illness, global warming, or what shall I wear at the Davidson's tonight?

A friend of mine had a worry sheet on which were listed 26 worries. I can't remember them all but the last one, and most neurotic of all, stays in my mind. "Having nothing to worry about!" As far as I'm concerned talk about worry keeps you from living.

My initiation into the discomforting world of worry began in childhood with the vague threat of the bogeyman. Perhaps I never actually saw him but I know I saw his shadowy profile plenty of times as he creaked and rustled. In adult life he transformed himself into a body called the Inland Revenue.

Approaching my teens the nightmarish problems of spontaneous combustion and public lavatory mirrors tormented my mind. Would wearing asbestos underwear cure the first agony, and would breathing hard on the mirror eliminate the two-way unease of being watched as I stood at the urinal?

After I passed my driving test the thoughts of metal fatigue plagued my reasoning power. Would the front end stabilising link-bolt on my car suddenly develop iron poor blood and snap while driving down the M6? If a terrible accident resulted, would I then go through eternity with the people I'd killed? And worse, what if I didn't like them?

The worries were numerous and often foolish. Would I speak better Italian if I ate more pizzas? If I wrote a story, would words that tumbled about my head and struggled to find their way out then become totally incomprehensible? Where do puppeteers really put their hands? And so on.

Being the product of a family retail clothing business, my adult life was tainted by the onset of a declining standard of dress. I worried whether "fashion police" would be created to hand out "fashion summons." Can you imagine leggy young women being evicted from shopping malls because their skirts were too short? OK, so can I! Would men be defending in court the right to wear tight bikini shorts which betrayed their endowments? And would size 16 women who squeezed into size 12 pants suffer the same consequences as men who displayed BBCS (Bare Bottom Cleavage Syndrome)?

A few years later I was told my brain cells were dying

by the millions. I began to feel them going belly up after a day's hard work. Worse still, they weren't being replaced. If things go on like this I estimate I won't be able to go to bed without a map. What will happen to my learning capacity? Will my brain attic get full and then, for each thing I learn, will I have to forego something else to make room? What if, for instance, by learning the capital of Latvia you forgot how to zip up your trousers? What if, at the next party you're at, you walk around all evening saying, "Riga! Riga!" while everyone wonders if you're trying to make a fashion statement with your flies undone?

Having realised that angst is created when you can't get your sports car roof up and your golf handicap down, I'm now a devoted reader of the "Angst Review", a magazine launched a decade ago out of sheer anxiety. The subject matter ranges from: "Does meat tenderiser work inside as well as out?" and "Will putting your foot on a line while playing hopscotch at the age of seven affect your pension?"

If I appear to have something on my mind and have a harried care-worn expression, please don't take it badly. Don't make me an object of compassion, just pass on your thoughts and let me do the worrying for you.

ONCE UPON A TIME THE CUSTOMER WAS ALWAYS RIGHT

When I was in retailing some years ago, the phrase throughout the shopping world was: "The customer is always right." Today, it seems as if Customer Service is always right. Indeed, you can spend all day waiting on hold for Customer Service to prove that customer service is serving you in the way you don't want.

My phone call is important to them. They have told me this many times in a sincere recorded message. They can't wait to serve me and to prove it, they will answer my call just as soon as they finish talking to the rest of the population. If our planet has turned into a global village I seem to be treated like a yokel who can be totally ignored.

But there is an alternative for Joe Public - the helpful company option route.

Press 1 for Accounts and Billing Problems.

Press 2 if you want Technical Support.

Press 3 if you require New Product information.

Press 4 if you need Defragmentation information. (Do I need what?)

Press 5 to speak to someone who knows nothing about the previous four, and is unlikely to answer any query to my minutest satisfaction. The complaining world is locked into a situation where it is impossible to get help when they're connected to button 5, and it's impossible to get help when they're not connected to button 5.

Why is there no button 6 for Complaints and Replacements?

I know it's my own fault that I needed to speak to Customer Service. I bought something that I expected to work when I used it. Now, instead of using the expensive gadget, I wait on hold listening to snappy "lite" jazz music they play when they're not telling me how important my call is to them.

While doing this, I got an idea. You know those telemarketing people who always phone you at meal times? I'm talking about the ones whose strongest muscle is the tongue and who never come right out and say they're selling something. Lately, they've been sneakily using the bizarre term "courtesy call" to describe what they're doing which is specialising in the promotion of prurience.

"Mr. Lomax," they'll say, "this is just a courtesy call to do you the courtesy of interrupting your dinner so I can ask you this question. Would you like to save 50 per cent or more on your long distance phone bill?"

What can I say but no? I always say no. Once I was weak and apathetic, but now I answer more robustly. I tell them that I want a big long distance bill and that I often place totally unnecessary calls to Outer Mongolia and that tiny Pacific Island whose name escapes me, just to inflate the bill. I tell them that if my long distance bill is not high enough to suit me, I deliberately set fire to a few ten pound notes. Then I hang up.

But of course, this doesn't stop them. The next night, they call again. That's how courteous they are.

This is how I see the problem. On the one hand, we have telemarketing people courteously calling us, despite the fact that everyone hates them and, to my personal knowledge, nobody in the history of the world has ever bought anything from them, and on the other hand, when we want to reach Customer Service we can never get through.

You don't have to move house for an essential service to create havoc. Electricity, gas and phone companies all use sophisticated computers which very infrequently resolve your problem. It's highly likely that as water pours from your phone, phone calls pour forth from your toaster and Terry Wogan drones from the Radio 2 tap as you turn it on, you'll be assured that your call is so important to them. Alas, you know, nobody seems to care.

Obviously what corporate Britain needs to do is round up all the employees in the Telemarketing department, force march them over to Customer service, and order them to remove the immobile figures of the Customer Service employees, many of whom apparently passed away without anyone noticing and, ANSWER THE PHONE ON A PERSON TO PERSON BASIS.

At least it should prevent the toaster burning my ear as I talk to the now totally aware and considerate Customer Service Department. Sadly it's so long ago since I punched in the numbers I've forgotten what I rang the company for in the first place!

YEAR ROUND ITCH

Personally, I've no objection to the fact that all human beings have skin - but, what biological function is served by itching? At this very moment there's a spot on my back, exactly midway between my two shoulder blades. It's the only spot on my body literally impossible to reach with any of my extremities. Therefore, it itches. It's most fortunate that at my advanced age I prefer a more mature form of recreation - scratching.

I don't think there is a single month of the year when there's not something out there destined to make you scratch yourself in a quivering, impotent frenzy. Your embarrassment is fulfilled when you're sitting in a public place, making grasping motions like a demented baboon as your body moves to rumba-like rhythms with not a note being played.

To help the itchers of Britain I've designed a painfully illustrated ITCH Calendar with monthly close-ups which I trust won't detract from the carefree rapture of your life.

In JANUARY a picture taken through a microscope of a speck of cat dander.

For FEBRUARY an irremovable designer clothing label will be portrayed. It will be located somewhere inspired, like the left armpit when you've got your right arm in a sling.

MARCH will feature an enlargement of a winter holiday sunburn.

For APRIL - yes, you've guessed it - it's pollen time. Just make sure you refrain from ever leaving the house or breathing.

The MAY segment is .... oh, goody! .... devoted to poison ivy and nettles.

JUNE will display in full colour enlargement with Latin sub-titles all the summer insects that bite.

JULY will illustrate a close-up of a sunburned torso exposed to intense radiation lying prostate on a sandy beach.

While AUGUST will show in magnified depth all the insects, some of them "smushed" beyond recognition, that can possible lay eggs in your clothing.

SEPTEMBER will picture all those insects that don't seem to understand that their entire span should only be a matter of weeks - and, they're still active, even in September.

OCTOBER will highlight a Halloween costume made of some incredible weird synthetic fibre which, naturally, itches. It's as well to note that this is the month that the human epidermis doesn't respond well to most indoor heating systems.

For NOVEMBER, you'll be treated to the sight of a family gathered round a bonfire all wearing wool garments. This natural fibre will insinuate itself into the consciousness off all the assembled family during the course of the evening ... fibre .... by fibre .... by fibre.

DECEMBER, as befits the season of goodwill, will be the most ambitious page in the entire calendar. It will focus on a depiction of a utopian society where nothing ... absolutely

NOTHING, itches. There will be no clothing, no sun, no chemical-laden skin care products, no insects, no stinging plants, no pets and definitely no allergies.

The front cover of the calendar will exhibit the Killer Tags, those little pieces of sharp-edged, plasticised fabrics manufacturers put on the back of shirts, sweaters and slacks. They are difficult to remove because you're not supposed to tear them off as they bear important instructions like: "Wash in cold water. Line dry. Made in Singapore."

So enjoy your year of the itch and remember our daily slogan - when you're in a nutcracker situation, you know you're among friends when you can scratch ANYWHERE that itches.

NOT SO GREEN FINGERS

Anyone can grow a large, healthy garden full of splendid vegetables and flowers. But it takes a special person to grow one thing and do it really badly. As you perhaps have guessed, I am that person.

Most people who are "good" gardeners have had (or so they tell me) no special training. "I just picked it up," they insist glibly, which to my mind puts gardening in the same category as telling dirty jokes - in the sense that you need to have a flair for it, and you don't get taught it at school.

It would appear that "good" gardening requires multi-hours of dedication and focused thinking. By this, I mean around the clock, including lying awake at 4 a.m., wondering if your hard work will still be alive at 7 a.m..

Most plants know these feelings. If I were to think of a single word to describe the average plant, it would be ....

suspicious! As plants are a completely different species from you and me, it doesn't take a genius to realise that the development of "legs" in children is normal and in plants is bad.

I've a convoluted feeling about plants. The occasional one rises up and blossoms, most lie sullenly for ages then when I yell at them, they take umbrage and go off to someone else's garden and bloom there out of sheer spite.

Following a series of outside disasters I've decided to concentrate my horticultural efforts on indoor plants. My grandfather used to pat plants. An aunt used to sing to hers. I feel more in tune with this comforting and melodic approach to plant improvement.

Throughout my childhood, grandfather patted his plants proudly, stroked them as he passed, spoke softly to them as he ensured their roots were watered. Roses, delphiniums, tomatoes and lettuce were the main beneficiaries of his patient affection. Of course, he also gave them tit-bits of horse manure, fertiliser, compost and a secret Victorian mulch. But, if you asked him, he always attributed their health to the communication he had established with them. On my frequent visits I observed this and assumed, in my childlike innocence, that his plants could hear and respond to him. Only when I grew older and more cynical did I begin to seek other explanations. Of course it was the fertiliser. Of course it was the weather. I mentioned this to my grandfather. He just smiled.

Later in my life, I started to ask around. Do plants have feelings? Can human emotion affect them? Do they respond to touch? If you shout at a begonia, does it shrink back? If you croon to a daisy, does it sidle up close? And, would it really be wise to sing rap to radishes? Sadly my grandfather is not here to answer such questions. But, I know how he would have answered me.

He would have put two geraniums on the window-sill, talking to both but touching only one. When both plants flourished my grandfather would swear that his kind words and heartfelt feelings were "leaked" from one plant to the other. To prove it, he would take one geranium and put it in total darkness in the pantry. Lo and behold, it would wilt, and I would be impressed. And he would smile knowingly.

My auntie May went one better. "To make plants grow," she said, "you have to love them enough. You have to sing to them." Modern theories of carbon dioxide exchange and electromagnetic radiation were rebuffed by auntie's rendering of "Honeysuckle and the Bee". As her voice was more chesty contralto than strident soprano, the carbon dioxide she exhaled was so voluminous it promoted plant growth in the entire street.

My grandfather and auntie had one thing in common. They were touchers. No, not of each other, that would never do. They worked on the premise that a touched plant is a healthy plant in spite of a growing feeling in the horticultural world that a regular touching significantly reduces the height of plants.

Auntie May always thought of her plants as excitable. That's why she never kissed my uncle on his return from work in front of any plant. "You'll never know what they'll get up to when we're asleep," she warned.

Whatever the truth of these views, I'm sure that plants help people with their emotions and feelings. The knowledge that there's a clear relaxation response in people exposed to gardens and gardening is not new.

My grandfather knew it as he hummed the bars of "Lily of Laguna", my auntie May knew it as she warbled "The Last

Rose of Summer". As for me, I'm trying to establish my green fingers with various silky renderings. But sadly... "It don't mean a thing if you ain't got that swing."

ELUSIVE EQUALITY ON THE FAIRWAYS

I sense an undercurrent of anger out there. A group of people are openly insulted and treated with disrespect, contempt and hostility. I venture with trepidation into a blatantly sexist topic.

It was all my wife's fault. She bounced into the kitchen the other day and said: "Have you ever seen a woman throw a golf club when she makes a bad shot?"

My memory remained blank.

"Have you ever heard a woman scream filthy four-letter words on a golf course?"

My memory begins to rise from inertia.

What had upset my wife was an article in a golf magazine giving advice to the growing number of women who've taken up the game.

"I've never seen an article on men keeping their temper tantrums under control."

She had a point. After all it's common knowledge that when a man butchers an important shot he's expected to cry out as if undergoing abdominal surgery without an anaesthetic.

"Go right .... right, you lousy (bleep)."

In its worst form the disease is expressed thus: "Oh, (bleep, bleep, bleep), why the (bleep) did I ever take up such a (bleep) stupid game? (Bleep) it forever."

A friend of mine unfailingly follows a botched shot with an ear-splitting "Billy .... Billlyyy .... Billllyyyyeeee!" His regular partner, Tom, turns his rage on outside forces of evil. "Those (bleep) seagulls. They always start their noise in the middle of my backswing. Why the (bleep) are birds allowed on the course? And those (bleep) church bells don't help either!"

In my experience women count all their shots and sink even the shortest of putts while being far more civilised golfing companions. They're far less of a nuisance on the course than men who perpetuate golf's three great sins. First, slow play. Second, cheating and lying. Third, telling really bad dirty jokes.

The fastest players are women and old men because they don't waste a lot of time twisting themselves into what they believe is a classic stance when they look like constipated hunchbacks. The average male hacker acts as if a curving metre putt is not worthy of his incredible skill, while he considers all his second putts to be gimmies. Worse, most men act as if waving someone through would leave them impotent for life.

Sadly we live with temper outbursts being part of the female stereotype. In films, a macho man will say to an angry woman: "Has anyone ever told you that you're beautiful when you're mad?" I've yet to recall any woman saying: "Has anyone ever told you that you're handsome when your eyes are bulging, your teeth are grinding, and you're shouting obscenities?"

If you don't believe me just watch any mixed four-ball on the golf course. Haughty male words to their long-suffering female companions don't change much over the years.

"Pick your ball up and let's go. There's another four-ball coming up behind."

"Hurry up, we're holding up play."

"Hit another one. We don't have time to look for a lost ball."

"Knock it away, you can have that."

Women can testify that a man will just pick up her ball himself or kick it back to her, as if her two metres putt isn't worth the bother. Then, HE will stand over his own putt, half the length, as if the Open at St. Andrews is at stake. All thought of the approaching four-ball are banished from his mind. When HE slices wildly in the rough, HE will entreat everyone in sight to look down every rabbit hole for the errant ball. The four shots HE took to get out of the ensuing bunker are not counted in the "hurry up" procedure.

A mixed foursome partner of mine, renowned for her forthrightness, once said of an offensive male golfer: "I'd like to tell him to take his ball and shove it where it definitely would be an unplayable lie." I couldn't have put it better myself.

The Lady Captain, never one to verbally hold back, once complained to me about her husband, a worthy man but of dubious golfing merit. "The only time in his life he broke 90, he did it by moving the ball out of the rough and away from the trees, giving himself every putt under two metres, and forgetting to add two fresh air shots on the first tee. And then he had the gall to yell at me about keeping my head down. This from a man with three chins, and who hasn't seen his feet in ten years! When I told him I wanted a lesson from the pro, he hinted that he could tell me all I wanted to know. I just had to tell him I already knew how to hit a ball into water, into sand, into bushes but not into the hole." With that the Lady Captain walked away briskly looking for a pouting but loved husband and now, in my eyes, a most unworthy man.

"It's their patronising attitude I can't stand especially when you hit the hole from a greenside bunker," said one of my club's single figure handicap women. Her friend Betty turned to me in disgusted tone: "You know, everywhere I play I look around to see some male golfer standing by a tree or a bush relieving himself. Emergencies I can understand but it seems most men think it their solemn duty to wet down the foliage, I wonder how they'd react if a woman did that?"

Ah! That's another golfing story in a game where equality can prove to be so elusive. I'm glad my wife brought the subject up, but I might not be when I get on the first tee next week. My five handicap will be savaged beyond belief and my behaviour will have to be impeccable.

GOD ON TRIAL

Occasionally, very occasionally, I reflect upon my standing in the cosmos. Sometimes I wonder about spiritual underpinnings but then my secular humanity overcomes these thoughts and I revert to normal. I'm the type of man hot-gospellers warn you about.

That doesn't mean I'm an absolute atheist. Heck, I'm not certain about the existence of a googly much less God. I suppose that makes me an agnostic of sorts.

Although I was largely unchurched I was encouraged, through hellfire and brimstone, to be a Primitive Methodist in my formative years. There was no antipathy to religion at home. My parents preached manners, tolerance and kindness.

I remember joining the Royal Air Force and having a mental battle to insert the correct answer to - Religion: .... I usually chickened out by putting Methodist although I had no faith and was educated at a multi-ethnic Church of England Grammar School.

Judging by my own experience, schools have been woefully remiss in teaching religion as pure history while ignoring the great art it has generated. After all, whatever I may believe, religion is a pre-eminent cultural force for good and evil in the history of human affairs. But, of course, it's not up to me. The holier-than-thou attitude always prevails leaving me out on a limb in support of one unified church should belief come to me. Yet, as a realist, I appreciate that support for various creeds will never die as religion is a crutch for those who lack reality; those who are helpless and those who are easily influenced. Historically, those who respect and fear a religion, end up being completely controlled by it. It's so easy to be indoctrinated in what can never be disproved.

If you'll forgive my tangent thoughts, I think it's time that all of us get together and sue all those known as "God." The grounds .... negligence. The God of your choice allegedly fathers an entire universe, spends biblical times behaving in a way that could have earned a restraining order, then wiles away the last couple of millennia totally incommunicado.

If a God had any sense of propriety he could at least make an occasional personal appearance. Press the flesh in the world's shopping malls. Do talk shows. Host this, host that. Why not? He'd be perfect, the most natural multi-talented media personality you could ever imagine.

I was never quite with the concept of one preacher who once thundered at me: "My God is a jealous God!" What a thing to say. What an example to set. The same preacher's cry of "God is love", suggested he had a hypocritical bent. My retort of: "If absolute power corrupts absolutely, where does that leave God?" left him testily silent.

Another thing. I'm not easy with the gender. A woman friend of mine is convinced God is a man as he doesn't listen and never phones back. If there is someone out there, why can't it be a She? So long as the word God stays and not Goddess I can live with it. After all, I prefer a touch of dignity in a deity.

I also find it difficult to have a belief when there's so much pain and suffering in the world, and, I lack more than a little respect when I total the amount of misery, corruption, cruelty and death perpetuated by followers of all religions throughout history. The way religion has been used by the rich and powerful to control and influence the weak and uneducated is a disgrace. I only know that the tenets of my life were drawn by excellent parental guidance based on accepted historical doctrines for good.

A fine example of the turn off I get from religion occurred in a recent earthquake. A church collapsed but although no one was killed, several of the congregation sustained serious injuries. The only thing left standing was a plaster statue of the Virgin Mary. The bishop regarded the statue's survival "as a sign of God's love." My view is simple and clear cut. If God, in all his infinite wisdom, drops a concrete roof and tons of masonry on his true believers, but spares a lump of modelling compound, it's time to question priorities. If I have to be composed of plaster to command attention in the universe something is wrong.

By the way, if God arrives in answer to the summons I would like to explain that he's not in charge of the weather, the outcome of football matches, car crashes or problematic marriages. He should set it straight once and for all that illness is not punishment, but actually God's version of bingo, with winners listed daily in the obituaries. And what if God says that Hell not only exists but is full? Do new arrivals get to work on Hell 2?

Take no notice, I've asked questions all my life and the older I get, the more I ask.

See you in the agnostics lounge. Sometime. Not too soon though.

WHICH IS YOUR FORK HAND?

In ancient Rome the lower classes used four fingers and a thumb to pick up food, the upper classes, two fingers and a thumb. Today, kids worldwide, and for the past thirty years, have held the fork and knife in unbelievable ways. They hold the fork with a fist and the knife like a saw and they shovel food in. It doesn't matter to them which way they hold their knife and fork. They eat which way they can.

The Britons and Americans however, are still at war. This time over the "correct" way to hold the knife and fork. "We whipped the Brits twice to eat as we wished, not as they deemed proper," said an American friend. My English friend was unimpressed by such colonial effrontery. The debate over what is the correct way to manipulate these flatware tools will no doubt continue for centuries to come.

I was raised that throughout a meal, I had to keep the fork prongs down in the left hand, and knife in the right with first finger pressing on top. I did it because it was both logical and labour-efficient, and my mother told me to do it that way on pain of death. It also made me feel like a sophisticated, continental regular guy.

Then I went to live in America where the fork is all powerful and the knife an occasional instrument of convenience. Consider the way most Americans wield a knife and fork while eating the cooked flesh of a dead beast.

Step One: With fork in left hand, knife in right, a slice of food is cut off.
Step Two: The knife is put down and the fork is transferred

	from the left hand to the right.
Step Three:	The morsel is speared with the fork and transferred to the mouth.
Step Four:	The fork is transferred from the right hand back to the left hand and the knife is picked up with the right hand.

What a lot of wasted motion. And don't ignore the needless din of cutlery clinking against plates after every bite as excess gravy dribbles off the knives onto the white damask tablecloth which can be quite disgusting. Particularly if like me, you came from a family in which gravy is considered a beverage.

Now, compare that laborious process with the way those who have been educated beyond the bounds of commonsense do it.

Step One:	With a fork in left hand and knife in right, I slice off a piece of meat.
Step Two:	With fork in left hand and knife still in right, I stab the piece of meat with the fork and transfer it to my mouth.

That's it. Two steps. No clanking of flatware. What could be simpler, except picking up the meat in bare hands and gnawing off a hunk, which good manners prevents me from doing unless I'm eating alone at home?

There are other advantages. With the knife and fork where logic dictates they should be, you can be infra dig and use the knife to scoop peas and other tricky stuff up on your reversed fork. This allows you to get more food to your mouth with fewer trips by the fork. The bad news is, you probably eat faster and get indigestion. But having the knife in your right hand throughout the meal ensures that you're always in a position to defend yourself and your food, should some thief leap out of nowhere and try to steal it. This has not happened to me yet although my mother said it would, but the way society is going, she may well be right.

To sum up, using the most efficient knife-fork technique allows me to consume food with a saving of approximately 46.4 per cent in time and effort. An American should think about that. Assuming they eat two knife friendly meals a day (Americans eat so much, statistics reveal that 2 out of every 4 people are 1 person) during their lifetimes they will have wasted several months of their lives needlessly shifting the fork back and forth, picking the knife up and putting it down.

The custom of American eating was the way everyone ate until about 1840. In 1852, a French etiquette book published that, if you wanted to eat in a high-class manner, you wouldn't switch the fork to the other hand. Before long, Europeans of all classes adopted that style thus ensuring they didn't look as if they'd just got off the last turnip truck.

Where do I stand on this Transatlantic conflict? I'm a firm believer in BOTH styles. For a stir-fry or rice dish, I use only a fork in the right hand. When I have to cut something, I use both knife and fork like a good European. I also believe the American style is more dignified, slower and more complicated, as opposed to the quick, shove-it-in European method. Efficiency isn't a virtue when it comes to stuffing food in your face. I've never once heard a doctor say: "You're not eating fast enough."

The word etiquette somehow implies dignity abounds. Here I'm writing about how to get grub from the plate to our chompers. It makes me feel quite subversive.

To zigzag American style or stay put the European way? There are pluses and minuses to both. Above all, having witnessed debris of an unbelievable nature on plates worldwide, I feel it's more important to eat neatly, cleanly and courteously with as little noise as possible as I speak here for the silent chewing majority.

A nagging thought remains. I don't want to be on my deathbed and cry out: "Where did all that time go?" and hear the reply, "You squandered it juggling all that bloody silverware you fool."

HOW TO STAY MARRIED

Recently I came across a heart warming story about an anniversary celebrated by Nina and Yuri Titov, a happy couple living in one of those unpronounceable republics that used to be part of the now extinct Soviet Union.

When they quietly married to the sound of rubber wedding bells, Nina was 17 and Yuri a mere boy of 16. But the marriage is obviously working to some degree as the Titovs have been together now for 100 years.

Imagine. One hundred years! Long past their golden and diamond anniversaries, and heading to their petrified wood jubilee. A century of his snoring and her hearing burglars downstairs. A century of him telling her to roll over and be quiet and remember they don't have a downstairs. A century of "for richer, for poorer, in sickness and health, to love and to cherish, till twin beds do us part."

Seeking tips on how to make a long term marriage work, I conducted the following interview with the Titovs. I started with the obvious question: "How can you possibly have stayed married for so long?"

Nina: "We owe it to mutual tolerance, shared respect

and studying the trade union movement on our honeymoon."

Yuri: "We owe it to collective deafness. I'm deaf in my left ear, Nina in her right. I stay on her right and neither of us has heard a word the other has said since 1951. I also stated at the outset that we were going to exist on my wits."

Nina: "I knew from the very first that was not a lot to go on."

"What sort of personality differences have you had to adjust to in 100 years?"

Nina: "Yuri's like the optimist who, as he fell off a 30 storey building went past the ninth floor thinking .... "Well so far, so good."

Yuri: "My Nina is such a pessimist. She goes around all day looking up, afraid she'll be hit by a falling optimist."

"Any other tips for building a sound marriage?"

Yuri: "I insisted that when I talk, Nina was there to listen. However, I did allow Nina the luxury of raising her hand if she got finished first."

Nina: "I never raised my hand because he spends so much time with his dog, he speaks fluent Doberman and I could never understand a word he said. The deafness excuse suited us fine."

Sadly, our interview ended abruptly when both the Titovs began throwing 100 years of accumulated dinnerware at each other while muttering Russian unorthodox words of tender distress like: "If you think marriage is a 50/50 proposition, you don't know the half of it." It was illuminating to see what happens when masculinism and feminism collide to create the volatility of life, the exquisite passions and the troublesome tensions.

Later, while treating their injuries, they did offer four basic rules to follow. First, always insist on an equitable split of domestic responsibilities. In their case, Nina did the cooking while Yuri ate the results. Second, if you avoid wild parties, dangerous activities, fatty foods and excessive sex and debauchery, you'll die anyway. Third, never stick to honesty when a good lie will suit you better. (This rule was absolutely essential when you were reared under a communist system but it has now become an intrinsic part of existing under capitalist ideologies.) Fourth, when in a marriage indifference and anxiety meet, to prevent apathy and fickleness prospering, avoid any serious conversations.

Yuri also appreciated that sooner or later, all married men will be asked this question by their wives. "Tell me the truth, does this dress make me look fat?"

Yuri could not emphasise enough how critical it is to reply in the proper manner. Whatever you do don't say:

1. "Yes."
2. "Fat compared to what?"
3. "No" .... because even if you tell your wife no she doesn't look fat, she'll say, "Oh, you're just saying that."

So, men of Britain, as you lie awake at 2 a.m. asking yourself what is the right answer, remember the old Russian proverbs devoted to the Titovs and their 234 descendants. An annual truth makes a worthy marriage, and they who stay in hot water will never get cold feet.

THERE'S A GULF ON THE GULF

Just down the road from where I live in Fort Myers, is

the pampered community of Naples. A mere 26 miles away, this trendy, sophisticated and elegant conurbation has Florida's largest per capita income of £46,000. In other words, money is no object for the majority of folks who live in this upscale coconut palmed resort founded in 1887.

This spreading community, now approaching 70,000 inhabitants, seems to have everything and more. A place where only the best will do, an area where shopping treasures and dining pleasures flourish on avenues where an endless stream of anonymous bronzed forearms rest on the doors of expensive convertibles.

To promote the town, a staff of 17 plus 9 contributing writers publish "The Magazine of Naples". This super glossy free magazine is published eight times yearly, has 258 pages and weighs a fraction over 2 pounds. Four items in the last edition reflect its subject matter: Women of Style, Vista de Flores, See & Be Seen, Have It All.

Believe it or not, 224 advertisements commit themselves to the Magazine's pages. 72 are trying to sell new homes, 44 declare their fine furnishings are the finest, 20 divulge the contents of fine art galleries, 18 offer costly private medical and dental care, 16 are selling pricey haute couture clothes, while 11 declare they have the most exquisite jewellery imaginable. Of the others, 5 are selling high-priced cars with the theme that "Jewels and Jags Go Together", and 2 promote First Class air fares and Women Only travel which appeal to the excess of wealthy widows who turn heads day and night with the line, "My husband used to ....", and strike up conversations as they pat their pedigree Bichon Frise or Soft Coated Wheaten Terrier.

Naples offers a wide range of dwellings from beachfront condominiums to luxurious estate homes, and from country club living within a gated community incorporating deep water access, to ultra-luxury residences where your nearest neighbours are feathered. There are so many resort choices, a buyer can't go wrong. You can purchase a multi-million dollar version of the simple life or an enchanting place where living like royalty is not reserved for kings and queens, albeit without a castle. You can buy your passion, vision or goal from £1 million upwards. If you have an abundance of money you can contact two agents who specialise solely in selling homes over £2.75 million.

You appreciate that "with every moment that passes by, someone else is acquiring the lifestyle you deserve," could ring true for you. Location choice is endless .... white sandy beaches near whispering surf or rolling fairways and velvet greens touched by Gulf of Mexico breezes. Another ad saucily asks, "What do you call a five star hotel where you may kiss the concierge?" "Home!"

As for the interiors, the choice is endless. How about decorating a huge circular ceiling with cypress beam accents? Or, for the kitchen, installing a polished, hand-hammered copper hood above a granite-topped island? You can chat in front of a real Mexican shell stone fireplace while your spouse plays in a clubby aura games room or activates the state-of-the-art media room.

You can enhance your furnishings with a masterpiece of global art as Naples is one of the top art destinations in the United States with over 47 galleries open for business. The height of the season is an art-filled delight centred on the Naples Museum of Modern Art. In February alone, just under 100 exhibitions, talks and shows are presented varying from the Winter Wine Festival to An Evening of Passionate Jazz, and from an intimate dinner theatre to dazzling dance at the

Philharmonic Centre for the Arts.

Naples is not short of the most amazing procedures offered by the high-billing medical and dental professions. Not just common o'garden breast implants and liposuction, but plastic and reconstructive surgery involving facelifts, chin and jaw implants, brow and necklifts along with anti-aging facials. Laser wrinkle reduction can make the body salon and spa even more appealing. As a perfect set of teeth are so essential to the American psyche, seeing a cosmetic dentist in Naples definitely gives a new meaning to the phrase: "Putting your money where your mouth is."

The opportunity to purchase red, white and blue-blooded fashion is endless. A fashion show with lunch at the Ritz-Carlton where married women circulate and single women mingle, is a good starting point. Armani, Gucci and Versace surround you even while shopping for fruit and vegetables in the local markets. As for the bizarre ritual of dinner parties where you are buttonholed for 3 to 4 hours by total strangers..... you are meant to like a dinner party in the same way you like flowers, music and sunsets. The food is simply epicurious and makes you long for a themed buffet at the Underwater Grill.

Fabergé abounds and diamonds outshine each other as you merge with women for whom marriage is now a distant threat. As few things restore the soul like the breath of sea air, a mere male might dream of becoming dependant on rigging his prohibitively priced yacht for the regatta. Harnessing the wind with the euphonic rush of heeling would surely make it all worthwhile. If all else fails, there's always the Croquet & Lawn Bowling Club to satiate latent anglophile habits.

If I live in virtual reality, Naples is a virtual garden of lavishness amid scenes of serenity and fiery sunsets. This part of south-west Florida is cool, very cool, but with only one perennial problem. I must stop parking my 1997 Dodge sedan between all those new Porsches, Audis, Jaguars and Mercedes. It quite lowers the tone.

A NOSTALGIA AND REALITY MIX

When you've supported Bury Football Club for over 60 years, do you long for the past and reject the present as an aberration? Or, do you ignore the past and look forward to the future, as ever, with false hope?

Like many other Football league clubs, the object of my life long obsession has struggled both financially and on the field for many years. If I lived my life again, would I still choose to support the Shakers? Of course I would, as any self-respecting boy would support his local team through thick and thin. Times have changed however.

I can remember the days when there were so few spectators, you could hear their hearts beating, and their brains thinking they shouldn't have been there on that sodden, windswept finger-numbing afternoon. Saturday afternoons on which you refused to renounce hope and belief although on more than a few occasions the team played with an intensity deficit. My mother's weekly words seemed to be: "Remember Gordon, all losses are character building." The team certainly had loads of characters, but it used to take a whole day to restore my natural equilibrium after a defeat.

It was a golden age of looking to fulfil your dreams. Supporting such lost causes seems to be a cruel form of madness. I was, according to a neighbour, "bloody daft", because who really cared except me and a few other diehards? Stoicism in the face of perpetual setbacks has never seemed to me an admirable part of the national character.

One thing has not changed. Football is supposed to provide an escape from real life, not more of the same. The modern game has changed in one aspect however, forever. The influence of money on this peerless game.

I'm wearying of multi-million pound footballers demanding fans to idolatrously applaud their skills. Although I can occasionally see close, hard fought games between near equals, I want to believe that championships are won by hard work and skill, not bought by the highest bidder. I want to believe players play because they're in love with the game and not just the money. I desperately want to believe in small town teams. I want to know that an underdog can still win because I want to root for that underdog. Except for the odd miraculous occasion, lower division teams are perpetually destined to fail while the likes of Arsenal, Manchester United and Liverpool are overwhelmingly destined to win. The gap between the pound sterling haves and the bank overdraft nots grows ever wider.

After all, the game itself isn't much different. The players still foul and spit for 90 minutes, but in an age when we worship the cult of celebrity, arguments rage as to whether footballers play too much or too little. Cards on the table. I don't appreciate pampered players who want a seamless delivery of off-field services to ensure success. Today, every player has an agent. I must say all sports agents aren't corrupt, it's just that 95 per cent of them give a bad name to the other 5 per cent. This can lead to a player saying: "I'm getting £2 million plus bonuses this season, but even if I was getting only £1 million, I'd be out there playing for the sheer joy of it." "I'm glad to know that," says the supporter on Social Security, and my grandfather who, as a former oppressed professional, got £6 only when he played plus £2 extra for a win and £1 for a draw. The players of yesteryear walked or biked to the match, while today, the celebrity multi-national footballer's new Ferrari is covered with puddles of drool deposited by envious supporters.

Super egos and super pay cheques hinder the development and the spirit of our national pastime. At the top levels, this much faster game, constantly trying to reach higher standards of skill, is still one of elation and heartbreak. At national level, journalists and supporters have had to face up to the distressing thought that they now have a foreign national manager who is more intelligent than they are.

Stories, the glue of football life, still abound. Hero worshipping and the cult of personality is strong.

"I was in the gents the other day," a friend related, "and I peed right next to David Beckham." Really. I don't think I've ever wondered who I was standing next to when my urine was flowing. One player talking about another at the start of the season said, "Charlie's the kind of player who improves as the season goes along, so the manager told him we'd already played nine games." One quixotic reporter working for the Manchester Evening News Football Pink told me, "Fred's body was so squat and compact, he could pull a hamstring in his ear!"

In former days, a director once complained that he couldn't get a transfer-listed player because: "He always wants to play for a team in red shirts to obscure the blood he's losing." In vogue today are the nutritionists, personal coaches, business advisers and golf instructors especially for those players exhausted through training too hard. Clubs used to have committees, now they are limited companies run by MD's, CEO's, CA's, and even ACEO's. These officers are like bidets. You don't know what they do or what they're for but they add a touch of class.

I'm a lucky man. I've been to three Cup Finals but if I wanted to go to the next one, I'd probably find the bank wouldn't approve the loan. I don't suppose things will change much in the future. The rich clubs in well-populated areas will get richer and the poor clubs poorer. The game is not the one I grew up with, but as everything changes, I've grown to accept it. Where once I read and believed in barefaced facts and glossy accuracies, today I've learned to accept bare-faced innuendo and glossy inaccuracies.

I realise I'm still running in the self-indulgent marathon of hoping my home town team will survive both financially and on the pitch. It's as much reality as I can take on a Saturday afternoon at quarter to five at this stage in my life.

DEBUNKING HISTORY

A recent study showed that senior school students " do not know basic facts about British history." I hate to labour the point, but this is something like the 1,066th consecutive study showing that young people are not cutting the academic mustard.

This revelation makes us older folks feel great. We go around saying to ourselves: "We may be fat and slow and achy and unhip and have hair sprouting from every known orifice, but at least we know the basic facts about British history."

According to the study, "more than half of the schoolchildren between the ages of 13 and 18 do not know the intent of the Magna Carta or the chief goal of British foreign policy after World War II."

Isn't that shocking? Of course it is, but to be fair, I have to admit that, for most of the past 60 years, almost nobody knew what our foreign policy was. It was a secret. For a while there, in the 1970's, the only person who knew anything about our foreign policy was a certain Prime Minister, who kept it hidden in a secret compartment in his underwear, refusing even to show it to the Queen during an audience, although he occasionally brought it out to impress dignitaries and spies at glittering state banquets.

In fact, we now know, thanks to recent news reports, that none of our post-war Prime Ministers really knew what our foreign policy was because MI5 (motto: "Xenophobic Aspirations Honed Here") was passing along false information about the Russians. There's an excellent reason why MI5 did this, but if I told you what it is, they'd have to kill not only me but all you readers out there.

Basically MI5 led Prime Ministers to believe that the Russians were this well-disciplined, super-advanced military power with all kinds of high-tech atomic laser death rays, whereas in fact the Russians, if they'd actually fought us, would have had to rely primarily on the tactic of throwing hard frozen vegetables. So we spent zillions of pounds on items such as nuclear submarines in case we ever needed to sneak over there by launching missiles on the Moscow branch of McDonald's.

But I digress. Back to the issue in hand, which is the intent of the Magna Carta. Displaying ignorance of this kind would not have been tolerated by Mr. Hindley, the senior history master at my school. We learned history the fun way. Too many of today's pupils regard the study of history as an opportunity to imbibe institutionalised amnesia. Mr. Hindley brought an orange to class and peeled it with only his left hand while telling us that this was a habit of Robespierre's as he signed death warrants in the French revolution with his right hand. (The more intelligent amongst us thought it must have been a blood orange in 1792 to symbolise the dripping guillotine.) We also learned history the hard way, being subjected to surprise bi-weekly quizzes in which we had to write 200-word essay-style answers to questions on topics we knew virtually nothing about.

The best way to prove history is a distant mirror and to reveal the intent of the Magna Carta is to recreate word for word my blether and blather offering to Mr. Hindley.

"The Magna Carta is without a doubt, one of the most important and famous historical happenings to be set forth in simple written form. And yet, by the same token, we must ask ourselves: Why? What is the quality that sets this great charter - the Magna Carta - apart from all other charters? There can be no question that the answer to this question is: The intent. For when we truly understand the intent of a charter such as the Magna Carta, or for that matter, any other charter, only then can we truly know exactly what that charter was intended to accomplish as far as charter intention is concerned. This has been an issue of great significance to historians and human beings alike throughout the long history of this great country that we call simply, the United Kingdom, a country that has produced more than its share of famous parchments and great heroes, and, yes, educators of the calibre of my history teachers, who in truth, perform leadership duties of Herculean responsibility while answering the call to perfection. They do such a superb job of preparing the young people of tomorrow for the time, when we finally reach 200 words."

See what I mean, young people? You have to have exam passing waffle at your finger tips. Thanks to my solid academic training, today I can write hundreds of words on virtually any topic without possessing a shred of relevant information, which is how I became a media success.

So I urge you to work hard at school and learn your history, because one of you could be the next Winston Churchill, the inventor of the steam engine in 1215 or should that be quarter past twelve?

TASTEFUL MUSIC

In an effort to make the arts just a bit more accessible to the unwashed, I recently attended a combined buffet and classical music evening. I know my body flows with rhythm and in my teens I was secretary of my school's Classical Music Society as well as the Jazz Club, but this was something new to me. Visiting the Hallé yes, but bribing people with food to boost attendances at concerts didn't seem like cricket somehow.

I have to admit it was the buffet and not the music that lured me in. Listening to a selection of larghettos and allegro moderatos isn't really high on my list of things to do at this stage in my life. But, there was a bonus, I'd be sitting at close quarters with cultured people. I attended on the presumption that there aren't a lot of the human family who can simultaneously appreciate Debussy, canned meat products and Havarti cheese in one mix. Everyone around me was totally unaware of course that Shostakovich gives me flatulence and taking it in a sporting context, his music always loses when I'm about.

The organisers had an unusual rule. After every piece more food was served. That way the crowd doesn't thin out. The music opened with four ladies playing a Rossini work on a flute, a clarinet, a horn and a bassoon. It was titled Quartet Number 4 in B-flat Major for Flute, Clarinet, Horn and Bassoon, which doesn't leave musicians much choice in the selection of instruments.

Everything was very informal. No dinner suits, no excessive jewellery and no deep cleavages like they have at prestige symphony concerts. The musical selection was nice and pleasant. No one did anything gauche like snoring or clapping in the wrong places, but I did notice someone's arm slip off his arm rest onto his partner's thigh and tap in time with the music. Quite out of place.

My favourite, the attractive bassoonist, performed well. The instrument has a certain fascination for me. For all the world it looks as if the player is drinking lemonade through a silver straw out of the side of a war surplus bazooka.

The petite lady next to me turned to me with a knowing look. "I'm always ready for the horn, aren't you?" she whispered. "Too much bassoon and the mind tends to wander." Before I had chance to reply, she leaned ever nearer. "It's lovely to see some young faces here." As I'm balding and long past fifty it felt like reincarnation was on the way. Was mutual harmony on the horizon?

There was a singular lack of showmanship in the performances and little to look at while you were listening. Perhaps that's why they dimmed the lights halfway through the allegro vivace. Perhaps that's what allegro vivace means.

Next on the programme, after a liberal helping of meat paste and hard-bake biscuits offensive to the human ear, was Lullaby for String Quartet for viola, two violins and a cello. After a quick switch to a more exhilarating rendering by Brahms, the musicians turned almost imperceptibly to a longer piece by Mozart. If Amadeus had been under pressure to finish his work before he ate his meat paste, you can bet it would have been a lot shorter.

The applause was enthusiastic with the petite lady on my right letting out a whoop of delight. "I'm so moved by Mozart. May I ask you a question? Are you wearing Brut?" "Well .... er .... perhaps too much?" I said. "No, no. I thought so. My husband used to wear it. He's gone now. I haven't smelled it in years," she said leaning ever nearer, "I do so hope to see you here again."

She just might especially if they can get the balance right between the hard-bakes and the quietissimos. But first the organisers must not assume everyone wants mayonnaise on their sandwiches. Further, the absence of English and French mustards conveys a narrow-mindedness that has no place in the arts.

Before I go again though, I might offer my services to work on the choreography for the polished bassoonist. After all adding another string to my bow might not be a bad thing.

VOCABULARY FOR SALE

You might be pleased to know that Sotheby's, the world famous auction house, will soon be handling the sale of my vocabulary. This major event will take place by special invitation only.

Like the government and the BBC, I can always use a little more cash than I happen to have at my disposal. As most of the popular methods of raising money like selling blood and robbing banks, are unappealing at my age, I've resorted to the sale of my most precious asset.

As I haven't got a Chagall to pull out of the attic or a

spare Sheraton chair to sell, I've taken stock and decided to put my vocabulary on the block. Immediately it became known, there was a buzz among collectors and wordsmiths about the refreshing mix of both crude and glib syllables on offer. The high quality of the thesaurus should only increase in value in years to come. The small gems of wit and wisdom blended with a neat assortment of foreign expletives and a previously unknown collection of humorous outback homonyms should also attract substantial bids.

The catalogue will divide my vocabulary by period and just to wet your appetite, here is a sneak preview of some of the priceless offerings of monosyllables and polysyllables that could be yours, along with descriptions straight from Sotheby's catalogue.

LOTS 1 - 202 INFANCY to TODDLERHOOD:

On sale are not mere "goos", "dadas" and "weewees", but those same words uttered with authority. Child development specialists are already mailing in their bids for the Lomax immortal "Salvanation Harmee" and his "Cowies an' Injuns" cry of delight at physical violence. These words could command upwards of £5,000 from those who specialise in TV and film related idioms.

LOTS 203 - 2,489 PRE-SCHOOL to UNIVERSITY:

This particular assortment is unremarkable in its scope, but does offer a representative glossary of clichés, puns and phrases for these developing years. Starting with "Get your hands of me" to "Man you're really movin'", serious wordists are presented with alternative expressions that may fill in certain gaps in their collections. Prefixes and suffixes, antonyms and synonyms used exclusively by the Lomax family will be tendered in job lots.

LOTS 2,490 - 3,011 THE BLUE YEARS:

Mr. Lomax regards this colourful group as the backbone of his vocabulary, without which he will be virtually speechless. His *#*#+*! is abusive language at its most grim and his simple ##**! is unequalled in its vehemence. Persons bidding on these lots will be required to either furnish identification proving they are 21 or bring a note from their parents stating that they already listen to rap lyrics, heavy metal music and political speeches on a regular basis. It was a time when Mr. Lomax based his verbal output on the typical British worker's farewell.

LOTS 3,012 - 4,686 THE PLEASANT YEARS:

Altogether utilitarian but somehow charming, Mr. Lomax has a way of saying "Hello, how are you?" that imparts the feeling that he cares not the least what the response might be. Also his "See you later" and "Get the hell out of here" deserve serious study for their use of inflection and pomposity. His doublets and his double entendres should not be ignored on grammatical grounds, while his single entendres are exciting especially to the etymologist with money to burn.

LOTS 4,687 - 6,202 HEREDITARY and ORIGINAL LOMAXISMS:

For those with a taste for the exotic, these root words coined by his ancestors and by Mr. Lomax himself, are not known to have been uttered by another human being. The lexicon includes the delightful "scrumptifying" in relation to skittish sexual foreplay, "tepwash" which portrays a cold, weak drink that turns warm before you can drink it, and "whoopsadink" that describes any machine that goes on the blink. The originality and subtle derivation of the Lomax vogue and nonce-words, maledictions and jawbreakers are alone worth the visit to the auction room.

Mr. Lomax will be in attendance to personally speak

and write the words as they're put up for sale. Sadly for the many British buyers present there will be no words connected with the weather. No matter how bad the weather was and in spite of the fact that 95 per cent of the population couldn't start a conversation without it, Mr. Lomax manages to live his life without any meteorological reference whatsoever.

For the record, Mr. Lomax doesn't intend to get rid of his entire vocabulary. A few words will be retained for occasional use. Not for sale are "damn and blast", "I'm sorry", "Hm, I know" and "Does anyone know where I put my ....", the basic verbiage necessary to negotiate the rest of his life.

THE PERKS OF AGING

Having just returned from the United States, I thought you would like to know that Uncle Sam gives away hundreds of millions of dollars in cash, goods and services to the over 55's regardless of their income or assets.

The fabulous freebies on offer include not only prescription drugs, free eye treatment and dental care, but free legal help. In addition, you can apply for:
1. A maximum of $800 for food.
2. A maximum of $15,000 to spruce up your house.
3. A maximum of $5,000 to help pay your bills.
4. $1,800 to keep you warm in winter.
5. $100 a day plus expenses to travel overseas.
6. $7 off your phone bill each month.

You can also have your own VIP tour of the White House without queuing like everyone else, and you can even get paid to spend your summers in the National Parks.

One other item caught my eye .... "Free and confidential

help with your sex life." Sadly, what is free and confidential is just the advice. The powerful 900mg. blend of sex boosting ingredients that will, make you an incredible lover at any age costs you $49 plus postage for 360 tablets.

Americans blithely assume that the old folks in the European "socialised" countries have far more perks than they actually have. How little they know!

To me, nothing seems more ridiculous than discounts and freebies for senior citizens, when, for the most part, people over 55 have far more disposable wealth than people in their 30's. It can be argued that every time has its problem. It has always been a bad time to be going to school, being a teenager, getting a job, being in your thirties, forties, fifties, sixties and so on, being in debt or in power, having children, taking out a mortgage and coping with the stresses of life.

As I'm no longer trapped in the kipper class, all freebies seem over the top for a man brought up in the austerity of war, with the constantly criticised but totally necessary National Health Service, and amidst the rising prosperity of the late 20th century.

I appreciate that I'm now at the age when my birthday cake collapses from the weight of candles and there is an often sudden attraction to take naps, but I don't feel I merit lots of extra perks just because I'm aging. Of course I won't refuse them, but do I need them? I still have that streak of independence that insists I can manage without perks and freebies. It's the fault of having the mind of a 25 year-old on a body well over 60.

I know we do things differently in Britain. When I have a doctor's appointment it's slightly annoying but most considerate of our instant communication age to be told: "The doctor would like you to know, he's just made a birdie on eighteen. He'll be with you in 15 minutes." I forgive him as he was the one who encouraged me to take up jogging so that I could hear the sound of heavy breathing again.

It's hard for me to believe that I was ever as thin as a 30" waist. And remembering some of the things I did in those days makes it hard to believe that I was ever that thin mentally. When I was young, age 40 seemed so ancient that I couldn't imagine what it would be like to be 40. Now I can't remember what it was like to be 40.

Age gives you an excuse for not being very good at things that you were not very good at when you were young. If you were good at something in your youth, the secret as you age is to do it yesterday when you were on form. I'm sure it was Fred Trueman, that great fast bowler nearing the end of his career, who when asked if he could still bowl as hard as ever replied, "Yes, of course I can, but the ball just takes longer to get to the other end."

Women may lie about their age to other people, but men lie about their age to themselves. Like so many people who are getting on in years, I'm fine .... so long as I remember that I'm not fine! Some people age like fine wine and others just turn to vinegar. Some look after their minds and bodies, some need side jets in the shower because their body has folds an overhead jet simply can't reach.

Someone asked me the other day at what age I started to lose interest women. I don't think I was flippant when I replied, "I don't know, but when it happens, I'll tell you." What I didn't volunteer was I still enjoy playing the old age game of adding up the combined age of my attire, although I still attempt to dress smartly (for the ladies, of course) and don't mope around in dishevelled clothing and let grunge overtake me.

We aging ones are not really smarter than the young.

It's just that we have already made the mistakes that the young are about to make, so we already know that these are mistakes and what the consequences are. In my aging process optimism has to be an essential part.. A friend in his fifties wants the highlight of his 90th birthday celebrations to be a surprise visit from his parents. That's my boy!

I've decided not to be envious of those extras my American friends get from Uncle Sam. I've just worked it out, I'm so far behind in the tasks I have to do on this side of the Atlantic, I'll never die!

My wife has the right idea. "You have 17 frowning muscles and 48 smiling muscles," she says, "at your age, favour the majority. If you use them, I'll massage them."

Good girl. That's why I don't need those expensive tablets.

MONEY-UP-FRONT

Any writer worth their salt loves to receive some form of payment for their creative work. The modern trend for publishers goes something like this: "As you must know Gordon, our freelance budget is virtually nil, but if you would like to submit a couple of articles about 800 words or so long, we'll see what we can do." In other words: "Send 1,600 words which will help to fill our profit oriented publication at no cost to ourselves." Sounds a good deal. For the publisher, yes. For the writer, no, except if vanity is the overriding requirement.

I'm a simple soul who happens to believe that the labourer should not only be worth his hire, but should share in some measure the profit created by that labour. Times change however. I understand that today in Japan women are actually paying money to nightclubs in order to take off all their clothes. As always, trust the Japanese to be on the cutting edge of all economic and social trends.

This new trend gives the impression of an uphill cash flow phenomenon. Rather than choosing careers for which we wish to be paid, we are now choosing careers which we must finance. It doesn't make much sense to me, but then I don't really understand how aircraft and strapless bras stay up either but they do.

My neighbour's son Rory is the first local participant in the Cash-Up-Front career stakes. He works as a saxophonist in his time away from resting and contemplating. He's quite a good musician but also needs the cash. Rory is currently employed by a very competent jazz band that calls itself "Have It Away". The club where he works shells out £140 a week for the six of them in the band. It doesn't take a Professor of Mathematics to work out that for the six of them to stay alive, the six musicians must be systematically replaced with either millionaires or Japanese instrumentalists.

That happened to the keyboard player when a Mr. Koji Tanaka appeared one night in the club and volunteered his services. In the process of refocusing the skill mix, Rory is next week interviewing a potential new guitar player. The first question Rory will fire at him will be, "What does your family do?" If the reply is, "We own half of Yorkshire", he will be hired because Rory liked the casual way he dressed.

The problem of the bass player solved itself. He went to a friend's house and jumped into the swimming pool. As he was high on drugs at the time he simply dissolved like a soluble aspirin. The choice of whether this action constituted a culling, a riffing or a downsizing is difficult to make

The next stage will be to find a drummer who has no

wish to be reimbursed. As this might take some doing, Rory might decide to do without a drummer and get the remaining members to snap their fingers a lot. This could be augmented by asking the audience to stand up and snap their fingers. At the end of the evening, the waitress, Rory's girl friend Cleo, can go round collecting small appreciations from them in cash or by Visa.

Rory, even with all this increase in income, is still not making enough money from his chosen career. He's making what those in the City call "reverse numbers". One way the band tried to economise recently was to rehearse at each other's house once a week. So, last week, they rehearsed at the Millionaire Guitarist's house in Yorkshire. and, being a millionaire, he lives at the top of a very high hill. On the downhill way home from rehearsal, Rory's rust-decorated van skidded on the wet road and rammed into a tree.

The repair to the van will cost almost £500. This means that if Rory kills the entire band and works religiously for the next fifty-two weeks as a soloist without buying food, clothing or petrol, he might break even.

At this point I've no wish to relate what happened at Mr. Tanaka's house. Suffice it to say, the cost incurred on the long-haul flight will be forever a setback.

I've yet to mention another of Rory's problems. The exorbitant extra costs incurred by advertising, phone calls, sheet music and toothpaste (you have to at least have presentable teeth when you smile a lot on stage) are quite debilitating on the poor lad. Rory sadly epitomises the man in the old joke who gets the job shovelling elephant dung at the circus, and complains to a friend about never getting the odour off his hands. His friend suggests that he get a different job, and he says, "What? And give up show business?".

I'm sure that there are many of you out there who have "real" jobs that are still costing you more money than you are taking in. Write to me, especially if you are Japanese and have the need to be vocationally relocated. I'll put you in touch with a now quite desperate Rory. All I want to know is how do those Japanese women afford the glitzy wardrobe?

WHO ARE "THEY" ANYWAY?

"THEY won't let you get away with that."
"THEY tell us all the fatty foods we eat will kill us."
"THEY say the difference between friendship and sex is a pint of lager."
"THEY say that if all the world's economists were laid end to end, they wouldn't reach a conclusion."

You hear about THEY constantly. On TV, radio, at work and virtually every conversation. The thing is, nobody seems to know exactly who THEY are. And just why is it so important to us to know what THEY think, anyway?

That little four-letter word is more complex than it lets on, representing everything from lazy language to the pangs of paranoia. Psychologists and linguists believe we all suffer from pronoun angst in this way.

The positive THEY is when your mother-in-law says, "THEY're all wearing it", referring to the salmon pink sweater she's just bought with buttons and little deer running across the chest for your birthday. The paranoia THEY is, "THEY'll never let that happen" in reference to some sinister conspiracy.

You never know when or where THEY will pop up. In fact, maybe you're one of the THEY. You're definitely a THEY if you work for the Inland Revenue, at the Town Hall, for Social Security or for any sphere of law enforcement. Anybody in a position of authority gets branded a THEY pretty quickly.

The problem is intensified when in print, as most people have a tendency to believe whatever they read and they use THEY as a general generic authority. Let me illustrate. Try this little thought experiment. As a member of the media - a THEY if ever there was one - how do you see me now? How am I dressed? Where am I sitting? To give me power and authority you might assume I'm wearing a smart suit and I'm sitting on a straight-backed chair at a mahogany table in an elegant office. But what happens to your image of me when I confess I'm wearing only brief shorts and a pair of socks, I'm totally unshaven and I'm sitting on a wobbly office chair surrounded by empty coffee mugs in a dimly lit stuffy room? Suddenly I'm not an authority. I'm now a me, not a THEY. My stock is low.

When we tell each other that, "THEY say it will rain at the week-end", we're summing up what we've learned. For goodness sake though, don't throw a THEY at an academic especially when it's paired with a tired old bromide. So, if you casually say to a professor, "THEY say all good things come to those who wait", he might shout back, "Who's THEY? Why do you say that? Do you have any evidence that such is the case?"

There are still more reasons for creating artificial THEYS. "THEY say to err is human, but to really make a mess of things, you need a computer." As a THEY, I'm doing my best to prove that's a correct supposition. What happens in general conversation is that THEY always appears when we're uncomfortable with somebody or some group. The paranoid and the bigot tend to use pronouns when they discriminate against a group. Minorities are called THEY as a way of avoiding things we don't like.

"THEY say the volume a person speaks into a phone is in inverse proportion to that individual's personal importance." and "THEY also say that batty laughter is just as important as superlative sex in keeping a marriage alive." THEY could well be right on both counts.

So it's best to watch your THEYS, as much as your P's and Q's, before you speak. Or at least, that's what THEY say!

POINT TO POINT CONVIVIALITY

"Bless the macaroni salad and keep us from salmonella. And let us not feel, tomorrow morning, as though our tongues has been used to sweep out the stables."

With these words the host sat down on his rickety campstool and oozed goodwill. It was the day of the annual point to point with eight races on the card. Tradition demands a picnic luncheon which lasts before, between, during and even after the races.

Spreading ourselves between the mass of Range Rovers, my wife and I observed with riveted interest the preferred etiquette of the occasion amidst the running commentaries which were numbingly banal when they weren't flat-out ridiculous. They all added to the stupor of the day.

Should the host and hostess offer the first toast? That honour should go to the person whose name appears on the newest car registration. If the car has been bought with a bank loan the owner of the next newest car is first to raise his or her glass. If the age of the cars is in doubt, the hostess should simply shout, "Whooooooeeeee! Get a load of that sexy jockey!" At that point her husband is usually expected to crush a full beer can to his forehead and offer a brief but quite tasteless imitation of the jockey.

How should guests be seated at the picnic? In a mixed party, M.A.'s and B.A.'s are placed around the wobbly tables according to net worth, doctors by the amount they pay in malpractice insurance, while teachers, B.Sc.'s and nuclear physicists by the number of weeks of unemployment

In passing, may I mention that any gatecrasher is dispatched to the nearest hostelry for pork scratchings. On his or her return the cars will have been moved or even painted. As the hosts bear ultimate responsibility for this unforgivable faux pas, it's their duty to provide surgical gloves to be worn when the other party guests are introduced to any outsider. An unwelcome couple will usually sense the hostility before it becomes necessary to throw unwanted and repaired food at them.

How should the hostess handle the problem of guests who imbibe to excess? It should be noted that most picnic drunks can be revived by leaning them against the front grille of any vehicle and blowing the horn in loud blasts. If a more vigorous method is required, it's the host's task to start an engine while the hostess clips, in vital places, two jump starter cables to the inebriate.

How can you tell a host, in a gentle fashion, that their menu is boring and not up to the standard of adjacent picnics?

Tactfully draw the host aside and quietly suggest some hot buttered scones, which can be warmed on an exhaust manifold. Fine wines can be decanted through an air filter provided the car has had a tune-up within the last 5,000 miles. Hot-toddied rum can be prepared in any Swedish made car simply by adding two sticks of butter and three fingers of Bacardi to the radiator.

At such events horse-play is considered second best to horse-power, and any mulish behaviour is deemed an insult to the host and hostess. Kinky liaisons are definitely frowned upon and are not to be excused as bonding experiences as a result of devouring two lime sorbets in quick succession.

It's absolutely not on to rehash the losing sequence by the oozing with booze host as he requests your advice for the last race. Suggesting that so far he's been betting on nags whose jockeys need horsewhipping over the fences is not a morale restoring line of action. That's no way to pay him back for dispensing boring, authoritative guidance on the nitty-gritty of life throughout the day.

As a final suggestion to ease the day along, using the correct forms of all verbs will avoid curious and crankish sentences. Bidding your adieu with a: "What a horse dealin', horse-faced day it's been," will certainly ensure your removal from next year's guest list.

As if you cared.

WHY MY WIFE GROWS YOUNGER BY THE YEAR

I feel like a daredevil today. And why not I hear you say!

So, in a spirit of complete recklessness I'm going to advise women over 50 how to look absolutely marvellous. Those under 50 can turn the page or pick up a pointer or two along the way. The groans having abated, I'll continue.

From where does this male presumption derive? I speak from years of experience watching women mature in my parent's fashion business and from observing my own wife and friends.

Whatever I say here I fully appreciate that being loved helps keep a woman young most of all. To that end I devised an annual allocation of alliteration which sets the tone for the month ahead for Team Lomax.

JANUARY, the month of CUPIDIC CUDDLES.

FEBRUARY, the month of SOOTHING SNUGGLES.

Let's be honest, 50 is that milestone age which causes women to wonder if not only their clothes but they themselves need remodelling. But it's not the beginning of the end, it's a challenge not a curse. Dismiss any feeling of rejection and don't yield to growing old gracelessly. Switch the mind and sail past the 50 years benchmark with style. After all, you wouldn't worry so much about what people thought of you, if you knew how seldom they did.

MARCH, the month of PULSATING PASSION.

APRIL, the month of FRENETIC FONDLES.

The hidden worry lingers however. Being invited out and choosing the right clothes is tantamount to selecting your last supper. You remember the old adage, you are what you wear, then turn to a wardrobe full of clothes which seems to proffer nothing exciting. You need to look smart but not threatening, feminine but not froufrou, professional but not butch. Suits are too prim, short skirts too young and long skirts and sweaters too dowdy. Your frantic delving turns your room into a retired home for burglars.

MAY, the month of EAGER EMBRACES.

JUNE, the month of ALLURING AFFECTION.

Be demure, remain calm. Help is at hand. Start with a wardrobe sort out. Keep only what fits and only the colours that make you feel good. Shorten skirts a margin, belt your shirt and accessorise in new and interesting ways. Eliminate any old-making clothes and wear those that are bright and fun. Cut out the high heels. The transformation will energise you.

JULY, the month of SKITTISH SCRUMPTIFYING.

AUGUST, the month of DEVINE DESIRE.

Try to look good by remembering it's not only what you wear, it's how you wear it. Your posture, your smile, your attitude are all so important. Get an uplifted hairstyle (always lighter never darker) with softness around the face to hide the odd intruding wrinkle. Do away with dark eyebrows, heavy rouge and false eyelashes. Use subtle colouring but always wear your favourite tone of lipstick.

SEPTEMBER, the month of SPARKLING SENSUALITY.

OCTOBER, the month of HARMONIOUS HUGGIES.

If you talk a little faster you'll sound younger and more vital - keep away from mumblers anonymous! Stay around younger people as much as you can, and get involved in their activities. How about tennis or aerobics? Make more time for the things you enjoy. And, don't be frightened of taking the odd chance or two into the unknown. Keep an open mind and don't get set in your ways. Look forward, never backward. As age is mainly in the mind not the face, your face will show few signs of aging.

NOVEMBER, the month of STIMULATING SQUEEZIES.

DECEMBER, the month of RAPACIOUS RAPTURE.

Creating self-esteem and confidence depends on how much you want it. To mature gracefully requires some effort. My wife's too busy to grow old. The years just flow by and she doesn't even count them. And, somehow or other, I ensure she laughs every day. One final tip. Don't forget the natural cure for arthritis. According to informed medical opinion sex stimulates the adrenal gland which secretes cortisone which relieves pain and swelling in inflamed joints.

"How old did you say she was? .... No! That's hardly

believable, she looks much younger than that! Are you sure?"

Which is your favourite month? Surely all twelve. Go for it girls!

YOU TAKE THE HIGH ROAD

Recently, my wife and I in an effort to explore this great nation's off-beat heritage visited the Scottish Highlands. Not a lot of people live there. I'd estimate that we met two-thirds of the population at our first hotel in Taynault. Sadly, the other third were still enmeshed in clan feuds, re-enacting old battles and practicing treachery.

A nice thing about the Highlands is that currently it has a low crime rate and is truly transformed from its cattle-thieving and savage clan war past. Many of the villages, gems in their own right, would prove to be about the size of a standard shopping mall, but with much less traffic. Occasionally, we came to a small town in danger of collapsing from the weight of all the animal heads and clan trophies hanging from the walls.

At first sight the Highlands appear to consist mainly of humongous stretches of beautiful scenery being munched on by shaggy Highland cattle. It was while out strolling one afternoon that we came upon a herd of such beasts that looked as if we should touch them only from the safety of an armoured safari Land Rover. There were about 50 of them, and they all looked up at us and started moving around in a suspicious manner, suggesting to us that they'd just that morning decided to quit eating grass and become carnivorous. Fortunately, no bulls were present. They were obviously away with other bulls drinking whisky and caber tossing, leaving the cows to moo contentedly and poop between the clumps of purple heather.

Rescue was at hand. The Highlands are full of large men in kilts who delight in danger and combat. Men who are weaned on the exultant clanging of swords and shields. Men who are patient and generous, yet steadfast and loyal. They have names like MacLean, MacGregor, Mackay and MacDonald. They relish dynastic arguments and valuing the merits of their chiefs cum liege-lords.

The typical highlander, always an imposing knee-weakening vision, was so big as a child, he could only play "seek" in the heather. Their tough Gaelic utterances are known to dry out your contact lenses from several metres away.

Hamish, who dismissed the cattle with aplomb, was such a man. His qualities were material to tailor a romantic mockery. He'd enough testosterone coursing through his veins to shift the balance of Nature. He spoke with keen devotion of Bannockburn and Killiecrankie, and the need to live frugally on barley and lentils. He dwelt at length on the merits of the Lochaber axe, the dirk and the claymore. We felt totally inadequate with counters of the virtues of the bow and arrow. It was blood and thunder versus silence and stealth. It was if Hamish had to keep our southern barbarian luxuries at bay lest they contaminate his native simple hardiness. At any second we full expected him to tread boldly off down the glen playing the bagpipes like a pied piper leading the cattle with tartans swirling in the breeze.

Known locally as the King of Fling, Hamish was also known for his unpredictable, creative and yet kindly temperament. The locals were proud of his odd talents like making a tasty barley stew, balancing sixteen whisky tumblers on his head and hopping 100 metres through the heather and fescue grass on one leg in 18 seconds. But, when all was said and done, did we really want to get near the soul of a man who was known to make Highland whisky from tree bark?

Hamish proved to be the type who has had a lot of interesting raw meat experiences some of which may even be true. "When you get older," he said, very significantly, "you know what's under the granite and who has the porridge." We both nodded sagely.

Hamish is also a poet, although he's modest about his literary ability. "I just think in Gaelic and write it down in English," he said, "and people south of Birmingham think it's poetry."

We walked on, then sat on a brae sharing untamed oats and listening to Hamish reminisce about battles of yore. He became extremely animated describing the skills of the schiltrons at Bannockburn. As he swooped, like a golden eagle, from subject to subject, he waxed lyrically about the bardic genealogies of the various clan chiefs. The heather in the glens of Sutherland and Caithness were turning bluer by the minute.

After a mere seven days in the Highlands we'd developed a lust for haggis and a true feeling for matters of the plaid and kilt. We sense a bond with the area and yet, deep down, we realised we were aliens. As Hamish implied as we said our goodbyes .... "When the phone doesn't ring, you'll know it's me!"

AM I NOW A SAILOR?

There comes a time in a man's life when he hears the call of the sea. My neighbour loves to sail and his initial aim in life was to quit his job and sail around the world, living a life of carefree adventure until an irate whale sank his boat and he was left on a tiny raft fighting with his wife over who drinks the last aloe after sun.

Sail befuddles me but not this man. In my view the only safe way to traverse an ocean is aboard a cruise ship the size of a major city. Even then you might be at risk through body expansion caused by taking in thousands of tons of high calorie food. Under existing maritime law cruise ships can't return to port until all their consumables have been converted into passenger fat.

When my neighbour appreciated my nautical terminology was limited to lee helm lag, hull displacement and the coefficient of drag plus hitting one rock equals zero progress, he recommended I buy a small power boat instead. Undeterred however, I asked him to show me the ropes, sorry the lines, and with a look of sheer terror on his face he agreed.

Soon I found that sailboats are the slowest form of transportation on Earth with the exception of airline flights out of Heathrow. Sometimes I suspect that sailboats never move at all, and the only reason they go from place to place is continental drift. As we tacked and gybed around the lake, I began to appreciate my luck. Gone were nasty things like salt water, tides, harbours and seaweed. I was kept busy doing things like untangling tell-tales, hoisting the main stizzen and mizzening the aft beam while constantly being passed by other boats, quacking ducks, retarded fish and icebergs.

After much luffing and puffing near shore, with hand on tiller I managed to plough into what nautical experts call the "bottom". Concealing his total disbelief, my neighbour suggested with a straight face that if I held on to a large pole called the "boom" and swung out over the water, my ensuing weight transfer might make the boat list enough to set us free. Most people aren't that stupid. My poor sweating flailing body instantly became a tourist attraction. The crowd on shore were laughing and pointing as Fuji increased its profits with this photo opportunity.

"It's unusually low water," someone shouted, "but I think she's moving." The Jaded Hussy was exhibiting no more flotation than Buckingham Palace. As I clung to the boom listening to my neighbour whimper, two thoughts penetrated my shame and pain:

1. If you have to die let it be in a noble cause.
2. Would I ever be able to borrow my neighbour's lawn mower again?

At that precise moment a gust of wind was enough to send the boom crashing towards the stern where it knocked my captain neighbour overboard. Miraculously the boat was free. I was alone and so was he. With the aid of a long boat hook and a pull on the seat of his trousers my neighbour came aboard. The cheering from shore was deafening as the fun nautical outing resumed in silence.

You might say my neighbour had the wind taken out of his sails but he rode the storm quite well, but it was sad to see in his eyes my demotion from potential master mariner to convicted galley slave in just a few minutes. Surely Drake couldn't have had these problems defeating the Armada? Definitely not, otherwise there would be a national bull-fighting programme, paella on every table and I would be a señor.

For consolation we plunged into the only food on board, six bags of potato crisps and four cans of now exceedingly fizzy oversweet raspberryade all registering in the "fatal snacks" column of life's eatables. Burping loudly my neighbour regained his sailorly poise, spread the canvas, brought Jaded Hussy into the wind and headed for home. Suffice it to say the conversation was brief and polite.

A few days later as I waved to my neighbour from my passing car I noticed he's now the proud possessor of a small 1.5 HP engine hanging boldly from the stern. He's obviously decided he doesn't need my help in getting back to port any more. As a potential English sea-dog I feel totally thwarted. Nelson wouldn't have treated me like that!

WE HAVE WAYS TO MAKE YOU HEALTHY

Can I get something off my chest? Besides the gravy stains, that is. The Ministry of Health has released yet another report that the British are getting fatter. The dangers of obesity are lurking everywhere, and for the umpteenth time warnings are issued that too much consumption of certain foods can be detrimental to your health.

Many years ago the British felt free to smoke, eat fatty foods, drink hard liquor and drive cars without seat belts, often all at the same time. Granted most of them died by age 40, but they were carefree and happy. Today, as body parts always make the news, we have vigilant health authorities notifying us daily that everything we put into our innards can be fatal.

One man who takes no notice is Cyril. He's an old friend of mine and he's 76 next birthday. Cyril is incredibly fat, like three of me plus a little chap with pneumonia. He's a natural power-luncher and he knows only two food choices: fatty meat and no thanks. Cyril wouldn't play golf if he couldn't smoke and drink beer - it's a pure labour of love handles. When he plays golf, the only sport with a halfway house, he believes that if you put on 5 to 10 kilos the ball will go at least 5 to 10 metres further. He's never had a problem hitting the ball out of and around his shadow. Cyril's views on the current PGA Tour having fitness trailers and locker rooms full of apples, oranges and carrots are quite unprintable.

Cyril and I were reared on a culture that deemed baked beans on toasted white bread was a splendid meal, while we automatically assumed that calories didn't exist in:
1. Any food used as a garnish.
2. Samples on offer in any food store.
3. Anything consumed while you're drunk.
4. Birthday cake on anybody's birthday.
5. The second and third helpings of cereal and ice-cream.

The problem, as I see it, is we went to different schools. Cyril's school, as it still does today, ensured that if you missed physical education classes nothing was said. At my school, PE class was compulsory and even attempting to evade attending was treated as a crime. "Your body needs a bit of sweat on it, boy!" The 45 minutes class was broken down as follows:

1. Changing into gym kit .... 3 minutes
2. Playing the fool .... 12 minutes
3. Trying to hit someone hard with a medicine ball .. 4 minutes
4. Being castigated for fooling about by Captain Turner (retired), our gym teacher, who was always late ... 4 minutes
5. Lining up in team lines .... 3 minutes
6. Team races in which the same team always won .. 2 minutes
7. Hurting one's private parts while vaulting appallingly .... 5 minutes
8. Changing back into school uniform while ensuring some individual remained naked and was last into French class for which he suffered detention ....12 minutes

It was no wonder that such training inspired a lifetime of fitness and ultimately ensured we won the Cold War.

Schools should teach pupils the skills they'll need to

stay physically fit for the rest of their lives. New school gyms should look like a health club. At the end of each term, simply assess kids on how well they learned to stay within their target heart-rate zone, mastered a new sports skill and improved their overall fitness.

I was schooled in traditional, now much outdated but still lingering, PE methods which often ended up benefiting only a quarter of the children in the class. Those who weren't athletes, or who didn't play team sports, were set up for failure. Three-quarters became prone to obesity, heart disease and related illnesses. The object of modern PE should be to instil a desire to maintain lifelong health.

Which brings me back to the government health warnings. How many cups of whole grain and how many helpings of vegetables and fruit does my body need every day? Two and five? As a nation we don't carry cups around with us nor do we encounter whole grains in the factory or office. In the real world we have to decide whether we want chips dipped in tomato sauce with two greasy pork sausages or a really large helping of chips dipped in tomato sauce with four greasy pork sausages.

Now, I'm not against farmers, but I do think, in return for all those subsidies, they should be required to spend 8 hours per week actively prevailing upon taxpayers from eating too much. The next time you go in a supermarket and put all those unhealthy packaged foods in your trolley, be prepared for the President of the NFU standing at the checkout shaking his head in disapproval. He'll smilingly give you a cup and a whole grain sample and tell you to start your shopping all over again.

For my part, that's how I'd handle the national health problem. As for Cyril, his dispensing of the cup and whole grain into the farmer's vitals would hardly match his delicate chip into the cup on the eighteenth for a red meat birdie.

TWO LEFT FEET

I'm married to a dance machine, a woman to whom the art of movement is life itself. Dancing with my wife is like simulating Beauty and the Beast, and I hold much sympathy with the view of George Bernard Shaw who thought "dancing is a very crude attempt to get into the rhythm of life."

But where did I learn to dance? Strangely not to music at a local dance hall but to the rise and fall of the crowd as I stood on tiptoes straining to see my football gladiators as a small boy. This "en pointe" technique transformed itself into the soft shoe shuffle to repel the winter cold. Knees bend pliés at half-time improved balance and prevented stiffness, but did not encourage balletomania.

I tender no excuses. My family had rhythm. My uncle was a dance band pianist of great flair and my father (known locally as the Waltz King) would tread a floor with anyone. He has been known to pirouette like a self-hypnotic spinning top around his shop's fashion dummies at the drop of a three-cornered hat. He always believed that a good leg is better than a good head, and looked with disfavour on anyone who claimed the band cannot play or the floor is uneven

My "dancing" established itself on the sporting fields of England where rhythm, tempo and style ensured more than a fair share of success. My school football coach not only demonstrated skills but encouraged athleticism way ahead of his time by supplying a constant stream of gymnastics movements blended with a welter of mixed complexities. He missed his vocation as director of tourism in the Seychelles.

The fact that most of his players used the same foot for kicking and the other to prevent themselves falling over was by the way.

Frankly I was embarrassed by my dance efforts and as the night of the annual school dance arrived, my knees rocked and rolled at the thought of leading my opponent - sorry, partner - to the floor. Backed by determination and a quick honing reflection as I passed a shop window, I offered tremendous variations on the pas de deux, a rustic clog dance and a cakewalk. I like to think my partner and I offered our fellow students virtuosity and syncopation mixed with witty and intricate steps, but I fear the end result was not the slightest threat to the skills of Fred and Ginger. Responding to a slippery floor we even had the temerity to slide ungracefully through the swing doors at the climax of the Gay Gordons. Our dishevelled reappearance proved to be the highlight of the evening.

If I'd been born in earlier times I'm sure I would have adapted easily to the unhurried minuet and the stately quadrille. I'm also certain that my performance would have enhanced the folk and country dancing scene as I always fancied myself with bells tied to my legs entertaining the peasants to an intricate Morris dance. And who knows where my interpretation of a jigging hornpipe would end?

My downfall happened when I was a guest speaker at a sporting dinner and dance. It became known to the organiser that my rendering of the rumba was a sight to behold. Little did he know. Fortunately, my wife, yet again, made me look wonderfully sensuous and excessively smooth. Perhaps having lived in Spain and moving to the lascivious but dignified sarabande and the lively farruca helped my cause. I only know that when the rumba calls I ooze basic rhythm and counter rhythms previously unknown to my body. Rhythms so enrapturing, they grip the audience like a vigorous demon.

As a man I don't have to decide how brief my cute tutu should be; if my jazz coloured tights are suitable for the Bolshoi; if I can match up to Salome or if my legs are long enough for the Folies Bergère. The challenge of Nijinsky and Bojangles lingers however, so deep down I have a great desire to be innovative, experimental and versatile. My pulse quickens and calories are burned up as I shimmy and cavort the floor. I make whoopee as I strut and chassé. My hope is that when I trip it's only the light fantastic. Oh! I can't help loving that girl of mine.

MAIDEN SHADES

The last thing this country needs is yet another government agency but lately I've become convinced that the nation can no longer exist without a National Colour Control Board.

If we had an NCCB I would be spared unsettling situations like the one last week when I bought a pair of trousers to match a brown sports coat. It began with the sales assistant asking me if I would be interested in something in taupe. I didn't want to appear the total idiot in fashion savvy, but neither did I feel the least bit comfortable saying: "Why yes, taupe is EXACTLY what I had in mind."

Because I had no idea what taupe was or any of those fuzzy shades that get foisted off on the unsuspecting public, I responded the way I do whenever I have to make a pivotal colour decision. "I'd just as soon see something in khaki." And that's what I wound up with, yet another pair of khaki trousers that won't quite match my brown sports coat.

Later I looked up taupe in a dictionary and discovered that it's a "yellowish-brownish-grey". But here's the worst part. It's called taupe because there's a species of mole found in France that is known as taupe. Now, I don't know about you, but I can't get real excited over wearing trousers that come in a colour that commemorates a half-blind foreign rodent that burrows in search of grub worms.

Apparently interest in the environment has heightened the popularity of earth tones and natural colours over the greys and grey-blues of previous years. We are now blessed with fjord, pascal and grain, in other words medium blue, yellowy-green and beige. In my opinion there shouldn't be any colour called ecru. I can tell you that ecru is white with a little brown in it. It is approximately the same colour as bath water in an old-fashioned boarding house. The National Colour Control Board would see to it that ecru, at the very least, became "muddy white". Verification and tone would make the NCCB an elite government body. The staff would be flush with enthusiasm and glowing with pride as they worked at fever pitch with not a stain on their character. At their finger tips would be explanations for colours such as celadon, quartz, loden, copen and kelp. Ready to be banned from the scene would be astral and rutabaga. Even that new hot colour mali would go - is it too much to ask that they just call it peachy-orange?

I've already had a preview of their first colour leaflet and their interpretive explanations. Amongst the latest shades are beach .. a granular neutral that brings to mind childhood nostalgia of a day at the beach. Artemesia .. a garden-inspired silver-green. Mosaic .. a blue-green inspired by Moorish tiles. Alkavert .. a cool natural look of a new leaf covered with morning mist. Bark .. a gnarled, blackened brown that anchors

the palette and replaces black as a natural backdrop. Muslim ..
an alternative to bleached white that is a basic friend to the
environment. Commeal .. a warm, subdued versatile yellow.
And finally, palomino .. a rustic, rugged lodge brown -
whatever that means!

To my mind the NCCB will have to be very careful. Their first issue looks like they've been taken over by the colour mafia. Gobbledygook is already permeating their first picks. We need to start worrying about these things and it will demand eternal vigilance on the part of patriots like you and me to see to it that good sense is applied when christening new colours. We must insist upon names with everyday significance.

In the meantime while the NCCB pontificates and deliberates my new shade of white will be known as "fish belly". My new light grey will traverse the world as "exhaust fume", a new browny yellow has a "battery acid" ring to it and my new pulsating shade of green is definitely "mildew".

I hope to get formal permission for their use in a few weeks but no doubt I will be way back in the queue behind all your creative and trendy offerings.

THE MOST DANGEROUS GAME

If you have a namby-pamby nature and would like to take up a nice relaxed sport, try ice hockey, rugby or boxing but leave tennis well alone. The only thing that compares to a game of tennis is the scene in a department store on the first day of the January sales when hordes of lunging shoppers, eyes glaring and credit cards poised, create a nerve shattering experience.

Have you ever been poked in the groin by the net crank handle as you stretch for a ball? It can turn a mighty man into a whimpering, snivelling midget. Many times in my tennis career I've been caught as I changed sides. Your knees buckle, your eyes water and for the next game or two you call out the score in a high falsetto voice. That's why many tennis players are childless.

No different to anyone else, I've been hit by the ball more times than I can count. And most of the time, where does the ball strike? Right again. Nine times out of ten it's right on your testimonials and your best leg of three.

Some years ago I was playing in a tournament against a good friend of mine, John Watson. Now John was built like Hercules only stronger, and he hit everything as hard as he could which was plenty hard, believe me. I stupidly put up a weak lob at point blank range and John's overhead came at me with the speed of a rifle bullet. I dropped like a prisoner before a firing squad. As I lay on the ground huddled against the pain in my family jewels, I croaked jokingly but meaningfully, "I'm cutting you out of my will." As my will was almost destroyed that wasn't at all surprising. Finally, I crawled across the tramlines and lay at courtside while everyone laughed and chatted about this and that. For me it was goodbye world.

Everything about tennis is dangerous. Nine stitches testify to being struck by racquets from both sides of the net. The court and its surroundings are waiting to snare you at the slightest opportunity to give you bruises galore and worse. Be it on grass, clay, wood, concrete or carpet, I've ripped, torn, pulled and strained every muscle, every tendon, every ligament and every fibre of my body as I've slipped, tripped, skidded and lurched my way around the courts. I've run and blundered into tables, benches, umpire's chairs, tubs of plants, flower beds, prickly bushes and copious fences and surround netting. The only soft landing that comes to mind is when I surprisingly appeared on the lap of a raunchy brunette while chasing a wide ball at set point.

The discerning reader will be aware that no mention has been made of falling yet. I've sprained ankles and knees, skinned my elbows and shoulders, and twisted everything that's twistable. Ice packs, plasters and liniment have vied with my wife for adoration. Having a tetanus jab was the result of bursting through the rusty back netting as I unavailingly chased a top spin lob. Emerging from the tangled mess I resembled one of Fagin's boys. Once hitting an overhead, I fell backwards and knocked myself out as my head hit the ground. Perhaps that's why I didn't become Prime Minister. I've fallen over the net, collapsed a net by leaning on it and tripped violently over the excesses of a frayed net. I do admit however, I wasn't hurt when a zip disintegrated and my shorts appeared below knee level as I sprinted from one side of the court to the other. Only my pride was dented.

The very act of hitting the ball causes both delight and trouble. The fabulous shots, the lucky net cords, the bad bounces, the brain sapping strategy and the physical excesses on the one hand. On the other, the back doesn't like many of the positions I put it in. The elbow is renowned for creating its own medical complaint, the knee doesn't relish a long series of magically quick turns, the toes and fingers are appalled by their blisters and every muscle has grown accustomed to the feeling of cramp. Under intense sun and questionable floodlighting I've had bugs in my eyes, collided with partners I didn't see and missed many a ball.

But, wherever and whenever I've played, I enjoyed every minute playing a marvellous game in front of spectators applauding like animated herbaceous borders. I wouldn't have missed it for the world.

THE DAYS OF YORE

Having just returned from the USA where I spend the greater part of the year and having reached the age when my features take longer to rearrange themselves each morning, I got to thinking about where I truly belong. As a worldwide citizen with a Danish wife, a son, daughter-in-law and two grandchildren in New Zealand and friends in many other countries, the answer is nowhere ... anymore.

The love of my wife Jytte plus the joy of many friendships are more than adequate compensation as they know no boundaries. They don't measure distance in miles or in the number of boundaries they cross. My friendships have transcended time, distance, language and culture. As the spirit of friendship draws people together any emotional baggage is far easier to sustain,

Strangely, one thing has not changed. I still follow the fortunes of the Shakers wherever I am. For those without a passionate sports persuasion perhaps it's hard to understand that Bury Football Club still harbours fond memories of Old Lancashire, a part of Lancashire that now serves allegiance to Greater Manchester. Old Lancastrians valued their reserve, maturity and traditions. Greater Mancunians value their enthusiasm, adaptability and new horizons.

Following The Shakers from afar doesn't make me a football fan, just a witness to an unfolding tragedy. I now understand that knowledge and empathy are not prerequisites of fandom but supporting football teams equates to ill-health and imperfection. At least years ago, the club used to revel in a higher echelons mid-table wasteland where more than a few supporters wore pained, bored expressions. Today, attendances have dropped so low in Division Three it looks like it is by invitation only. I seem constantly to be involved in a triumph of hope over experience. This is a bijou antidote to the days when urine trickled down decrepit terracing as fans feasted on pies of dubious quality washed down with sweet tea topped with floating leaves.

On reflection I'm not really at home anywhere, and I don't really fit in, now that my father has died, back in the north-west any more. I've now very little in common with one specific place but I am in tune with the wider world. I certainly feel more international than national. More modern than traditional. More a revolutionary than a conformist. Although born in a town full of factories and frictions I was schooled to seek wider horizons. Throughout life I've constantly lost touch with my own generation as I lurch towards youth and the future as a world citizen

But memory still serves me well.

In my teens, to leave the north was seen as an act of betrayal as well as folly. In the south they rode to hounds and went to Ascot; in the north we kept pigeons and raced whippets. Emotionally the north began in Birmingham and ended in Newcastle. The south was one place, one city. Devon and Cornwall were seaside resorts while Somerset and Kent were places working people went on holiday to pick fruit.

The real and only "down south" was London. You needed more clothes down south because people dressed according to the weather, whereas up north you wore the same thing, rain or shine and occasionally turned out like a pawnbroker's window. Nobody would ever dream of wearing underpants, possibly because such garments were only worn at weddings and funerals. A suit was worn only on four occasions - first interviews, first court appearances, and of course, weddings and funerals. Women became experts at enhancing their appearance with a sleight of hat. One activity that's been eliminated, with disastrous consequences to the moral fibre of modern youth, is the wearing of jock straps by those of a physical persuasion. Wearing such an item for a lengthy period, as any sporty, old Lancastrian male will know, could cause the wearer to be singing in a different section of the choir within months of the original activation.

    The air in my young days was always cool with an overcast sky, as if someone had turned off any possibility of summer. If you had a Baxi fireplace, any type of fridge or an inside loo, you had really made it. Marital differences up north were kept under wraps and the days of women with few legal rights, cooking, baking, cleaning and washing all day, then making themselves sexually available, are thankfully long gone.

    The north was a place where the noise of looms and loud machinery was turned into money, and a region where prudent wives developed a strong grip through counting the contents of wage packets. What the north had was a reservoir of latent talent which drained away down south over the years. Places like Suffolk, Dorset and Hampshire didn't count. The chasm between the north and south has always been economic in spite of media and government suggestions to the contrary. The concept of a divided nation in my youth still lingers and I suppose will never fade.

    In one way or another we're all in flight from our family roots and now that I've left the family Sunday dinner torture syndrome behind I can appreciate the past without rancour and with much affection but without the slightest need or wish to return to such spheres.

How life changes. I'm of the generation that if it's on your plate, you eat it, and if you order it, you consume it .... all. Once I ate chips fried in buckets of lard and consumed ham so thin you could see the grocer through it. Nowadays, supermarkets up north carry rocket, wild mushrooms, Parmigiano-Reggiano, crème freche, filo pastry and a dozen kinds of rice, of pasta and of olive oil. Today most restaurant customers drink wine which would have been unthinkable even in the 1970's. In those days a £5 dinner for two could include "1/2 giraffe" of wine. Women seldom drank, now they put away bucket-sized goblets of Chardonnay with an ease that makes the mind boggle.

The humour and straightforwardness are what I remember most about my old stomping ground.. You know you're in Black Pudding country if:

1. You identify a Manchester accent as southern.
2. You're frostbitten and suntanned on the same day.
3. "Down south" really means Cheshire.
4. "Summat to eight" is a meal and not the time of day.
5. "Ayup" means "'Ello", "'Ow are you?", "What's this?", "'Ang on a minute!", "Bloody 'ell", "Get 'orf!", or "Summats wrong!"
6. "Pop" is a drink and not your Dad.
7. You caught a fish in the Irwell and it glowed in the dark.
8. You can pronounce "Athanaeum" but can't spell it.

I seemed to be my mother's energy while she was my calm. Her words of advice are countless and four observations stick in my mind.

1. "Someone might be stupid but there's no excuse for not being clean."

2. "Never get into a fight with ugly people because they've nothing to lose."
3. "It doesn't matter so much where you are but in what direction you're facing."

Last, and perhaps the most important.

4. "Work hard, never give up and believe in yourself."

Misunderstandings were commonplace. Our next door neighbour told my mother that "the Countess of Ayr was coming to tea." The neighbour lost face when it turned out to be merely the County Surveyor.

Religion and politics often clashed. I quickly learned that decisions are made by people who turn up and that argument tests the strength of someone's position. Coming from a Methodist background tinged with a Rechabite soul led to me renouncing the evil drink and even coffee and tea until I was in my late twenties. Bedecked with socialist and liberal thoughts made my journey through school and later life easier to bear. Reality taught me that religion is purely a superstition and that the principal cause of religious hatred is religion as all religions have a separatist idea at their very core. That idea is exclusion: the "othering" of the unredeemed. The study of history also taught me that more than a few religions diminish the individual and create cowed cultures. The northern social life also reflected that people are uncomfortable with other people who have a greater certainty of belief. Experience has revealed and cemented my early thoughts that the spirit of friendship draws people together more than any doctrine.

As an only child, attending school was idyllic. Not only was I taught things of great value to my future life but I enjoyed it immensely. The meanings of words became clearer and helped me to understand the real world. For example, "scheduled" meant "hoped for", "strategy" was a sales pitch for "low cunning", "a frank discussion" was in reality "a bloody argument" and "analytical projection" was simple "a guess". My economics teacher, a man with a great inflationary feeling, revealed that: "Statistics are like a bikini. What they show is interesting but what they conceal is vital."

I still smile when I recall my classmates history essays in which they stated: "St. Teresa of Avila was a caramelised nun" and "The British defeated the French from 1793 to 1815, but at gastronomic cost." Mr. Senior, our history teacher and also the Headmaster was not amused.

It's cause for reflection that I'm now part of a mobile phone-owning peasantry in which the length of the call is in inverse proportion to the meaningful content. And yet, I've no doubt that the days of yore were good but the days of widening horizons were, are, and will be even better.

When I'm gone from this world it will irk me considerably that I won't know what the next one, two, three thousand years of human advancement will bring. I've always looked forward to change ... long live tomorrow's world!

TO MY EXECUTOR

Recently I read about a vintage car fanatic who was buried in his old Ford. My first reaction was to condemn the lamented car lover for being excessively eccentric but then, the more I thought about it, the more I found myself admiring the fellow's resolve to have the final details carried out in style. Perhaps we all ought to put down on paper our every little wish regarding our ultimate exit from life which is, after all, only a sexually transmitted terminal disease.

The first object is to keep a tight rein on the funeral

director. If he even begins to suggest that the background music be something like Handel's Largo, some dreadful hymn, or even "The Impossible Dream", then you have my permission to throttle him immediately. Just go through my CD's and pick "April in Paris" by Count Basie and "Misty" by Erroll Garner. Play any melodic jazz and the "1812 Overture" .... loudly! "Capriccio Italienne" and "Rhapsodie Espagnole" .... louder still! Ensure the mourners (all four of them) move like Tina Turner and sing like Ella Fitzgerald. Once they're in the groove keep it going with Oscar Peterson's "I Want To Be Happy" and the Ray Charles rendering of "Hit The Road Jack".

I know it's customary to be laid out in a nice suit but I'd just as soon be wearing my sponsored tennis kit. My wife has always said I had nice legs so why hide them at the point of departure. If you've got it, flaunt it!

If you insist on putting me in a suit make sure it isn't made of polyester. For one thing the creases would never come out and for the other I'd hate it to last longer than me. The last thing I want to be is the object of some future archaeological curiosity. You can imagine the scene. "Check the label Fred, it's probably another one from the 21st century who died after that big M & S suit sale."

Do however unfasten the top button on my shirt as I've never liked tight collars and ties. There are no fond and priceless possessions that I feel compelled to take with me, but I've never been too far away from a tennis racquet, golf clubs, Brussels sprouts, ice cream, choolate and an ever flowing ballpoint.

At the modest ceremony please remove anyone who lavishes praise over my remains but never bothered to do so while the living, breathing me was in circulation. How dare they imply that death becomes me in a way life never did? I've no idea who might officiate at my send-off, but may that person choke on their words if tempted to utter: "To a better place he goes." How the hell can anyone know that? Besides, I've had such a fantastic 24-carat lifestyle nowhere else could possibly be any better, and even if there was, who wants it perfect anyway? For all anyone knows I might just have been reincarnated as a ferret to venture into any sexy place I choose.

Let anyone stand up and say anything about me that they want, but if their eulogy should quote from the Desiderata or anything sickly that reeks even vaguely of a Hallmark Greeting card, then kindly throw things at them until they shut up. Furthermore, if anything that rhymes winds up on a piece of granite, I'll come back and haunt the perpetrator.

You've got the picture. No weeping, no wailing, no gnashing of teeth and certainly no black veils or sombre clothing. Match my life and enjoy every minute. I appreciate that things could get a little boring but please do NOT, under ANY circumstances, talk about the weather. That would really tick me off. Suggested topics: Sport, jazz, humour, chocolate and ice cream recipes plus anything to do with the future. The more people raise their eyebrows in surprise the better.

One other thing. Please no hearse and limousines blocking traffic in a procession at funereal pace. I'd like to be carried off in something red and fast. Just strap the coffin on the roof and hit the accelerator. Ask the police for special dispensation to have a quick .... and I mean quick .... burst of speed down my final road. If they won't give it, make sure you break the speed limit as I'm certain to leave enough to pay the fine.

The last salute by survivors and friends rightly overcome by grief, sentimentality and sustaining libations should be: "What a life!"

What granddad first gave me

Hot English mustard on a Bury Black Pudding